Catholicism and Democracy

Catholicism and Democracy

An Essay in the History of Political Thought

Emile Perreau-Saussine

translated by Richard Rex

in memoria aeterna erit iustus
ab auditione mala non timebit

PRINCETON UNIVERSITY PRESS
Princeton and Oxford

First published in France under the title *Catholicisme et Démocratie: Une histoire de la pensée politique* © 2011 by Les Éditions du Cerf.

English translation © 2012 by Princeton University Press
Published by Princeton University Press, 41 William Street,
Princeton, New Jersey 08540

In the United Kingdom: Princeton University Press, 6 Oxford Street,
Woodstock, Oxfordshire OX20 1TW

press.princeton.edu

LIBRARY OF CONGRESS CATALOGING-IN-PUBLICATION DATA

Perreau-Saussine, Emile.
[Catholicisme et démocratie. English]
Catholicism and democracy : an essay in the history of political thought /
Emile Perreau-Saussine ; translated by Richard Rex.
p. cm.
Includes bibliographical references and index.
ISBN-13: 978-0-691-15394-0 (alk. paper)
ISBN-10: 0-691-15394-9 (alk. paper)
1. Christianity and politics—Catholic Church. 2. Democracy—Religious
aspects—Catholic Church—History. I. Title.
BX1793.P4613 2012
261.7—dc23   2011030644

British Library Cataloging-in-Publication Data is available

This book has been composed in Minion

Printed on acid-free paper. ∞

Printed in the United States of America

1 3 5 7 9 10 8 6 4 2

Contents

Foreword

Political theory is among the most demanding of the humanistic disciplines. Excellence is achieved only by those who not only know how to frame philosophical questions but are also adept in historical enquiry and able to learn what they need to learn from their colleagues in political science. And because, unsurprisingly, the habits of political thought vary, often subtly, from one national order to another, they have to be aware of the differences between political cultures in respect of what is taken for granted and what is not. When therefore someone who had developed this relatively rare set of skills and sensitivities is taken from us prematurely by death, we not only mourn the loss of his human qualities but also grieve for the intellectual loss, for having been deprived of the kind of colleague whom we most need, if we are to understand the politics of our past and present. So it is with our mourning and grief for Emile Perreau-Saussine.

His education had been in key part an initiation into a tradition of distinctively French liberal political thought, in which a respect for English thought and English political experience was generally taken for granted but sometimes without a due sense of how very different from each other English democracy and French democracy, English liberalism and French liberalism, are. But Perreau-Saussine had both learned from and transcended the limitations of his education. What he had acquired were the abilities of an interpreter, someone able to throw new light on a political theory or event or cast of mind by showing how it appeared from a hitherto unfamiliar standpoint. So it was with his view of my work in his first deservedly prize-winning book. That he was so much at home in the English language as well as in French was of course an indispensable part of this. But what mattered as much or even more was his political imagination, his capacity for understanding both sides of a quarrel and how the partisans of each side viewed themselves and their opponents.

These gifts and talents served him well in the writing of this his second book, a book that, happily for us, he completed not long before he died. It is a book that will be important for both its English-speaking and its French readers, but for different reasons. Let me focus first upon its importance for English-speaking readers. The issues that were and are posed by the history of antagonism and reconciliation between the Roman Catholic Church and the forces of modern secular democracy have never had anything like the importance for English politics that they have recurrently had for French politics, and it is not difficult to understand why. The Catholic Church had ceased to have any significant political influence in Britain by the end of the seventeenth century, well before the long and slow movement from eighteenth-century oligarchy to twentieth-century parliamentary democracy had begun. Insofar as Catholicism invited serious political consideration, it did so only because of the part that it played in making the problems of Ireland so intractable. Popular hatred of Catholicism was, of course, sometimes a useful political emotion—witness the Gordon riots—but it too steadily diminished. And during the nineteenth and twentieth centuries, progress toward electoral democracy and the integration of Catholics into British political life went hand in hand. Indeed, the identification of a majority of Catholics in Britain with the labor movement for much of the twentieth century became one of the salient features of British democracy.

Hence, G. K. Chesterton's ardent commitment to both democracy and the Catholic faith became less and less surprising to his British readers. In France, in the same period, it was otherwise. There were those notable few who agreed with Chesterton in championing both, such as Charles Péguy, but the democratic tradition in France was defiantly secular, anticlerical, and for the most part anti-Catholic, while many of the French Catholic clergy and laity were deeply suspicious of democratic republicanism. What we have to learn from Perreau-Saussine is that the history of the relationships between the democratic republicanism of the French state and the Catholic Church is far more than a history of antagonisms and partial reconciliations. It is also a history of unpredictable and unintended transformations in which the deprivation of its secular powers, often construed as a defeat for the church, turned out to be a liberation of both Catholic hierarchy and Catholic laity. What followed were a series of episodes that resulted in a reconciliation of the church with democracy, even as Catholics continued to recognise that "democracy, like all political systems, could go wrong."

The interest of the story that Perreau-Saussine has to tell is in the details. And that interest is very great. He provides us with new and illuminating accounts of the significance of Vatican I and Vatican II . He throws light on the relationship between political change and spiritual change in the life of the church. And such figures as Maistre, Lamennais, Tocqueville, Comte, Littré, and Péguy all find a place in a narrative that is interestingly different from those in which they have hitherto been assigned a part. So this is much more than a political history. It should be required reading for Catholic theologians and perhaps for certain kinds of political atheists. Most important of all, this book is itself a further contribution to the same controversial history that it narrates, a contribution by someone who found himself at home in both of the traditions that he was discussing. And, therefore, it too is inescapably controversial.

A foreword is not a book review, so that although one of the great merits of this book is its provocative character, I shall resist the temptation to note here the occasional doubts that I would have wanted to express to the author or the questions that I would have been anxious to put to him. But I do so with unusual sadness, since I shall never learn what he would have had to say.

ALASDAIR MACINTYRE
University of Notre Dame
London Metropolitan University

Catholicism and Democracy

Introduction

Representative democracy and liberal Protestantism seem to have a natural affinity. Like liberal Protestantism, representative democracy entails the relegation of belief to the domain of the private, the individual, and the subjective. It privileges not truth as such but the individual's freedom to search for truth. People can pick and choose for themselves from sacred texts in their quest for models and rules of conduct to adapt to contemporary needs. Individualism entails a desire for autonomy that often seems incompatible with submission to religious authorities. From being forces that shaped entire societies, religions are reduced to merely personal preferences. To believe is no longer to belong. This affinity with liberal Protestantism gratifies liberal Protestants and reassures agnostics, but it disturbs both those Protestants who are not liberals and those believers who are not Protestants—starting with Catholics.[1]

The theological drift of democracy is not exclusively in the direction of liberal Protestantism. It also tends toward pantheism, to the idea that God is All and All is God.[2] In putting everyone on the same level, its doctrine of social equality undermines the sense of individuality. The citizen is absorbed by the people, the people by humanity, and humanity itself by an indifferent and undifferentiated Nature. The finite is swallowed up in the vague and nebulous infinite. Sensitivity to difference and to particularity is dulled. The sense of the person is lost in the totality, and the dignity of the individual person becomes meaningless. This pantheistic tendency appeals to environmentalists and to the most radical democrats, and it is welcome to those totalitarian ideologues who find their own freedom a burden. However, it disturbs those believers who uphold the Christian concept of the person and of personal salvation along with the broad outlines of Genesis: for if God created the world, then the world is not God. The tendency toward pantheism is particularly disturbing to Catholics, whose traditions sensitize them to the importance of hierarchy, order, and form.

In this book, I set out to show how the Catholic Church has responded to these two contradictory yet complementary challenges, the upper and nether millstones of liberal Protestantism and pantheism, which, under more or less totalitarian regimes, have squeezed it to the point of persecution or driven it to the point of civil war—for example, during the Vendée (1793), or in Mexico

(1926–29) and Spain (1931–39). How has the church adapted to liberty and equality? To what extent has it turned threats into opportunities?[3]

My analysis is organized around the two great councils that, for the Catholic Church, bestrode the last two centuries: Vatican I (1870) and Vatican II (1962–65). I intend to show that the First Vatican Council was just as "modern" as the Second Vatican Council, and even that the latter reasserted aspects of tradition against the former. I intend to show that the two councils represent in effect the two poles between which the Catholic Church oscillates in the age of democracy, but also that these two poles are complementary and can be successfully integrated within a single perspective. By analogy with the "Gregorian Reform" of the eleventh century and the "Counter-Reformation" of the sixteenth century, I speak here of a "Vatican Reform." I argue that the contemporary Catholic Church is blending the work of the two councils into a coherent program of Vatican Reform on the basis of which it can go forward.

The First Vatican Council set the seal on the renewed affirmation of the importance of the papacy in the democratic age. Under the Ancien Regime, Catholics were for the most part nationalistic and attached little importance to the papacy. But with the end of the "confessional state" and the destabilization of national religious identities came a shift in allegiances. Catholics now looked to Rome as the center of a religious identity that was no longer rooted in national traditions. Vatican I defined the doctrine of papal infallibility. Yet though reactionary in several ways, it nevertheless represented an adaptation to political deconfessionalization. There was an element of liberalism in the triumph of ultramontanism. (By "ultramontanism" is understood the ecclesiastical tendency to look *ultra montes*, beyond the mountains—that is, the Alps—toward Rome, emphasizing the superiority of popes over bishops.) Catholics would never have turned to the papacy in this way had they not in effect agreed with liberals that there was something irreducibly secular about the modern state.

Vatican II completed the work of Vatican I. The council fathers of Vatican II gave explicit, albeit measured and conditional, recognition to the merits of democracy and liberalism. They abandoned the concept that the state as such had specific duties with regard to God. They ceased hankering after the confessional state and acknowledged the right to religious liberty, making it the cornerstone of Catholic political thought. They emphasized the political role of the laity and abandoned the idea that political life ought to be predicated on close collaboration between civil and ecclesiastical hierarchies.

It is not my intention to rewrite the history of the councils, for their story has been well enough told.[4] I intend rather to put forward a history and an interpretation of Catholic political thought in the age of democracy, concentrating on the case of France and on the now somewhat forgotten history of Gallicanism—the doctrine that, in contradistinction to ultramontanism, set a high value on political life and on the milieu of the nation. There are two reasons for this.

In the first place, it was France that set the tone for Catholic political thought between 1650 and 1950, when the church was, more or less, adapting to what we call the "modern world." In the history of France, we see clearly the tensions that elsewhere remained hidden. France was at once the epicenter and the laboratory for the process. In Spain, Quebec, Italy, and the United States, for example, the debates were neither as wide-ranging nor as profound. It was France, more than anywhere else, that saw real reflection on the relations between Catholicism, nationalism, liberalism, and democracy, because it was France alone that was at once a great Catholic nation, a cradle of the nation-state (unlike Spain or the Habsburg Empire), and the stage for the Revolution. The crisis of the Revolution called forth the most powerful and the most extreme analyses, ranging from the political theology of Joseph de Maistre to a homogenizing Jacobinism and a republican anticlericalism. Over the past few centuries, the most substantial, the most engaged, and the most influential Catholic political thought has been that of France. Demographic shifts within the universal church and internal change in France have latterly combined to bring that intellectual primacy to an end. The internal arguments of American Catholicism now hold center-stage, but that is a recent development. Previously it was in France that religious, political, and intellectual life came together with unparalleled vigor, conferring a more universal significance upon the events of the nation's history.

Second, the tension between Vatican I and Vatican II, between the two poles of the Vatican Reform, plays out at the level of the universal church a tension that first arose in the heart of political and ecclesiastical life in France. The forces that shaped developments within the Gallican church came to shape the universal church. The Catholic Church was caught between two paradigms to which it neither could nor should conform if it were to remain Catholic: that of a church organized on a purely national basis; and that of a church entirely separate from the nation-state, autonomous and self-sufficient under the guidance of the papacy. This book is therefore especially concerned with the history and varieties of Gallicanism, because, within the Catholic Church, Gallicanism is the preeminent tradition of distinctly *political* thought. Gallicans have always insisted on the autonomy of the temporal or secular power. It was within the matrix of Gallicanism that, from the high Middle Ages onward, the secular tradition took shape. This Catholic tradition, which has attracted surprisingly little attention from professional historians, has nevertheless played a crucial role in the development of the framework of modern politics: the liberal and democratic nation-state.

My project is thus situated at the intersection of several intellectual disciplines: the history of ideas, religious and political history, ecclesiology, and political philosophy, with a particular emphasis on the last of these. It seeks to complement the fine work that has already been done in these various areas.

Neither church historians nor historians of political thought have yet attempted a "history of Catholic political ideas in the democratic age." I aim to fill this gap.[5] I do not presume to paint a complete picture: that would be an impossible task. Thus, I scarcely touch upon "social Catholicism," nor do I deal with papal policy as such. I can only hope that the reader will accept my oversights and omissions as the necessary price of a welcome brevity. The authors whom I have picked out for analysis have been chosen for their representative character and because they offer the clearest and boldest arguments. It goes without saying that I confine my view largely to Catholic authors. However, the Catholic Church envisages itself precisely as church, and not as sect; as a church that aspires to embrace all, even pagan philosophy. So I have no hesitation in drawing where appropriate upon non-Catholic and non-Christian authors. If the history of the church is, as the church likes to think, the history of Truth, then it is better if it is not confined to the presbytery. The church encompasses the life of nations, and its horizon is the unity of humanity made manifest.

I

A New Role for the Papacy

THE ORIGINS OF VATICAN I

1

From Bossuet to Maistre

The Civil Constitution of the Clergy

The breach between religion and what we call the modern world dates neither from the birth of the state nor from the Declaration of the Rights of Man, but from the Civil Constitution of the Clergy and the oath associated with it. Enacted on 12 July 1790 by the Constituent Assembly, the Civil Constitution sought to integrate the Catholic Church into the Revolution on a Gallican basis. The organization of the church was to be mapped onto the new political organization of the kingdom. The Assembly reduced the number of episcopal sees from 135 to 82, aligning the diocesan boundaries with those of the new administrative "departments." Moreover, it provided for the election of parish priests and bishops by, respectively, the district and departmental electorates. This assimilation of the ecclesiastical system to that of the civil administration was meant to ensure a harmonious relationship between the Catholic faith and the new order established by the Revolution. Where once the people had been answerable to their parish priests, and the priests to their bishops, the Assembly meant to subordinate priests and bishops alike to the people. The aim was to replace the descending thesis of the Ancien Regime with the ascending thesis of the Revolution. In fact, the principle of election was by no means unknown in the tradition of the Catholic Church, which had given it an important place in its internal arrangements long before secular bodies followed its example.[1]

Almost inevitably, the alteration of the political order had consequences for the church. Reorganization of the civil power entailed reorganization of the ecclesiastical power because they were so inextricably entangled. In the "society of orders," divided into its three estates of clergy, nobility, and the common people, the church held its place as of right. Indeed, the church held pride of place, for the clergy officially constituted the first estate. The abolition of the system of estates changed everything. Henceforth, society was to be composed of equal citizens. The clergy, wrote Siéyes, in a pamphlet that celebrated and hastened the coming of the new regime, "is not an order, but a profession."[2] As long as the clergy constituted an order, its authority was inscribed in the very nature of society. Once it became a profession, the social and political grounds of its authority were shaken. Hence the Assembly's plan to introduce elections for bishops and priests, in order to furnish them with a new basis of legitimation.

Democracy entailed a radical transformation. The society of the Ancien Regime was a complex web of privileges and corporations. Aristocratic by nature, it was in theory organized around a vertical chain of command that ran from top to bottom of the social scale with manifold ramifications. Social equality under a democratic regime brings about an entirely different system. Society is divided into two parts: the state, which rules; and civil society, which is ruled. If the state rules, then differences between citizens have no relevance in the political domain: citizens are, as such, equal. The existence of the state makes estates redundant: the abolition of the estates makes the state necessary. Society is no longer directed by clergy and nobility but by an abstract and impersonal state, which strips nobility and clergy alike of their political functions and leaves society equal but at the same time atomized and depoliticized. What ties together the two parts of the new order is the myth of "representation." Government is reckoned legitimate when it "represents" the will of the governed. The political life of a democracy is a delicate system of exchange between state and civil society, undertaken in order to ensure the smooth working of this representation. But this leaves the church in an ambiguous position. Where does it stand? By reducing society to its constituent private citizens, the state's imposition of individualism jeopardizes the freedom of intermediate institutions and of organized religious bodies. The Civil Constitution of the Clergy set out to address this problem.

Hierarchical societies are "corporate societies" that assign a quasi-political role to the head of the family, to the intellectual, to property, and to religion. The separation of the state from civil society effaces these intermediaries. Representation relates the abstract individual immediately to power. There is no political role as such for family, property, learning, or religion. For the democrat, "it is essential that there should be no subordinate societies within the State."[3] The monism of political life in a democracy is markedly less favorable to the church than the ill-defined pluralism of predemocratic society. The church therefore struggled to find its place in the new regime. Whether it was a matter of popular sovereignty or state sovereignty, it left the church out on a limb, for the church was neither the people nor the state. The Civil Constitution was designed to get around this problem by identifying the people *qua* citizens with the people *qua* Christians, so that citizens participated as of right in the life of the Catholic Church.

Rejected by the pope, however, the Civil Constitution became a bone of contention. In 1791 almost half of all parish priests refused to swear allegiance to it. Until then, France had hoped to forge some consensus on this issue through the efforts of the Assembly. But faced with the oath, a considerable body of Catholics turned against the Revolution. The clergy split into "patriots" and "non-jurors." In the Vendée, contention soon erupted into civil war.[4] The Civil Constitution of the Clergy, which meant to establish harmony by aligning the ecclesiastical system with the civil, achieved the exact opposite. It hardened attitudes as much among revolutionaries as within the church and brought Catholicism into alliance with the Counter-Revolution. The Constituent Assembly's policy, which sought to reconcile the church to the new regime, actually opened a deep gulf between them. Adept in so many other respects, in this matter the Assembly committed a blunder of the highest order. We need to explore just what it was the Assembly failed to grasp.

In providing that parish priests and bishops should be elected on, respectively, a district or departmental basis, the Assembly sought to introduce an element of democracy into an institution that had hitherto been organized on apparently aristocratic principles. In the Catholic Church, however, the people are not accorded the competence in religious matters that they may have in politics. On the one hand, the people as citizens are not coextensive with the people as believers. On the other, the Catholic Church enshrines a nondemocratic principle insofar as it is organized around an apostolic hierarchy based on divine right.

In order to harmonize the religious system with the political system, the revolutionaries declared that all citizens should have a vote in the "chapter," that is, that they all had a right to vote in the elections for parish priests and bishops. But from the moment that the Declaration of the Rights of Man recognized religious liberty (article 10), there were citizens who were not Catholics. Their participation in appointing priests was hardly going to be acceptable to the church. Hence the observations of Boisgelin, archbishop of Aix, the spokesman for a large section of the episcopate, in his speech of 29 May 1790:

> In the plan you are putting forward, bishops are to be elected by the same people who elect the members of the departmental assemblies, and these electors are themselves the elected representatives simply of the citizens in the political system, and not of the body of the faithful. Departmental assemblies might consist partly or entirely of non-Catholics. The electorate might not include a single priest or bishop.[5]

What would happen at places such as Montauban or Nîmes, where there were large numbers of Calvinists, or where the electoral assembly was dominated by a revolutionary club bitterly opposed to Catholicism? Before article 10 it might have been conceivable to select clergy in this way, but not after.

Boisgelin therefore suggested reserving the election of bishops to the clergy. But the Constituent Assembly found in Robespierre a powerful voice for its egalitarian principles:

> The nomination of bishops is an exercise of political power. So to privilege the clergy over other citizens in this process is to ride roughshod over the principle of political equality, which is the foundation of the

Constitution. It amounts to granting the clergy special political influence and reconstituting them as a separate body.[6]

Robespierre's case was reducible to the idea that establishing any public body within the nation introduced divisions between citizens, ran the risk of fostering faction, and entailed blatant inequality. Equality presupposed a direct relationship between the state and the individual, as well as the exclusion of any intermediate bodies that might introduce tiresome differences and thus in effect resurrect the old hierarchies and privileges. This argument, rooted in the ideas of Rousseau and the Jacobins, had considerable appeal and was not without a certain logic. But it was hard to reconcile with the liberalism of article 10 of the Declaration of the Rights of Man. It left the French church in disarray.

The first article of the Constitution of 1791 recognized the right of everyone "to practice the religion to which they subscribe." Yet its authors went on to persecute recalcitrant priests whose only offense was to refuse an oath of allegiance to an ecclesiastical system they could not approve. An opponent of the oath posed the following pointed question:

> In your wonderful Declaration of the Rights of Man, you have proclaimed with a great fanfare that opinion, even religious opinion, should be free: so why do you compel me to take an oath against my opinion and my conscience?[7]

As Mme de Staël remarked, "This was simply to substitute political intolerance for religious."[8] This brings us to the heart of the contradiction that lay within the revolutionary program. The democratic principle could be integrated with the idea of a national church only if the population was exclusively Catholic. But from 1790 the revolutionaries aspired to an absolute democracy incompatible with the liberalism they espoused elsewhere. Democracy was beginning to turn against liberalism.[9] At the same time, recalcitrant Catholics enlisted under the banner of liberalism. Bishops opposed to the Civil Constitution demanded and secured the secularization of the civil administration, so that in matters relating to births, marriages, and deaths, Catholics were not obliged to have dealings with clerics who had taken the oath. The law to this effect, passed on 20 September 1792, was a concession extorted from the extreme revolutionaries, who wanted a national religion, by those Catholics who remained loyal to the Holy See and who therefore set out to boycott the "constitutional" clergy.[10]

The revolutionaries' identification of the people as citizens with the people as believers had already run up against one major obstacle: not all citizens were Catholics. But there was another problem: not all Catholics were French citizens. The Catholic Church was an international body whose universal aspirations were most obviously expressed in the roles it ascribed to the papacy and to general councils. The Civil Constitution challenged this universalism by stipulating that the pope was merely to be notified of episcopal appointments.

This was a logical consequence of the doctrine of popular sovereignty. If there were to be a dispute between the people of France and the Holy See, who would decide? According to elementary democratic logic, the people. So it was enough to notify the pope. There was no need to seek his approval or advice. From the Catholic point of view, though, the Civil Constitution entailed Protestant or Presbyterian consequences. One of the clearest outward signs of the unity of the church was being erased, and that unity itself was being reduced to a mere formality. No wonder the pope drew the line.[11]

But there was yet another reason why the church could not accept the revolutionary logic that equated citizens with believers. The Catholic Church embodied a principle that was anything but democratic. It was not for the faithful to decide on the organization of the hierarchy, for that had been laid down by Christ.

> The National Assembly wanted to give the Gallican church a constitution conceived in the same spirit and on the same principles as that of the state. But it failed to realize that the principles of the Catholic faith are entirely different from those of the new constitution. The basis of that constitution, the fundamental principle from which all else follows, is that power is derived from the people and must be conferred by the people. The fundamental principle of the church, in contrast, is that everything it possesses, all its powers, were given it by Jesus Christ, and that its authority is derived from God himself.[12]

In the Catholic Church, teaching authority, jurisdiction, and the power of ordination lay in the hands of the bishops. They were teachers, expounding the faith; priests, leading public worship; and ministers, exercising ecclesiastical government. The Civil Constitution of the Clergy had to be ratified by authorities competent under canon law to do so. In the absence of papal agreement, it needed at least a national council of the church. There were churchmen in the Constituent Assembly, but they were not present in their ecclesiastical capacity. An assembly that had been convened on an estates' basis might have been able to commission the clergy to undertake reforms. But the Constituent Assembly explicitly repudiated the whole notion of a society of estates. That, after all, was the very foundation of the Revolution. The democratic principle, by challenging the whole notion of estates, fatally undermined the competence of the Assembly in religious affairs.

At the start of the Revolution, a substantial party among the clergy looked favorably on the new ideas and took an enthusiastic part in the revolutionary movement. The church's counter-revolutionary turn was thus by no means inevitable. Fearful of alienating the Constituent Assembly, the bishops were ready to make concessions, while the papacy's fears of losing the "eldest daughter of the church" made it equally flexible. But the Civil Constitution went too far. The Assembly had failed to realize that applying democratic principles to the church would raise insurmountable obstacles. It unwisely pursued the mechanical transfer to the ecclesiastical domain of a system devised for the political domain, and thus sparked off conflict between church and state. Freedom of religion necessitated a degree of deconfessionalization of the state and a corresponding curtailment of their own power that the revolutionaries were unwilling to contemplate.

To summarize, democracy means the sovereignty of the people. It therefore called the authority of the clergy into question, as the clergy did not derive its authority from the people. The Civil Constitution of the Clergy was an attempt to solve this problem by providing for the election of the clergy by the people. However, the implicit identification of the people as citizens with the people as the faithful was unacceptable to the church because it could put the appointment of priests into the hands of citizens who were not Catholics and because it excluded from the process any Catholics who were not also citizens (first and foremost, the pope). Moreover, the Constituent Assembly was setting about a structural reform of the Catholic Church without proper authority. The church regarded its own constitution as a matter of divine rather than human law. For the Assembly to ignore these issues of canon law was a major political blunder.

The Civil Constitution of the Clergy was not simply a blunder, however. It was a deeply revealing moment. The hubristic reforming ambition of the revolutionaries went back to the democratic ideal itself. Under the Ancien Regime, politics was essentially a matter for a small number of groups and individuals. For the vast majority of the population, life was largely apolitical. The Revolution brought the masses into the political arena. It was a political Pentecost, a civic epiphany that sparked off an explosion of activism. The coming of democracy and representative government saw a broadening of the base of politics unprecedented in the history of the church, and this inevitably caused problems in the religious domain. As a result of article 10, fellow citizens were no longer necessarily fellow believers, and national unity was no longer predicated on religious unity. The church hierarchy was caught off balance by the claims of the laity.

This sudden politicization was all the harder for the church to assimilate because Christianity has a marked tendency toward the apolitical. Christianity aspires to reach all people. Envisaging itself in universal terms, it does not concern itself greatly with the particular characteristics of political institutions or with the varieties of forms of government. Nationalists charge the church with failing to show proper concern for the nation. Monarchists criticize it for pandering to the people and democrats criticize it for compromising with kings. Christianity is for citizens and slaves alike, as much for those excluded from power as for those with their hands on its levers. A slave can be as good a Christian as any citizen.[13] From a democratic or republican point of view, Christian universalism looks like political indifference, and that indifference in turn looks like a complacent acceptance of the political apathy that tyrants love to foster. From Machiavelli to Rousseau, political philosophers alert to this tendency have been prompt to heap reproaches on this apolitical tendency in Christianity:

> Why are people today less passionate about liberty than the people of ancient times? For the same reason, I think, that people today are less stouthearted: namely, if I am not mistaken, a difference in upbringing founded on a difference in religion. Our religion, in effect, having shown us truth and the right path, leaves us with less regard for worldly glory.[14]

The more the faithful turn toward contemplation and pursue humility, the more they subordinate the interests of this life to those of the next and appear as bad citizens, incurring the obloquy of republicans driven by the call to action and the lure of national glory—the values that underpinned the French Revolution.

Christians likewise could feel ill at ease in the world of democratic self-determination, which they saw as a hubristic enterprise, a Promethean bid to emancipate human freedom from the will of God. The politics of self-determination could easily lapse into love of self at the expense of love of God.

"This revolution, properly understood," wrote Joseph de Maistre, "is nothing but the expression of a vicious pride that oversteps all bounds."[15] Much later, Jacques Maritain was to condemn the political application of the concept of sovereignty. In a book that presented itself as a democratic manifesto in contrast to Maistre, he argued that neither the state nor the people could properly claim sovereignty, which was an attribute of God alone.[16]

Writing during the bicentenary of the Revolution, Jean-Marie Lustiger, cardinal archbishop of Paris, observed of the Civil Constitution of the Clergy:

> In the final analysis, the dispute turned on the question of whether there is some "absolute" that is manifested and embodied in the human institution of the state. . . . For those who affiliate themselves unconditionally with the agenda of the Revolution, national sovereignty is ultimately that absolute. . . . The sovereign state cannot tolerate citizens appealing to any other tribunal. But the religious conscience does precisely that in appealing to God as the foundation and guarantee of all freedoms.[17]

Political life is bound up with an affirmation of the value of the self with regard to which the church is often ambivalent. Religious life is predicated on the submission of the self to the will of God, whereas political life is predicated on the right and the duty of the self to govern itself. The believer prostrates himself in the dust before the Creator; the citizen stands up for pride in political freedom. Military victory, the precondition of independence and thus of national pride, is therefore subject to contradictory evaluations. Saint Augustine relativizes its importance: "What does it matter . . . if some are victors and others vanquished?

I see nothing in this but the empty glamour of human glory." Rousseau, on the other hand, waxes indignant at this indifference to political glory, denouncing Christians because "they know better how to die than how to conquer."[18] The Revolution, which liked to conceive of itself in the neatly turned slogans of Rousseau, readily harnessed republican passion to military endeavor with mass conscription and the rhetoric of a nation in arms. Turning first on their king and then on their neighbors, the revolutionaries mobilized potent yearnings for empire and liberty.

The audacity of the Civil Constitution of the Clergy is testimony to the extent of revolutionary politicization. It shows the representatives of the people eager to take the church in hand and to assert their freedom, indeed their sovereignty, in the field of ecclesiastical organization. It shows a tendency, in clearing a new space for a *Civil* Constitution of the Clergy, to minimize that which is God's and to maximize that which is the people's. It shows a desire on the part of the people to participate actively in the life of the church as *lay* people. In short, it amounted to a crude intervention by a politicized people into the life of a church that was at home in a less politicized society and therefore felt threatened by this newfound determination of the people to take decisions for themselves and by themselves. The authors of the two key speeches justifying the Civil Constitution, Jean-Baptiste Treilhard and Armand-Gaston Camus, claimed with entirely democratic insolence that the Assembly could go even further. "A state can decide whether or not to permit a religion," wrote the former; "We certainly have the power to change religion," wrote the latter.[19] Political self-determination trumped dependence on the true God.

The Civil Constitution therefore faced the church with two particular challenges: the first was *homogenization*, a corollary of democratic equality; the second was *politicization*, bound up with the assertion of political sovereignty. Catholics as such were not opposed to national sovereignty. On the contrary, Gallican tradition predisposed them toward it. But from their point of view, national sovereignty was balanced by an integral relationship between church and state, by an identification of the state as essentially Catholic that was summed up in the slogan "une foi, une loi, un roi" (one faith, one law, one king) and in the epithet "Most Christian" that formed part of the royal title. In this perspective, it was the Revolution's repudiation of that Catholic identity that upset the theological and political balance and rendered it unacceptable. It was this new move on the part of the Revolution that explains the shift in Catholic political thought from the Gallicanism of Bossuet to the ultramontanism of Maistre.

All nations could reckon themselves "chosen" by God in some way or other. Since Christ, Israel no longer had a monopoly of divine election. However, even if all nations were "chosen," Israel alone could boast the promise and the covenant. As Fénelon rightly said to one of his many correspondents, "You tell me that God will protect France. But I ask you, where is that promised? Do you have any guarantee of miracles?"[20] From the Christian point of view, Fénelon was clearly correct. But only in the wake of the Revolution did Catholics truly realize it. In the midst of the revolutionary persecutions, the feeling took hold that God no longer protected France in the same way and that French national life was corrupt. The identification of France with Israel and of the king of France with King David lost all credibility.

The Autonomy of the Temporal Power in Relation to the Church

In 1682, at the high tide of absolutism, the Assembly of the Clergy issued a "Declaration of the Clergy of France on Ecclesiastical Power," whose first article read as follows:

> Popes have received only spiritual power from God. Kings and princes are not subject to ecclesiastical power in temporal matters. They cannot be deposed by virtue of the power of the head of the church, nor can their subjects be released from their oaths of allegiance.

After this declaration was issued, no ecclesiastical authority (pope, council, or bishop) had any direct or indirect temporal power either to depose a prince or to release subjects from their obligations of obedience. This constituted "political Gallicanism," the doctrine of the French monarchy: the king of France held his kingdom from God alone and recognized no superior on earth. Though as a Catholic he was a subject of the pope, as a sovereign he owed the papacy nothing.

Despite being condemned by the Holy See, this doctrine did not cause French Catholics any problems. Indeed, the fact that a doctrine condemned by the Holy See could be held so resolutely by French Catholics is itself the best illustration of what Gallicanism meant. Some articles in the 1682 declaration were contentious, but not the first, for in France there was a strong vein of hostility toward theories that ascribed direct or indirect temporal power to the pope. The Gallican position was that papal jurisdiction was entirely spiritual and that the scope of papal action did not extend outside the spiritual domain.[21] Clerics—even the Jesuits, who were in theory the most committed to papal authority—were of one accord on the monarch's total autonomy in the temporal sphere.[22]

As its name would suggest, political Gallicanism operated on statist or royalist principles. For the officials of the parlements, lawyers dedicated to royal service, it was a matter of defending national sovereignty against papal "interference." The felt need to keep the French church under the control of the secular power out of sheer political prudence is clearly set out in the following extract from a Gallican text published in 1723:

We believe that the doctrine of the ultramontanes tends to disturb the common peace and to put the life of the sovereign in jeopardy. Discontented subjects will call the prince before an ecclesiastical court. If, once excommunicated and deposed, he continues to exercise his power, then according to them this will make him a tyrant and a usurper. Then theologians will step forward to argue that it is not simply permissible but positively meritorious to free the people from his control. And desperate fanatics will put their teaching into practice. There are plenty of examples.[23]

Gallicanism was pretty much a given, for it was intimately related to the birth, growth, and self-assertion of the French crown and state. Aware of the dangers that could arise from conflict between church and state, Gallicans made a sharp distinction between the spiritual and the temporal order even as they asserted the supremacy of the state in the temporal. They insisted on the independence of the civil power from the spiritual.

It is easy to see why the French monarchy saw advantage in promoting a political Gallicanism that asserted royal and state sovereignty so decisively. But why was the Assembly of the Clergy so willing to subscribe to such a theory? The answer is summed up in a single phrase: *French Catholics tended to see no need for Roman threats or sanctions in order to behave in a Christian manner.* This is the impression given by the most illuminating author of that era, Bossuet (1627–1704), who not only drew up the declaration of 1682 but also justified it in a substantial work that was itself condemned by the papacy, the *Defensio declarationis.* Bossuet is the point of reference for Gallicanism, the writer who provided its fullest and most coherent theological justification.

Bossuet dedicated an entire and eloquent chapter of his *Politique tirée de l'Écriture sainte* (Politics derived from Holy Scripture) to the subject of "love of country," going so far as to say that "there can be no happiness for a good citizen when his country lies in ruin."[24] There could be no better illustration of Bossuet's own profound patriotism than his magnificent prose, which remains among the most accomplished examples of the French—the *national* language—of the classical era.[25]

In Bossuet's view, "the Gallican church has produced the most learned, the most holy, and the most illustrious bishops there have ever been."[26] The scriptural roots of his political theology were sunk into the books of Kings at the expense even of most of the rest of the Old Testament, not to mention the New. He did not dwell overmuch on the political implications of Genesis, Exodus, or the Babylonian Captivity, or on that of the Crucifixion or of the Apocalypse (Revelation). Bossuet saw in the absolute monarchy of Louis XIV the biblical kingship of David and Solomon, for he had a strong sense of the history of France as that of a chosen people, an elect nation. France was indeed, for him, "the eldest daughter of the church," and therefore had a crucial place in the divine plan: French history was written by the hand of God. The identification of Louis XIV with the kings of Israel arose not from anachronism but from an absolute assurance of divine election, which put the autonomy of the nation-state on a theological footing.[27] An elect nation could be envisaged as enjoying guarantees that protected it from error at a fundamental level. Upheld directly by God, such a nation was sure of its ground in its essential orientation: it had no need of the helmsmanship of an Italian pope.

Bossuet was the theoretician of absolutism who worked out a theology that marked the coming of age of the state. Scion of an eminent office-holding dynasty distinguished by its loyalty to the crown, he furnished a political theology for a state that had attained full self-consciousness: *l'Etat, c'est moi* (Louis XIV). The comparison of the king with King David had been used at the time of Philip the Fair to assert royal sovereignty, and it was to emphasize their indisputable authority that the French kings had, since the fifteenth century, adopted the style "Most Christian." The assertion of the sanctity of the French nation and of its kings yoked together two complementary logics, one religious, and one political. The confessional character of the state brought the benefit of harmonizing a political commitment to national autonomy with a religious commitment to the public espousal of the Gospel message.

Called by God to his royal duties and crowned in Reims Cathedral, Louis XIV did not worry about the divine right of the pope because he had a divine right of his own to set against it.[28] The concept of the "divine right of kings" had two complementary elements.

First, it served to subordinate the church to the state. In conferring sacral status upon the temporal power, it allowed it to rival the spiritual power. "The royal throne is the throne not of a man but of God himself," wrote Bossuet.[29] How could any bishop or theologian have the impudence to contest that kind of authority? As the new David, the king felt no need to bend the knee before the Successor of Peter. To assert its own authority, the secular power had to distinguish itself from the ecclesiastical power, but it needed a complex strategy to achieve this. Essentially, the state had to imitate the church that it aimed to dominate, investing itself with a comparable aura of sacrality. The jurists who laid the foundations of the modern state did so by refusing to allow the church a monopoly of God and grace. They traced temporal and spiritual power alike to the same divine origin in order to prevent the spiritual power from claiming any absolute or exclusive primacy. They blurred the distinction between priest and layman in the person of the king and sacralized royal power in order to set secular power on an equal footing with ecclesiastical. In effect, the monarchy stole the papacy's clothes, transforming the mysteries of the church (*arcana ecclesiae*) into mysteries of state (*arcana imperii*).[30] Secular power and religious authority exchanged attributes in a paradoxical process through which differentiation was achieved by imitation.

Second, the divine right of kings held the crown and the state in a firmly Christian orbit. It was precisely a *divine* right, heavy with Christian symbolism and specific constraints. The divine right of kings did not release the king from his obligations as a Christian. On the contrary, his temporal supremacy made moral and spiritual demands upon him. The church reached an understanding with absolutism partly because it had no real choice, but partly because the state's political supremacy was balanced by its commitment to the church.

> A Christian state is itself a portion of the universal church spread through-out the world, and in entering that church the state undertakes to obey its fundamental laws, which exist irrespective of that state's membership.[31]

The Gallican church could tolerate the protection and control of the state precisely because the state recognized Catholicism as its official religion. In affirming the intimate relationship between the spiritual and the temporal domains, the king was obliged to be orthodox in his theology. He gave his backing to canon law. He stood, sword in hand, at the entry to the sanctuary, sworn to uphold the liberty of the church and to banish heretics from his dominions. He endowed priests and monasteries. For the church, the "secular arm" guaranteed the defense of the faith and obedience to the rules of ecclesiastical discipline. The laws of the church in effect formed part of the laws of the state: what the church judged evil, the state judged evil.

When the archbishop of Reims poured the holy oil onto the forehead of the king, he made him the Lord's Anointed, the Vicar of Christ in temporal affairs, the "bishop in externals."

> The anointing consummates the action, because the people want none but a Christian and a Catholic king.[32]

At the moment of consecration, the archbishop asked the king, "Do you wish to be the guardian and protector of the churches and their ministers?" The reply was, "I wish it."[33] Church and state subsisted in perfect harmony, because their members were the same. Whoever was outside the Catholic Church was by that very fact excluded from public life. Heresy was punishable by the state as a crime akin to treason. Parish priests kept registers that recorded the condition of subjects. Ecclesiastical tribunals regulated matrimonial matters, because marriage was regarded as a sacrament.

The assertion of the sanctity of the French nation and of its kings yoked together two complementary logics, one religious and one political. Gallicanism had the advantage of reconciling, up to a point, royal and Christian imperatives in the love of country. Exponents of political Gallicanism could hardly be indifferent to the welfare of a church that was so integral to the history of the nation. Exponents of ecclesiastical Gallicanism, likewise, could not be indifferent to the body politic that guaranteed the social context within which the French church worked. Of course, French kings were not saints (or not often), and there was no shortage of tension between church and state. Kaleidoscopic maneuvers saw ultramontanism and the three varieties of Gallicanism (emphasizing respectively the rights of kings, parlements, and bishops) spin in an ever-shifting pattern of short-lived alliances and rivalries. Their struggles were often ugly, but never without rules. Gallicanism as a system maintained a delicate balance. The bishops secured more for the papacy than the lawyers were happy to concede, and they granted more to the king than was to the liking of the curial theologians at Rome.[34] If the pope had some grievance with the king, then he could refuse to fill vacant episcopal sees. If the king was unhappy with the pope, then he could stonewall papal bulls and decrees, which could not take effect in France until registered by the Parlement and formally "received" by the episcopate.

The papacy's chief concern was to ensure that the Gallican church did not declare unilateral independence, and papal policy therefore combined stern warnings with endless patience. The French kings, for their part, had little to gain from schism. The Concordat of Bologna (1516) had long since given them most of what they wanted. Francis I's victory at Marignano in 1515, which left him in control of the duchy of Milan, had put him in an excellent negotiating position with respect to Leo X. The Gallican church stretched its virtual autonomy from Rome as far as it could without actually sacrificing its Catholic credentials, for it aspired to be genuinely Catholic as well as genuinely national. The inevitable disputes were played out on the tacit understanding that nobody wanted an outright breach.[35] The religious and political authorities were too closely connected not to feel, despite their incessant squabbles, the overwhelming importance of mutual accommodation. Not even the most rigorist of popes could afford to lose the largest, liveliest, and most learned church of that age.

The opening article of the declaration of 1682 might have seemed to imply a total separation of religion from politics, so robust was its assertion of the autonomy of the temporal power within its own domain. But in practice the papacy had little cause for concern. In a report of March 1682 on the issuing of the declaration, the papal nuncio made this revealing comment on the first of its four articles:

> I doubt whether, under the present circumstances, one could find a single Frenchman who would not accept it. Yet, all the same, if a heretic were (God forbid) to become king, then a good many of those who now uphold the independence of the temporal power would soon start to insist on the exact opposite.[36]

French Catholics may have recognized in law the temporal autonomy of the king, but they unambiguously reserved the right to challenge the legitimacy of a monarch who fell into heresy. The independence of the temporal power protected the king against the pope all the more effectively because it did not separate politics from religion. The point of Gallicanism was not to marginalize the church but to give the political life of the nation-state a role in the economy of salvation. Bossuet dwelled so emphatically upon the Old Testament precisely because he found in it the model for a people and a political system under the guidance of God.

The intimate union of church and state deftly combined religious and political logic to keep the partners together. It guaranteed a degree of stability. The absolutist confessional state drew its strength from the blending of national self-interest with the religious sense of a divine calling. Despite their mutual differences, political and religious varieties of Gallicanism were perfectly suited to the era of Catholic absolutism. If he was a Gallican, the Catholic was therefore nevertheless a patriot and felt no tension between his patriotic duties and his religious obligations. The bone marrow of Gallicanism was the identification of Catholics with the life of the nation. The public role of the church, which lent a Catholic tone to the entire nation, nurtured this identification.

Catholics accepted the autonomy of the temporal power on condition that this autonomy was balanced by the loyalty of the temporal power to the church. So, after that lengthy digression, it is easy to see why the Revolution caused such immense problems. By separating the state from the church to some extent, it upset the delicate balance at the heart of absolutism. It shattered the theological and political economy of the Ancien Regime. It called into question the covenant that held political and religious interests in balance. The "patriot" clerics who were sympathetic to the civil constitution harked back to Bossuet and the concept of France as an elect nation, but for others the civil constitution posed notorious difficulties.[37]

The Constituent Assembly, which had directed the French Revolution during its opening phase, had gradually stripped the king of his absolute power, transforming a king by divine right into a constitutional monarch. Article 3 of the Declaration of the Rights of Man states that "the foundation of all sovereignty resides essentially in the nation." But in putting an end to absolute monarchy, the Assembly was at the same time putting an end to the politics of religious uniformity. And article 10 therefore stipulated that "no one can be troubled for their opinions, not even in religion." A decree of 24 December 1789 made non-Catholic Christians eligible for any public or military office, and this measure was extended to Jews on 27 September 1791.

Under the Ancien Regime, disputes between church and state nevertheless rested on a fundamental accord: the officials of the state were all Christians. Church and state comprised the same people. Civil authorities were independent of the ecclesiastical authorities, but they had to reach an understanding with each other because both sides belonged at once to the church and to the nation. Tussles between kings and bishops were, if not quite family affairs, then at least quarrels among insiders. After article 10, however, church and state were no longer strictly coterminous. While there was as yet no formal separation along the lines of 1905, there was a measure of disengagement. The laws of the church no longer had a purchase on the state. With the acknowledgment of religious freedom, the laity as such was no longer necessarily "on the inside." Now there were also lay people "on the outside."

The entire structure of the Ancien Regime was thus called into question. The king's power was no longer derived directly from God but from the nation and its representatives. Full membership of the body politic was no longer predicated on the Catholic faith. Church and state were no longer composed of the same people. The French were no longer, at one and the same time, subjects of the Prince and sons or daughters of the church. The church lost its fiscal privileges and its right to petition over its grievances. Its vows were no longer enforceable in public law. Matrimonial matters were now for civil tribunals. Heresy no longer constituted a crime. Canon law had nothing to do with the state. Thus, the recognition of religious freedom entailed a degree of disestablishment for the church. Despite the repeated requests of the clergy, the Constituent Assembly refused to declare the Roman Catholic faith the state religion, first in February 1790 and then again in April. In justifying this, one of the Assembly members remarked that "the new principles of the constitution require us to show due consideration for the freedom it grants in religious opinions."[38] The vote on article 10, six months later, prevented anyone from exaggerating the confessional character of the state.

For Joseph de Maistre (1753–1821), the clash between church and Revolution was no accident. It was inscribed in the very essence of the Revolution: excessive self-assertion. France was recreating itself not in the image of God but in rebellion against him:

> Forgetfulness (I will not say contempt) of the Supreme Being brings down an irrevocable anathema on those human deeds that bear its mark.

This "forgetfulness" was nothing other than the acknowledgment of religious freedom, seen in this perspective as a grave mistake. Revelation was now just one opinion among many, competing with them on equal terms. The basis of the social order was thus jeopardized by what would soon be termed "theological liberalism": the reduction of faith to a matter of personal choice whose content was diminished to the extent that the individual subject gained the upper hand. The insistence on political freedom, at both the individual and the collective level, was a challenge to the very basis of the authority of the church: it was the hubris of revolt. "The distinguishing feature of the French Revolution," wrote Maistre, "what makes it an event unique in history, is that it is evil, radically evil."[39] The Revolution was not to be celebrated: it had to be expiated.

Maistre positioned himself in the lineage of Bossuet, regarding France as a chosen nation—though chosen, now, to suffer for the sins of Europe. In his *Considérations sur la France* (1796), he expounded the sufferings of France amid persecution and political disaster in terms of the loving chastisement of a justly wrathful God. However, this new version of French exceptionalism itself threatened to undermine the classical order. As long as the French church could claim, in Bossuet's formulation, "the most learned, the most holy, and the most illustrious bishops there have ever been," it had a fair claim to its autonomy from Rome. But once national apostasy became its distinguishing feature, its claim to national ecclesiastical autonomy began to look less plausible.[40]

Once the revolutionary state had turned away from Christianity, French Catholics were not prepared to turn with it. Instead, they found another focus for unity: the papacy, pretty much the only institution that could fill the void left by the state. The Gallican church had lost its state role. It no longer enjoyed the political credit that enabled it to protect the nation against injustice and breach of God's law. The nation, in turn, no longer looked to the church for moral guidance or to furnish meaning for its political existence. France was no longer "the eldest daughter of the church" and was therefore no more to play, as such, a central role in the Christian world. Exploring in greater depth the ideas that he had sketched out in *Considérations sur la France*, Maistre worked out a thorough critique of Gallicanism (*De l'Eglise gallicane*, 1821) and a telling defense of ultramontanism (*Du pape*, 1819).

The revolutionaries certainly appreciated the political advantages accruing from the close association of church and state: witness the Civil Constitution of the Clergy itself, which sought to perpetuate the old link in a new guise. But they did not mean to put that association at the heart of their new order, and that was the fundamental problem facing Catholics. Why did the revolutionaries reject the old alliance of church and state? There were two reasons. First, they did not wish to pay the price in religious intolerance and persecution. Many revolutionaries had unhappy memories of the Jansenist persecutions or, worse still, of the persecutions of Protestants. Second, they felt that purely spiritual constraints upon the freedom of action of an absolute monarch were not an adequate guarantee of good governance: there had to be temporal constraints as well. But before considering this second point, it is worth dwelling a while on the first.

The Alliance of Church and State as a Matrix of Intolerance

Louis XIV had persecuted the Jansenists because of the unpleasant scent of liberty that hung about their movement. He had successfully lobbied Pope Clement XI for a papal bull to condemn them: *Unigenitus* (1713). In the wake of that bull, the Jansenists became opponents of both absolutism and the papacy. They therefore argued both for the primacy of the temporal power (against the pope, as author of the bull) and for limits on the royal prerogative (against absolutism). Some historians have traced one of the roots of the French Revolution itself to the alliance of Gallicanism and liberalism that marked the Jansenist movement.[41]

The persecution of the Jansenists was not Louis XIV's finest hour, but neither was it the greatest blot on his name. For in 1685 he had revoked the Edict of Nantes, and unleashed the "dragonnades" against recalcitrant Huguenots. Protestants fled the realm in huge numbers, and France lost a substantial fraction of its commercial elite. The kingdom threw itself into a policy devoid of humanity. The France of Louis XIV yearned for greatness, but there was no greatness in this. And the policy posed some fundamental questions. If the more Catholic a king was, the more absolute he was, could he be king at all if he was not Catholic? Were Catholics obliged to recognize the sovereignty of Protestant kings? Again, if the Catholic character of the monarchy was jeopardized by the existence of a Protestant minority, was it not necessary for the nation to persecute that minority in order to safeguard its Catholic identity and thus also to defend the sovereignty that went along with it?

The Edict of Nantes, promulgated in 1598, had extended freedom of conscience to those of the Reformed faith, along with a limited freedom of worship and a measure of political equality with Catholics. These concessions were guaranteed militarily by the allocation to the Huguenots of a hundred fortresses and strongholds. There were also judicial guarantees in the form of "bipartite tribunals" composed of both Catholics and Protestants. The Edict of Nantes had two slightly different aspects. Primarily it was an edict of toleration, providing for peaceful coexistence between two religions that had been locked in mortal combat. But it was also one of the cornerstones of absolutism, for in effect it raised the king above both sides. As legitimacy could not come from below, from the concord of Christian subjects, it had to come from above, from the Prince, whose will was therefore made supreme. The preamble to the edict emphasized the concept of the state, which it set out to restore to "its original wealth, power, and splendor." The edict embodied the political philosophy of Jean Bodin, whose *Six livres de la République* (1576) offered ideas for the bolstering of the state that were taken up by royal publicists from the 1580s. Toleration and absolutism could be separated only with some difficulty, because it was the raising of the king above the two sides that made him a kind of umpire, capable of keeping the peace between them. With the religious unity of the nation shattered, the sacredness of the body politic was realized only in its head. In the absence of religious unity, it was for the head alone to sustain political unity.[42]

Although the edict of 1598 made the state in certain respects more the guarantor of public order than the guardian of the faith, the mystical aura which allowed the crown to carry out its public functions retained a deeply religious tinge: the crown claimed divine right. Absolutism combined a political logic that subordinated the urge for religious uniformity to the political imperative of peace with a religious logic that grounded the primacy of political considerations on a basis that was itself religious. The tension between these two logics meant that the Edict of Nantes was always liable to be called into question. Absolute monarchy, precisely because it was absolute, labored under no self-denying ordinance in matters of faith: rather the contrary. The Revocation of the Edict of Nantes in 1685 was not so much the reversal as the dialectical converse of its original logic. Placed over and above society by the edict, the king was for that very reason in a position to rescind even the edict itself. Although the edict presupposed a degree of separation between church and state, the absolutism that it engendered enabled the king to set the religious course of the nation. The Edict of Nantes rested liberalism on a foundation of absolutism. Louis XIV simply deployed the absolutism against the liberalism. His purpose? "La gloire," his own glory: he dreamed of the conversion of the heretics.

Despite the brutality of the "dragonnades" and the inhumanity of a policy that forced "converts" to receive sacraments in which they scarcely believed, not a single leading Catholic spoke out to condemn the revocation. The church backed a policy that it thought was in the interests of the souls entrusted to its care. If some bishops, such as Bossuet, forbade their priests to make new converts take communion "in a spirit of hypocrisy and dissimulation, without devotion or respect,"[43] this was not out of humanity but for fear of profaning the sacrament. For all that Bossuet was more concerned than Machiavelli for moral edification, he had not a word of criticism for Louis, whom he thought worthy of comparison to Constantine or Theodosius. Machiavelli, indeed, had shown more humanity in similar circumstances, denouncing the "holy cruelty" which had ordered the expulsion of the Moors from Spain.[44]

The lack of humanity of which Bossuet is just one example alerts us to the blind spot at the core of the absolutist confessional state. The identification of France as a new elect nation went so far that it precluded awareness of extremes of evil that it therefore accepted unwittingly. For Bossuet, Gallicanism was paving the way for the conversion of the Protestants. The return of the Reformed community to the true church would be made all the easier by the privileges the bishops claimed in their relations with the papacy. "Depapalized" by Gallicanism, the French Catholic Church should seem more appealing to the Huguenots, who had never had much love for Rome. From this point of view, Gallicanism ought to have struck Huguenots as the acceptable face of Catholicism. But, from another point of view, Gallicanism could mean religious uniformity and persecution.[45] By yoking French national identity so tightly to Catholicism, Gallicanism raised the stakes of intolerance by implying that Protestantism had no place whatsoever in the king's dominions. "In those days, a man's first duty was to be religious, with obedience to the Prince a close second. The tension between these two obligations caused huge problems. Thus the Prince, be he Catholic or Protestant, wanted religious conformity from his subjects so that the two duties would become mutually reinforcing. Subjects wanted a Prince of their own religion so that they would not face a painful choice between two rival authorities."[46]

The Revocation of the Edict of Nantes involved a complex of political and religious considerations that can scarcely be disentangled. The security of the state was not threatened by the survival of the Protestant minority, which was no longer in any position to put up armed resistance, and which, in any case, had regularly demonstrated its loyalty to the crown. But the king, at the head of the most powerful and prestigious nation in the Western world, would brook no opposition of any kind. The spirit of liberty that marked Jansenism served to render it suspect in his eyes even though the Jansenists professed absolute loyalty to the Catholic Church. Louis XIV was a monarch, and he intended to be so "absolutely": the Huguenots were the victims sacrificed on the altar of absolutism.

The Revocation of the Edict of Nantes shows that liberalism cannot successfully be based upon absolutism, because an absolute monarch is rarely liberal. It is unwise to leave the liberty of the subject hanging on the goodwill of a sole ruler. This was the truism that led the revolutionaries of 1789 to challenge absolute monarchy in demanding liberty. It was evident to them that the key to good government was not a confessional state but a stronger parliament in a system of political checks and balances. It seemed to them more rational and more effective to set constraints on the exercise of power by means of representative democracy than by the merely moral obligations of religion.

The Edict of Nantes had been made possible by emphasizing the primacy of the political. In his speech at the assembly of notables at Saint-Germain, which in 1562 promulgated one of the first edicts of pacification, Michel de l'Hospital had explained that "we are concerned here not *de constituenda religione, sed de constituenda respublica* [of settling religion, but of settling the state]: and many people may be *cives, qui non erunt Christiani* [citizens without being Christians]: someone who is excommunicated does not cease to be a citizen."[47] From 1570 onward, all the edicts of pacification invoked the same formula, inviting the French people to "live peacefully together as brothers, friends, and fellow citizens." Shared political interests made possible a truce between the warring parties and a degree of peace. Henry IV's apocryphal *bon mot*, "Paris is worth a Mass," demonstrates the primacy of politics over religion. The Edict of Nantes, then, asserted the autonomy of politics. But this declaration was ultimately inadequate because everything rested on the person of the monarch, as the revocation was to make clear. The revolutionary solution after 1789 was to make liberalism depend on a broadening of the base of politics, the politicization of the people, and in particular of the minorities, who were now given the chance to be heard and to defend their interests. This was the revolutionary option: what we now call "liberal democracy."

The Inadequacy of Spiritual Constraints and the Need for Temporal Constraints

The affiliation of the crown and state to a church had a cost: intolerance. But its advantages had been thought to outweigh its disadvantages, for in theory it placed upon the monarch spiritual constraints which should have guided him on the path of good governance.

Before the Revolution, canon law was one of the sources of civil law. Divine law was one of the sources of positive law. Interpretation of these sources obviously took place within the national context but also within the context of the universal Catholic Church, which therefore imposed real constraints on the absolutist system. For Richelieu, for Louis XIV, and for Bossuet, Gallicanism could never go to the extreme of schism, a prospect that would have horrified all three. The political logic of national autonomy could never justify the transmutation of Gallicanism into a French version of Anglicanism. The assertion of temporal independence did not mean religious separation. France stayed within the universal church and accepted the authority of general councils.

The great Gallican declaration of 1682 comprised four articles. The first pair concerned political Gallicanism, while the latter pair were more a matter of ecclesiastical Gallicanism.

> These four articles came down to two principal points: the temporal power was independent of the spiritual power; and the position of the pope within the church was not so supreme as to put him above canon law, to put his determinations regarding the faith beyond question, or to render him in all cases immune from earthly judgment.[48]

Ecclesiastical Gallicanism was not a matter of politics (in the narrow sense) so much as of a specific ecclesiology: according to the teaching of the Council of Constance, a general council was superior to the pope, and the pope was not infallible in questions of faith unless his determinations were approved by the bishops, who had as much right as he to pass judgment in such matters. The declaration deployed conciliarism against ultramontanism. Conciliarism had two aspects: one particularist or national, and the other universal. At the Council of Constance, voting had been carried out by "nation" in a way that made the council a sort of parliament of the temporal powers.[49] The French church envisaged itself as a relatively autonomous body, with the freedom of action appropriate to its prestige. Conciliarism took account of the nation as a political reality. However, it too remained within the ambit of the universal church, and the nationalist logic of absolutism was therefore moderated by spiritual constraints.

In making the monarchy akin to an ecclesiastical office, the jurists, theologians, and publicists of the Ancien Regime set the Prince above both his people and his nobles, but at the same time they fixed him within an essentially Christian moral universe. This can be seen in Bossuet, who certainly did not promote the liberties of the Gallican church in order to render it a mere tool in the hands of a cynical state. It can even be seen in Richelieu, who was far from being the unscrupulous Machiavellian of traditional portrayals. If Richelieu used religion to consolidate the authority of the state, he never lost sight of the Christian perspective and of the interests of the religion to which he was personally very deeply committed.[50] Louis XIV was certainly an absolute monarch, but in theological matters he knew that his role was that of pupil, not teacher. He remained a layman, a son of the church.

In the words of a historian of canon law, "It was, on the one hand, the nature of the theocratic office which supplied the strength of the king, but it was also, on the other hand, that same office which placed severe limitations on the king."[51] *Non est potestas nisi a Deo*, wrote Saint Paul, "There is no power but from God." Paul's bold statements in Romans 13 have generally been understood as inculcating the duty of obedience to civil authorities, but this obedience is predicated to a certain extent on the respect shown by the civil authorities themselves for divine and natural law. Even an author such as Bossuet, who sometimes seems too indulgent toward absolutism, insists on the moral and spiritual limits to royal power. The *Politique tirée de l'Ecriture sainte* was composed while Bossuet was responsible for the education of Louis XIV's son. It shows that he was anxious above all to instill in the future monarch a sense of his duty to God. The *Politique* stood squarely in the tradition of the "mirror for princes," reworked with a strongly anti-Machiavellian thrust to counter immorality and irreligion in politics.[52] There is nothing in it even remotely akin to the doctrine of *salus populi suprema lex* (the good of the people is the ultimate law). Bossuet justifies the state, but he does not justify *raison d'Etat*. Absolute monarchy, in his view, does not allow monarchs simply to do whatever they like (*ab legibus soluta*, bound by no laws). Kings remain bound by fundamental laws. Bossuet affirms the distinction between "absolute" and "arbitrary" power.[53] Absolute, paternalist, sacral—royal authority nevertheless remains subordinate both to reason and to revelation.

In showing that a political system could be derived from scripture, Bossuet sought to show that a good political system meant a Christian political system, and thus that Christianity was not so apolitical as Machiavelli had suggested. Toward the end of the dedication of the *Politique*, Bossuet announces with a fanfare that "those who believe piety is political weakness will be proved wrong." Book V of the *Politique* is of particular importance in this regard, for there Bossuet paints a picture of the prudence, skills, intelligence, powers of concentration, and insight into the human heart that are required in the ideal Prince:

> Under a skillful and well-advised Prince, nobody dares to do wrong. It is as though he is ever present, as though even thoughts . . . cannot be hidden from his gaze.[54]

Bossuet expatiates on the superior intellectual qualities of the wise, on the mental capacities that accompany the Christian virtues. In his hands, King David becomes considerably more pious than the Davids of other authors—such as Machiavelli, Bayle, and Voltaire.[55] So Bossuet insists, against Machiavelli, that the Prince has no need to sup with the devil.

That all changed with the Revolution. Thereafter the emphasis was on temporal, not spiritual constraints. Above all, the revolutionaries set out to establish representative government accompanied by a declaration of human and civic rights. The best way to bridle the power of the state was no longer through its confessional character, through the Christian moral education of the Prince and the recognition of the authority of general councils, but through empowering the legislature in order to control the executive. The best way to keep the government on the straight and narrow was to limit its role to the protection of private property and individual rights. This represented a radically new understanding and organization of political life.

This change raised a whole series of questions, which I list in no particular order. While the church had recognized the legitimacy of a state that accorded ~~privileged status~~, what reason did it have to recognize a state that no longer accorded it such privilege? Why should the faithful obey a state that was no longer bound by divine law or revelation? What was the metaphysical framework of a state when that framework was no longer provided by religion? What goals would it be pursuing if it was no longer pursuing goals set by the church? If "the principle of all sovereignty resides essentially in the nation," is the judgment of a nation necessarily more reliable than that of a church which reminded monarchs that they were answerable to God?

The deconfessionalization of the state has often been seen as one stage in the advent of "modernity," as a release from a dark and barren age. Many liberals of more or less secularist outlook were delighted to see the state released from the constraints of an official belief system. Notions of progress and of the rise of individual autonomy seemed natural concomitants of the secularization of the public sphere. But observations of this kind are somewhat one-sided. It is easy to forget that revelation imposed on the state moral constraints that served as guarantees for its citizens. By continually recalling the Gospel message, the church could restrain, hinder, or even thwart wicked plans, or policies that fell short of the demands of elementary justice. As I noted earlier, notwithstanding his absolutism, Bossuet was opposed to arbitrary government: he was an anti-Machiavellian. This is not to say that Christianity prevented injustice or tyranny. But it furnished a moral framework and substrate of fundamental laws from which a Christian state, to the extent that it remained Christian, could neither easily nor completely detach itself. This is a point that should be obvious to us of all people, after the era of totalitarian atheist regimes whose barbarity was part and parcel of their repudiation of Christianity. Such regimes sought to throw off not only the political shackles of pluralism and constitutional government but also the moral constraints of religion. The sense of the sacred which the church communicated brought with it a sense of moral limits. The secularization of the state seemed to offer it the potential for action without limits. Challenging the political or quasi-political role of the church opened the way to a potentially totalitarian political monism.

The ideologues of the Counter-Revolution were particularly alert to this danger. Unable to conceive of politics separate from religion, they could make no sense of the idea of political constraints that were not at the same time religious constraints. The revolutionary achievement struck them as essentially evil, not to say absurd. In their eyes, the Revolution simply opened the way for novel forms of tyranny, and they saw no cause for rejoicing in that. Joseph de Maistre felt keenly that the deconfessionalization of the state posed political questions that it did not answer: "Now . . . everything comes down to force, which is as much as to say despotism on one side or rebellion on the other—the divine stamp has been effaced."[56]

It was necessary to bridle the state. Maistre admitted readily enough that in this the liberals were on firm ground. But in that case why talk of the rights of man rather than the rights of God? Why look to the fickle people rather than to the Holy See, which was so much more trustworthy?

> If it is absolutely necessary to set legal limits on sovereign power, I wish with all my heart that the interests of humanity would be entrusted to the Supreme Pontiff.[57]

A papal power of veto over the actions of sovereigns would be the best solution. It was wiser to require papal intervention to release subjects from their oath of allegiance than to let subjects decide for themselves, unless you actually wanted anarchy. Maistre bolstered his case with an argument from history: "Bamboozled by the propaganda of the *philosophes*, people think that popes spent all their time deposing princes," but this was not in fact the case.

Awe-struck by the momentous changes that the Revolution had set in train, Maistre saw no future in clinging on to Gallicanism, whether in its political or its ecclesiastical guise. So he looked to Rome for the moral and spiritual guidance that an apparently dechristianized state could no longer offer. He was surprised by what he saw as the inconsistency of the revolutionaries:

> I take the liberty of informing my contemporaries that there is a flat contradiction between their zeal for constitutionalism and their rancor toward the popes.[58]

His contemporaries were saying that it was essential to limit sovereignty and to be on guard against absolute power, that power had to be shared, and that inalienable human rights should be a counterpoise to state power. At the same time, they were stripping the church, and in particular the papacy, of effective power. For Maistre, these were contradictory impulses, as the best way to bridle the state was to trust the church. Maistre wanted to entrust the safeguarding of the interests of humanity to the papacy, or at least to a collaboration between papacy and monarchy:

> If the France of today, humbly submissive before divine authority, had received her excellent king at the hands of the Supreme Pontiff, do you not think that she would at this moment be somewhat more at peace with herself and with others?[59]

Representatives of the papacy ought to be involved in the great international congresses, and the pope should resume his role as arbitrator in international relations.

In his *Considérations sur la France*, Maistre sang the praises of the "ancient French constitution" and emphasized that the French monarchy had an intrinsically "theocratic element."[60] For him, the revolutionary urge to wipe the slate clean was essentially unhealthy, a way for the wicked to disencumber themselves of the conventions that formed the framework of all public life. He denounced the Enlightenment rationalism that sought to detach practical reason from the particularity of context, as if it were desirable, or even possible, to emancipate oneself from all national and religious traditions. For Maistre, no great institution was the product of a plan. It was not reason, but religion, that was fundamental. In doing away with privilege and utterly transforming their laws and their political system, the French were not so much casting off their yoke as tearing down their defenses. Those who established the republic had rushed ahead "with no idea what they were doing."

Joseph de Maistre condemned not the way that popular sovereignty was being used, but popular sovereignty as such. He condemned not the excesses, but the very principle, of democratic revolutions. He stood for religious constraints in preference to the purely rational political constraints advocated by the revolutionaries, for neither human rights nor representative government struck him as effective options. The reason for this was quite simply that Maistre did not believe in rational political constraints. For him, only religious constraints were real. Natural law and positive human law were simply inadequate: only divine law would do. His writings are therefore more exercises in political theology than political philosophy.

The French Revolution through the Lens of Political Theology

For the revolutionaries, freedom was the human vocation. It had to be presumed that humanity was worthy of this high calling and was therefore good. Rousseau, the high priest of this theory, rewrote the biblical narrative of the Fall. It was not "necessary to suppose humanity wicked by nature when one could trace the origin and rise of wickedness."[61] Evil had entered the world not because any particular man or woman had intended it but by a disastrous mistake, the establishment of private property, which entailed a choice between self and others, and led to an endless series of divisive mutual comparisons. Above all, evil had not entered the world through one man, Adam, but through the social order. Man was innocent: society was guilty. We were evil because we had been *alienated by society*. Evil came not from individuals but from society, so it was society that had to be changed. Evil was to be eradicated not by means of edifying sermons, nor by a social pressure that would ensure a minimum moral conformity, nor yet by an asceticism that would strangle unruly passions at birth, but by social transformation. Rousseau wrote his *Confessions*, but, in contrast to Saint Augustine, his intention was not self-reproach but self-justification. His explanatory system "functioned chiefly as a means of exculpation, as a plea of not guilty."[62] The root of evil was not the individual's tendency to seek equality with God but the tendency to compare oneself with others. The crucial relationship was no longer plotted on the vertical axis, with the Creator, but on the horizontal axis, with other people.

Alienated by society, people had to analyze their alienation and then exorcise it. Human beings were malleable, heavily dependent on their social context, and were therefore perfectible, by education or by revolution. Rousseau's big idea was that social hierarchy had to be abolished, that the inequalities which fostered limitless competition and loathsome self-love had to be eradicated. A regime of equality would prevent people from falling prey to the vanity that made them wicked and unhappy.

The counter-revolutionaries flatly contradicted this analysis. Examining human evil, they asked why one should grant liberty to those who would make the worst use of it. They did not dream of transforming society but took humanity as it was—or, at least, as they saw it—that is, as radically corrupted by original sin. In his *Examen d'un écrit de Jean-Jacques Rousseau*, Joseph de Maistre wrote:

> It is impossible, man being what he is, that he should not be governed, for a being at once social and wicked must be kept under the yoke.[63]

People were too wicked to be left at liberty, too perverse for it to be worth even consulting them, let alone making government depend on their consent. Maistre harped on the corruption of the will and human depravity in order to justify firm government and the absolute state. To the reactionaries, all authority was good, simply by virtue of existing: rulers were good, people were bad. What society needed most of all was neither liberty nor equality but authority, to ensure order from the top down. The idea of representative government promoting freedom and equality struck them as outlandish and unreal. A robust authoritarian regime was self-evidently preferable.

The objection, of course, was obvious. What was to preserve government itself from this universal corruption and depravity? Who was to guard the guardians? If all people were wicked, what miracle could keep the ruler from wickedness? Maistre was well aware of this problem, because he himself raised it against Machiavelli:

> The vile and abominable system of Machiavelli . . . has just one problem: how can one murderer stop another?[64]

If all people are evil, then so is the Prince! What good, then, is authoritarian government? Maistre's reply was summed up in one word: God. Where Machiavelli ruled out theocracy, Maistre maintained that all power was ultimately theocratic. God gave a guarantee to duly constituted authorities, which enabled them to bring a modicum of order to a fundamentally disordered world. Unlike the people, the ruler was capable of good, because God conferred this capacity as a special privilege on the powers of this world.

Although affirming the political dimension of papal authority tended to undermine the nationalist theory of the divine right of kings, Maistre was always anxious to avoid this implication. He had not thrown over Gallicanism in order to cut God out of the process of instituting kings. On the contrary, he retained the theory of divine right. However, he did this not so as to preserve the autonomy of the temporal order but so as to keep the authority of the state firmly within bounds marked out by the church.

> The Supreme Pontiff does not contravene the doctrine of divine right when releasing subjects from their oath of allegiance. Rather, he emphasizes that sovereignty is a sacred and divine authority that cannot be controlled except by another divine authority, albeit one of a higher order.[65]

For Maistre, authority was always ultimately divine in origin, and the relationships between different authorities resolved into a hierarchy of the sacred. In a fallen world shot through with original sin and dominated by evil, only the church and its authority could provide a guarantee, a sure and solid basis for order. In Maistre's thought, Catholic apologetics was inseparable from social realism. The "good Christian" and the "loyal subject" were two sides of one coin.

Reason without the aid of revelation was not an adequate guide. "What are we, feeble and blind as we are? What is this flickering light we call reason?" Our guide through life could not be reason alone, left to its own devices, but only reason in close association with revelation and thus with the church, the guardian of revelation. As Maistre explained in his *Considérations sur la France*, written in opposition to the Revolution, "All conceivable human institutions rest on a religious basis, or else they pass away. Their strength and durability depend on how far they are *divinized*, if we may put it like that."

> Politics and religion merge into one another. The priest and the legislator can be distinguished only with difficulty. Political institutions consist primarily in religious rituals and sessions.[66]

Following in the tradition of Maistre, Schmitt gave the title "political theology" to a book in which he set out a position akin to Maistre's, insisting on the political character of religion and on the religious character of politics. Politics and religion were virtually commutable or interchangeable. That was why, for another counter-revolutionary, the Vicomte de Bonald, a regular correspondent of Maistre's, "the revolution shaking Europe is much more religious than political; or, rather, in its politics, it aims at nothing more than religion."[67]

> Religion is the rationale of every society, for without it there is no rationale for either authority or duty. Religion is thus the constitutive principle of every society.[68]

In a similar vein, the Spanish author Donoso Cortès wrote that "every political or social truth is ultimately reducible to a theological truth."[69]

The autonomy of secular governments had to be confined to purely temporal affairs. In everything else their actions had to be subordinate to the supernatural ends of society, of which the church alone was the competent judge. Even if the state was not merely a tool in the hands of the church, even if the church did not directly appoint the agents of temporal power, even if canon law did not necessarily take priority over civil law, a harmonious relationship between divine and human law nevertheless remained indispensable. It was for the church, which was endowed with a special competence to judge even matters of this world, to guide the making of laws, to control education, and to furnish divine sanction for princely and governmental power.

Maistre, forcibly struck by the power of human passions and the depressing pageant of human history, did not believe that society could be founded on reason alone. The principle of political life was found not in rational argument but in received opinion and dogma. The counter-revolutionaries had nothing but contempt for the philosophical projects of those who reckoned themselves "enlightened":

> Human reason alone—what they, without knowing what they are talking about, call "philosophy"—cannot take the place of the foundations that they, again without knowing what they are talking about, call superstitious. Their "philosophy" is in fact an essentially destructive and disintegrative force.[70]

The counter-revolutionaries saw only an idle dream in the Enlightenment project for a society based on Reason. They flatly denied that humanity had "come of age" or "reached the age of reason."[71] Influenced by illuminism and by the theosophy of Saint-Martin, Maistre was not convinced that the people had challenged the authority of the priests in order to rely on their own unaided judgment. The secular order required a sacred foundation. Relegating religion to the private sphere threatened the social cohesion of the entire nation. Even assuming that the violent dechristianization of autumn 1793 did not reveal the inmost essence of the revolutionary movement—and few enough of the Catholic reactionaries would concede even that—the fact remained that the revolutionaries all agreed on the principles of 1789, and it was those principles that had overthrown the political and juridical position of the church.

For those members of the reactionary movement of which Maistre was the spokesman, the liberal separation of church and state was a scandal and a cause of anomie. The secularization of the state seemed to them impossible, for it meant an attempt to separate two things that could scarcely be clearly distinguished even on a theoretical level: religion and politics. Religious toleration seemed equally indefensible. For Bonald, "there can be no doubt that the toleration of godless men and their godless opinions, not to mention the patronage that has been extended to them for the past fifty years, has been, even on the merely political level, the primary cause of our national misfortunes."[72] Rulers ought to profess religion publicly, and their laws should punish irreligion and offenses against ecclesiastical discipline. What counter-revolutionaries found most offensive about the secularization of the state during the Revolution was that it deprived people of their only reliable guide in social and political life.

> When one reflects on the facts of human history; when one considers that all human institutions, from the great empires that mark the epochs of the world down to the humblest little club or confraternity, have a divine foundation, and that human power, left to its own devices, can confer upon its works but a false and fleeting existence; what are we then to make of the new France and the power that has given rise to it? I, for one, shall never be brought to believe that nothingness can be fruitful.[73]

The idea of a state without religion was to them just a monstrous and unnatural fiction, and in separating religious allegiance from political allegiance, toleration ran counter to elementary common sense. "Jews cannot be, and, no matter what, never shall be citizens in a Christian society without becoming Christians," wrote Bonald, forging an amalgam of Catholic antiliberalism and anti-Judaism that would prove distressingly successful.[74] Toleration was not a virtue but a vice. The Revocation of the Edict of Nantes was entirely justified, as religious freedom merely allowed heresy to prosper and religious indifference to spread.[75]

Louis XIV had been right to banish the Protestants but wrong in his Gallicanism. Maistre's mistrust of Gallicanism was integral to his political theology. For in asserting the autonomy of the temporal sphere, Gallicanism challenged the very notion of political theology. Maistre did not wait until the 1810s to become an ultramontane. He was developing his "antidemocratic and anti-Gallican thinking" as early as 1791, in reaction to the opening phases of the Revolution.[76] He took issue at one and the same time with democracy, Gallicanism and what would soon be called liberalism, all of which presupposed a natural dimension that could not be reduced to a supernatural (i.e., religious) dimension. In the interests of political order, Gallicans claimed that there was a clear-cut distinction between the temporal and the spiritual. Maistre met them head on, doing all he could to hold together what they insisted on putting asunder.

For Maistre, the revolutionary state was not a state that was indifferent to religion or incompetent to deal with it. Because human social reality was founded on religion, the assertion of religious neutrality on the part of the state was inherently mendacious, a mere mask for anti-Catholicism. Maistre wavered between four diverse explanations of events—atheism, Protestantism, Satan, and divine chastisement—but all four had one thing in common: a deeply religious character.

"Atheism," he wrote, "has in our times bound itself to the most energetically active principle, namely the spirit of revolution."[77] Counter-revolutionaries were prone to dwell on the more or less clandestine role in all this of men of letters, freemasons, intellectuals, and other such miscreants.[78]

But Maistre also aired the theory that the Revolution was a Protestant plot. The revolutionary state was not being "deconfessionalized" but "reconfessionalized," in the direction of a Protestantism whose insistence on the right of individual private judgment of scripture was the taproot of liberalism. In his *Réflexions sur la protestantisme dans ses rapports avec la souveraineté* (Reflections on the relationship between Protestantism and sovereignty, 1798), Maistre denounced Protestantism as not just a religious but a political heresy: it undermined respect for sovereignty and authority and fostered a rebellious spirit. For Maistre, "when authority commands, there are only three possible responses: obedience, remonstration, and rebellion—the last of these is called 'heresy' in the spiritual domain, and 'revolution' in the temporal."[79] Protestantism, like the Revolution, rejected lawfully constituted authority. Maistre saw Protestantism and democracy as closely related errors. The Protestant concept of "private judgment" was in his view the theological prerequisite for the declaration of rights of 1789. The discrediting of the ecclesiastical hierarchy and the discrediting of the temporal hierarchy rested alike on the logic of Protestantism, individualism, and democracy. I noted earlier that, for the reactionaries, authority was good simply by virtue of existing. The people were corrupt, but the rulers and priests were good. Maistre saw the Protestant primacy of private judgment and the liberal primacy of individual consent as constituting the matrix of modern individualism.

His third explanation of events was: "There is in the French Revolution a satanic quality that distinguishes it from anything ever seen before, and perhaps also from anything that shall ever be seen hereafter."[80] But it was his fourth explanation that carried the most weight, for he described the Revolution as a divine chastisement for the sins of France and indeed of Europe. "Never before has God revealed himself so clearly in any human event. If he has used the vilest tools, that is because he punishes in order to regenerate."[81]

To summarize, Maistre's attitude toward the Revolution came down to two considerations. One was the view that Catholicism necessarily goes with a particular kind of government, namely monarchy, which in turn implied that every attack on that form of government amounts to an attack on Catholicism. The other was that the only viable constraints on power are, ultimately, religious constraints. Political constraints such as human rights and representative government might make sense in theory, but they simply did not recognize reality. Maistre's radical opposition to the Revolution was derived from these convictions, which, in the absence of a "Most Christian" king, led him to turn to the "Holy Father."

2

The Collapse of Reactionary Ultramontanism

Napoleon's Miscalculations

Throughout the Middle Ages, Catholics had turned to the king in search of protection against a papacy that was seen sometimes as predator and sometimes as itself prey to the intrigues and machinations of Italian politics. The French state had long been regarded as a bulwark against the papacy's political ambitions. In the age of absolutism, when the state was more securely established and more confident in its own power, things began to change. Fénelon was alert to this in 1711:

> Rome wielded an arbitrary power that had a troublesome impact on local churches, with its preemptive appointments, frivolous appeals, burdensome taxes, and dubious dispensations. But we must admit that these abuses are now much diminished. Today the abuses come from the secular power, not from Rome.[1]

The change of front that followed the Revolution was therefore already present in germ in the reign of Louis XIV. "The king, in practice, is the head of the church in France, not the pope: freedom from the pope is slavery to the king," wrote Fénelon.[2] The Abbé Fleury, briefly a colleague of Fénelon's, had similar views. He was asked,

> Why do we churchmen not show more zeal in resisting the infringements of lay power on the church than the magistrates show in resisting infringements by churchmen? Why are we so complacent toward the rights claimed by the king, but so inflexibly opposed to those claimed by the pope? To all this I can make no response other than to agree that we do not act at all consistently; and that in these affairs, as in everything else, custom does not always correspond to right reason.[3]

These observations, valid enough for the Ancien Regime, became even more valid in post-revolutionary France.

Could those who had solemnly proclaimed freedom of religion in August 1789 claim the right, in the spring and summer of 1790, to impose their will on the church? The Constituent Assembly had no mandate for that, nor could it ever have, in view of what it had set down in the Declaration of the Rights of Man. The proclamation of religious liberty was in effect an assertion of the private nature of religious belief and should therefore have precluded the Assembly from meddling in the internal affairs of the church.

When society was envisaged in terms of the three orders—*orantes, bellantes, laborantes*: those who pray, those who fight, and those who work—the "state" was the business of the *bellantes*, the military aristocracy, whose task was to defend and protect those who worked and, even more, those who prayed. But with the end of the system of the three estates, with the Declaration of the Rights of Man, and with the abolition of privilege, there came a fundamental change in the very function of the state. The state was no longer charged with supporting the church in its earthly pilgrimage but with ensuring the right of each person to freedom of religion. This in turn deprived it of the right to exercise any special control over the *oratores*. In depoliticizing the church, the state abdicated its own right to intervene, precisely because the church was now excluded from politics.

Three consequences followed logically from the secularization of the state: that the clergy cease to constitute an order within the state; that the laws of the church cease to be generally obligatory; and that the state cease to interfere in formulating the laws of the church. The Constituent Assembly unhesitatingly drew the first two conclusions but shied away from the third.[4] It was possible to impose obligations on the church, but only if those were balanced by compensating privileges. One could levy taxes, but only in return for compensating benefits. It was inconsistent to deconfessionalize the state while still insisting on the state's legislative control over the internal discipline of the church. The problem first noticed by Fénelon and Fleury had now assumed massive proportions.

It is easy to see why the revolutionaries felt that the church was a political institution, for such had indeed long been the case. But article 10 of the Declaration of the Rights of Man broke the bonds that had held church and state together. Once it was partially secularized, the state should have shown more discretion, as it was no longer in such a strong position to interfere in ecclesiastical affairs. The superannuation of the old slogan "une foi, une loi, un roi" should have meant abandoning the old interventionist habits of the monarchy and not, as the revolutionaries sought to do, intensifying them.

One of the traditional moves in defending the Gallican church against papal intrusion was to counter with a king whose anointing at Reims equipped him with a divine right not a whit inferior to the pope's. This option was no longer available to the revolutionaries, who had replaced the divine right of kings with the sovereignty of the people in the Assembly, something akin to parliamentary Gallicanism. Unable to invoke a "Most Christian King," they had in effect to posit a "Most Christian" people and a divine right of peoples. The absolutist assumption of *cuius regio eius religio* (whoever rules the land decides on its religion) still prevailed, only now it served no longer to bolster the position of the monarch but to guarantee the sovereignty of a "nation" still reckoned to be

Catholic. Anxious to outmaneuver the king and prevent him from continuing to nominate bishops, the Assembly felt it had to turn to the people and replace royal nomination with popular election: hence the Civil Constitution of the Clergy. In order to weaken the king's grip on society, it recast the religious structure of the entire country. From the start of the Revolution, the problem of the jurisdictional competence of the Assembly was in a way the supreme political problem, because the revolution was just that: the replacement of one sovereignty by another, causing a struggle between rival sovereignties, that of the king and that of the Assembly, each impugning the other's legitimacy.

One of the members of the Constituent Assembly, Treilhard, proclaimed insistently that freedom of worship was essential. But nervous of mortgaging the future of the constitutional church, he baulked at the implication that priests who refused to swear the oath should nevertheless be allowed to lead worship. Hence his comically incoherent observation that "I regard freedom of worship as essential, as guaranteed by law, but I do not want to see two religions where hitherto there was but one."[5] The proclamation of freedom of religion implied a degree of distance between church and state that the Assembly did not adequately comprehend. Instead of withdrawing from religious affairs, the state felt that the democratic revolution authorized continuing intervention. Not for one moment did the revolutionaries envisage religion as an entirely private matter. When in 1790 the Assembly took it upon itself to bring the religious system into line with the new political order, it envisaged a sort of national Catholicism, independent from Rome and revitalized by the principle of popular sovereignty. It hoped to see church and state inspired with the same spirit so that patriotic fervor would become one with the Christian faith.

Yet having refused to declare that the state remained Catholic, the revolutionaries now set about a reform program more ambitious than anything ever attempted by the Most Christian Kings of the Ancien Regime: a program that presupposed a full identification of church with state and state with church. If Louis XVI had attempted something of that kind, there would have been outrage—"an outcry against such a grotesque infringement on the jurisdiction of the church."[6] And at least Louis had been anointed at Reims. From the moment that the temporal sphere severed its direct link with the spiritual sphere, it was going to become difficult, if not impossible, to enact a *civil* constitution for the *clergy*. The state could not at once abandon its confessional character and cling on to the prerogatives and privileges which that character had conferred upon it.

One of the leading advocates of the Civil Constitution of the Clergy, the Abbé Grégoire, maintained that the exterior organization of Christianity

> admits of modifications required by the common good, as and when they are proposed by the "bishop over externals," namely the sovereign—in this case, the national will.[7]

This astonishing sleight of hand shows how the authors of the Civil Constitution had to minimize the significance of the Revolution's break with the past in order to justify their policy. This they could achieve only by means of some very questionable reasoning. The Most Christian Kings, as sovereigns, had claimed the status of "bishop over externals," a title traceable back to the Emperor Constantine. The national will, as expressed in the Constituent Assembly, was sovereign. Therefore the Constituent Assembly was, in its turn, "bishop over externals." But did this conclusion really follow?

The *philosophes* of the eighteenth century and their revolutionary disciples "sought not so much to divorce church and state as to conjoin them more closely in a marriage in which the state had all the rights of the husband, including the right of chastisement."[8] That was the problem: the state arrogated to itself an authority that the church simply could not concede. The reorganization of the state certainly necessitated some reorganization of the church, as the two were so intricately entangled with one another. And one can easily appreciate why the revolutionaries thought that the church ought to form part of, and help to support, the political institutions of the state. Were the church not to lend its support to those institutions, then it might prove, if not its downfall, then at least a serious obstacle to its functioning. But it would have been wiser to make more concessions to the church and to take seriously the objections raised by the pope and the bishops. Formerly, the church had been happy enough to treat the state as its "secular arm." But it was less keen on a situation in which it found itself treated as the "religious arm" of the state.

Napoleon sorted out some of the contradictions of the Revolution, but did he address this one? In his *Histoire du consulat et de l'empire* (History of the consulate and empire), Thiers reckoned that there were four possibilities open to Napoleon in religious policy. First, there was doing nothing. But that would have been risky. After the revolutionary dechristianization and the deep split that broke out among the clergy between "patriots" and "non-jurors," it was necessary to reconcile the clergy both to the government and to each other, to restore peace within divided families, to reassure those who had bought expropriated church lands, and to provide comfort to the dying. Second, Napoleon might have made himself head of a French national church. But establishing a national church would merely have complicated things further, adding yet another element to an already volatile mixture. A new schism was certainly not the most obvious way to set about healing religious and political divisions. Third, he might have turned to Protestantism. But that would have been the riskiest of all and would have succeeded only in rallying the people to the defense of Catholicism against the government. Finally, there was the most reasonable option, to negotiate a concordat with the papacy.[9]

During the ensuing negotiations, the pope called for the recognition of Catholicism as the "predominant religion." Harking back to the debates of winter 1790, Portalis replied on behalf of the French state:

> The political situation of France does not permit what His Holiness requests. The Catholic religion, which is that of the imperial family and of the vast majority of the French people, is predominant in practice, but it is not possible to enshrine this reality in law without shocking public opinion, disturbing the state, and even compromising the very religion on which such official recognition might be bestowed. The Catholic faith should flourish by virtue of the moral and intellectual excellence of its ministers rather than by virtue of laws that would render it suspect of intolerance.[10]

For Portalis, it was simply not possible to turn the clock back to the pre-Revolutionary era. That would be bad for both Church and State. Religion could no longer be made the basis of the social order, nor could the Church expect to wield public jurisdiction. It would have to rely on the teaching authority of its words and example ('moral and intellectual excellence') to make its impact.

The system set up by the Concordat was a system of "recognized" religions, though this recognition was social rather than theological.[11] The civil authorities no longer had the obligation or even the right to inflict penal sanctions on those who breached the regulations of the Catholic faith. Such privileges as were conferred upon Catholicism were justified on grounds not of public law but of social fact.

> The protection afforded by the state is similar to its supervision. It is an exterior and political protection only, and it is not to be confused with the right that our ancient laws accorded the king as "bishop over externals" and enforcer of canon law. The state guarantees the church the free exercise of worship and the freedom to undertake its own organization and administration, but it does so not as though it were itself a Christian institution, nor in recognition of Catholic dogma as such, but as a magistrate. . . . The state's concern is not for doctrine but for peace and public order.[12]

The clergy, as such, no longer had a role in government. Indeed, it no longer had any political function, but was henceforth confined to the provision of worship. Alongside Catholicism, the Concordat also officially recognized Judaism and Protestantism and proclaimed freedom of conscience. For the papacy, the terms of the Concordat meant renouncing the claim to "indirect" temporal power as well as accepting the secularization of the state and retrospectively acquiescing in the Revolution's expropriation of church property. Jurisdiction over the clergy was ceded to the Council of State, while the policing of religious worship also became a matter of civil jurisdiction. According to Thiers, "this was the Civil Constitution enacted in 1790, subject to certain modifications that rendered it acceptable to Rome."[13]

Napoleon unilaterally added a number of provisions to the Concordat, the so-called Organic Articles, which were unacceptable to, and never accepted by,

Rome. The Organic Articles stipulated that all contact with Rome and all gatherings of the French bishops had to have government authorization. The temporal power asserted its right of veto over papal bulls and encyclicals, the activities of papal legates, and episcopal appeals to Rome. In short, to the horror of the Holy See, Gallicanism was back (articles 24–25).

The Organic Articles might have been a dead letter, simply held in reserve in case of conflict between church and state, a threat all the more effective for not being carried out. But Napoleon was not one to deny himself the opportunity of bringing church and pope to heel. He sought to impose his will on the pope, arresting him and detaining him for a considerable period. He tended to regard the bishops as "prefects in purple vestments," on the grounds that a priest was worth fifty policemen. As Portalis explained, the function of the episcopate "has too much to do with teaching and with all branches of policing for it to be exempt from the rationale which has conferred upon the First Consul the power to nominate prefects, judges, and teachers."[14] The ecclesiastical polity was resolutely episcopal and imperial: priests were under the control of bishops, and bishops under the control of the head of state.

Ballanche, like many Catholic writers, denounced Napoleon's casual attitude and "godless condescension":

> He seemed to think, at times, that he could control [the Christian faith] the way that the rulers of pagan peoples controlled pagan religions. He did not appreciate that those rulers were not out of step with the religious thought of their societies, and that, in a Christian society, religious thought cannot be anything other Christianity itself.[15]

Napoleon had fallen into the same trap that had caused so many problems at the time of the Civil Constitution of the Clergy. A power that was now essentially secular had once again trespassed onto the spiritual domain.

Napoleon thought to control the French church even though the state was no longer bound by the constraints of Catholicism. He revived the old customs of absolutism, but in the context of a largely deconfessionalized state. He wanted to keep in place safeguards against the abuse of privileges that no longer existed. Everything had changed: but he wished to keep a grip on the clergy as though nothing had happened. Given that the clergy no longer constituted an "estate" within the state, and that canon law was no longer temporally enforceable, the civil power ought to have abandoned interference in ecclesiastical affairs and scrapped the jurisdictional machinery of absolutism. But Napoleon used it even more systematically, and while he shut the church out of the state, he thrust the state into the church. The church knew it had no choice, but it resented bending the knee to an apostate regime. It was inconsistent to govern the church as though it was a state religion while refusing to acknowledge its supremacy as a religion on the grounds that it was the religion only of the majority, not of the entire population.

Like the Constituent Assembly before him, Napoleon had sought to conciliate the church but had succeeded only in alienating it. He hoped to secure the allegiance of French Catholics to the new imperial regime and to maintain Gallican traditions in the post-revolutionary world. In practice, all he achieved was to rob the church of precisely that national status he had hoped to preserve and to attach it still more irremovably to the pope, from whom he had aimed to separate it. The church refused to be governed by the "reverend fathers of the Council of State." In place of a diverse clergy, governed by a host of separate authorities and rooted in the localities through landownership, Napoleon substituted a unit of almost military discipline, cut off from all local ties and commanded by a single head. Subordinating his religious policy too crudely to his foreign policy, he understood neither the spirit of French Catholics nor that of the papacy. Some decades later, this is how Catholics recalled the indignities inflicted upon the head of the church:

> Napoleon held the pope himself prisoner for five years; he brought him from Rome to Fontainebleau in a locked carriage like a prison-wagon; he threw his chief minister, Cardinal Pacca, into a dungeon at Senestrelle, and when that prelate requested a breviary, they gave him a book by Voltaire.[16]

The humiliation of the church, reduced to a mere instrument of state, provoked a reaction among Catholics, who started to look toward Rome as a symbol of independence. It was Canossa in reverse, and it redounded ultimately to the papacy's benefit.

Napoleon, then, having wished to narrow the gap between church and state, had ended up widening it.

> If, on the one hand, his intelligence and self-interest enabled him to see the benefits he could derive from religion, on the other, his jealousy of any rival power led him to harass the very clergy that he was claiming to reestablish.[17]

The consequences of his policy were the exact opposite of his intentions. For his policy to succeed, he needed to stick to the Concordat as negotiated, not add to it unilaterally. He needed to show greater respect for the liberty of the church, to be more generous than he knew how. Instead, his authoritarianism overreached itself. His clumsiness speeded up the developments he was trying to slow down. He ended up making a mockery of Gallican "liberties," and thus destroyed them. If Maistre was dismissing Gallicanism as early as 1791, he was nevertheless still arguing then (as he would for several years) within a framework of absolutism. Even in the late 1790s, he continued to envisage religion within the framework of the nation. It was only the disillusionment brought about by Napoleon's policy that led to Maistre's ultramontanist turn. His anti-Gallican polemics were a product of the 1810s, emerging in the context of a correspondence with Blacas, a royalist who had close connections with Louis XVIII, in which he strove to dissuade the royal entourage from a Gallican restoration.[18]

The failure of Napoleonic Gallicanism was perhaps inevitable, for the Gallican church had been shaken to pieces since 1789. The policies of the Assembly and the Terror had unleashed a process that could hardly be stopped. The Concordat itself is evidence enough for this, as there seemed no hope of breathing fresh life into Gallicanism without papal cooperation. The French Catholic Church was so divided, disorientated, and internally and politically weakened that Napoleon had to turn to the pope for the legitimation he required for the restoration of the Gallican church.

Napoleon wanted to have a clean slate, to remodel the French episcopate from scratch. His plan was for the pope to require the dismissal of all existing bishops. But the pope would not accept this, and his representative did all he could to oppose it. Toward the end of his lengthy negotiations with Napoleon, Cardinal Consalvi resorted to a subtle argument, which he recalled in his memoirs:

> I decided to try an approach that seemed as though it should make an impact. I relied on the principles that they now professed in France. I suggested that the highly prized and much vaunted liberties and privileges of the Gallican church were going to suffer a setback unprecedented in the annals of French history. Ninety or a hundred bishops deposed all at once by an exercise of the supreme power of the papacy, should they refuse the voluntary resignation he demanded of them; deposed, at that, without due process or formal judgment, so that new bishops could be appointed in their place; if, I said, it could perhaps be justified in terms of the greater good at which it aimed, it nevertheless meant acknowledging a degree of papal power over the French church that would bring the whole edifice of Gallican liberties and privileges tumbling to the ground. . . . But none of this bothered the First Consul.[19]

The situation was not without its ironies. The papal envoy was explaining to Napoleon that he ought to safeguard Gallican traditions, while Napoleon was ignoring his warnings and taking a decision that would consolidate the new powers of the pope. In effect, article 2 of the Concordat provided for the Holy See, in consultation with the consular government, to redraw the French diocesan map. Article 3 required the bishops of the doomed dioceses to resign. Pius VII stripped thirteen recalcitrant bishops of their powers and nominated new bishops to the redesigned dioceses.

These moves gave rise to the schism of the "Little Church," in protest against the Concordat.[20] Some contemporaries saw in the redrawing of the diocesan map a "blow that was undoubtedly all the more shattering in that it was delivered by the government of the church."[21] Napoleon had, paradoxically, conferred on the pope new powers, beginning with that of deposing *en masse* the survivors of the old French episcopate. As Renan observed, not without a little malice:

> Napoleon's Concordat taught the pope that he really had the rights that he had never doubted he had, in particular that of suppressing an entire church with a stroke of the pen and then reconstituting it on an entirely new basis.[22]

The pope was no longer *primus inter pares* but had become the bishop of bishops, which he had never been before. Napoleon meant to reduce the pope to subjection, yet in effect he invited the pope to behave as an emperor would in his own domain. All in all, it was a strange episode in the age-old rivalry of pope and emperor.

Having thus been completely refounded on the basis of an agreement with the pope, the French church could no longer ground its claims to legitimacy on itself alone. Napoleon's solution, turning to the pope in an attempt to dispossess the pope, could not lay the foundations of anything lasting. The Concordat was a tombstone for the past, not a signpost to the future.[23] After the fall of the empire, the theologico-political thinking of the Catholics developed in new and unexpected directions. Not only did the Catholics become ultramontanes, but their ultramontanism, paradoxically, ended up spiced with a distinct tang of liberalism.

Maistre is usually portrayed as an absolutist and an enemy of liberty, and this is for the most part true. But it should not be forgotten that he was a constant defender of the liberty of the church against even absolutism.

> I am accused of endorsing ultramontane principles. What are these appalling principles? That the church should enjoy the full and free use of all the authority that she received from Jesus Christ. That the temporal power should be strictly forbidden from encroaching in any way on the jurisdiction of the church. And what, in contrast, are these liberties of the Gallican church? Nothing but the full and complete enslavement of that church.[24]

In his view, the vaunted "liberties of the Gallican church" were nothing but "a fatal capitulation signed by the church, by which she bound herself to submit to the outrageous encroachments of the Parlement."[25] At the heart of his critique of the Gallican church was the imbalance between civil and ecclesiastical authority, which was evident in both the Civil Constitution and the policy of Napoleon. Maistre's analysis centered on the role of the pope:

> The church of France has been justly oppressed and brought low at home, in exact proportion to the liberty that she sought to arrogate to herself

with regard to the Holy See; as she permitted herself to judge its decisions, hers are in their turn judged by the secular power.[26]

The enslavement of the church was directly proportional to its independence
from the papacy. Conversely, dependence on the papacy was the church's
liberty. The real "liberties of the Gallican church" consisted not in Gallicanism
but in ultramontanism. In this respect, Maistre was not so much a nostalgic
reactionary yearning for the Ancien Regime as a radical innovator.

Under the Ancien Regime, the state accepted its role as the "secular arm" of
the church because the bishops and clergy put their moral authority at the service of the state and because the state, in its turn, kept a close eye on what the
church did and what the church imposed upon it. Despite having to keep to
what the church laid down, the state nevertheless kept the upper hand. It decided on appointments to high ecclesiastical offices. Before allowing papal decisions and instructions to be implemented, the crown had them checked by the
Parlement, to make sure that they contained nothing contrary to French fundamental law or liable to cause a breach of the peace. By virtue of its role in en-
forcing ecclesiastical laws, the state had secured a say in their formulation. But
the Revolution put an end to the "religion of Reims." The church was no longer
prepared to accept the intervention of the state.

Thus, ironically, the reactionaries condemned liberalism in the name of the
liberty of the church. For them, the "liberals" aimed not at setting believers free
but at confining them to the private sphere, in such a way as to dominate and
marginalize the church. This privatization of belief was in their view a way of
securing the hegemony of a godless state power. This point of view is evident in
the *Syllabus of Errors* of 1864, beyond doubt the most notorious manifesto of
Catholic antiliberalism. Among his thunderous anathemas against the "modern world," Pius IX denounced the following ideas with particular venom. "The
ecclesiastical power ought not to exercise its authority without the authorization and approval of the civil power" (no. 20). "The civil power has a direct
negative authority in sacred matters even when that power is in the hands of an
infidel" (no. 41). Yet even as they opposed liberty in principle, the reactionaries
nevertheless invoked it. It is worth noting that the great ultramontane publica-
tions were all pleas for the liberty of the church.[27] One can therefore legitimately talk of a core of liberalism at the heart of ultramontanism. In practice,
despite the hopes of Joseph de Maistre, ultramontanism did not lead to caesaropapism in the temporal sphere, but to a rethinking of the role of the papacy that
focused on its authority in the spiritual sphere.

Félicité de Lamennais on the Atheism of the Law

For Catholics, the Restoration (1814–30) could have been an opportunity to resuscitate Gallicanism. Most of the Left remained attached to the Gallicanism of

the old parlements, and most of the Right to the Gallicanism of the Ancien Regime episcopate.[28] The Restoration itself sought to knit together once more the broken threads of Catholic faith and monarchical loyalism. It was a question of preserving whatever of the Ancien Regime could be salvaged. But how could you "restore" a regime predicated on continuity? For all their starry-eyed recollections of the Ancien Regime, in fact it was dead and gone. Louis XVIII sat not upon the throne of Louis XIV but on that of Napoleon. He owed his position to a kind of social contract: the Charter. The words "restore" and "conserve" are in a sense opposites. The baptismal name of the regime—the "Restoration"—was its death certificate. The Restoration regime wished to revive Gallicanism, but it failed because the very foundations of Gallicanism had washed away.

In 1818 a law was passed instructing householders to decorate their houses when Blessed Sacrament processions were to pass by. Some Protestants refused to obey this law and were taken to court. Their advocate, Odilon Barrot, recalled in his memoirs that:

> When their case was taken to the Supreme Court of Appeal, the issue was not the mere matter of municipal regulation that people had imagined, but the whole principle of freedom of religion; of the relationship between church and state; of the separation of powers; it was, in short, the Revolution in its most precious achievements locked in combat with the most reactionary aspirations of Legitimism.

Barrot had no trouble appealing to the principles of the Charter in making his case:

> The law in France offers protection to all beliefs and all forms of worship, and takes sides with none. The day it takes sides with one of them will be the day we have a state religion: other forms of worship will merely be tolerated, but will no longer be free. Freedom means equality before the law and the neutrality of the law.

Thus, he recalled what the regime was anxious to forget but could not ignore: that the Restoration, despite itself, had had to ratify the principles of the Revolution, and that this was the basis on which its own legitimacy rested. That much was clear to the opponents of the "ultra" tendency, such as Barrot and Guizot.[29] But it was also clear to those who, like the fiery Félicité de Lamennais (1782–1854), reckoned that neither Louis XVIII nor even Charles X went far enough in the direction of reaction.

Lamennais was horrified by Barrot's line of defense, and in a journal whose title summed up its editorial policy—*Le Conservateur* (The conservative)—he raised the stakes and scandalized his readers with this sensational statement: "So the law is of no religion: then the law is atheistic." Barrot's response, delivered before the Court of Appeal, was no less sensational and scandalous.[30] As he put it in his memoirs, "Yes, I exclaimed, the law is atheistic, and it has to be, if by atheism you mean neutrality." But Barrot had the Charter on his side, and this was precisely what horrified Lamennais, an advocate of a genuine alliance of throne and altar, not of a regime that in fact, almost shamefacedly, endorsed the principles of the Revolution, notably that of freedom of religion.

In 1825–26 Lamennais published a book, *De la religion considérée dans ses rapports avec l'ordre politique et civil* (Religion considered in its relations with the political and civil order), whose second chapter was entitled "That religion in France is entirely excluded from political and civil society, and that in consequence the state is atheistic." Rather than praising Charles X for audacity, Lamennais blamed him for pusillanimity. He regretted the fact that the Restoration kings owed their power not to anointing but to a Charter that specified their rights and duties in contractual form. Not only was the state no longer the defender of the true faith, but it officially recognized and even protected heretical sects. The church had conceded its teaching functions to the state university. It no longer officially held a monopoly on the guidance of souls. Births, marriages, and deaths were no longer under its aegis but, since 20 September 1792, had been recorded not in the parish sacristy but in the town hall. The French could be born, get married, and die without going anywhere near a priest. But what Lamennais did not grasp was that the secularization of the functions of the registry office had taken place at the insistence of the recalcitrant "nonjuror" clergy. He interpreted it as a sign of decadence. For him, *the Charter is the Republic.*

> The Revolution has succeeded in excluding God from the state and establishing atheism in the political system and in civil society. . . . From now on, what is religion to the government? What must Christianity be in its eyes? Sad to say, an institution fundamentally opposed to its institutions, its principles, and its precepts. In short, an enemy, and that irrespective of the personal sympathies of those actually in power.[31]

The law was atheistic because the state born of the Revolution aimed at establishing human sovereignty. It no longer looked to God. It looked to nothing beyond the will of the people and the consent of the individual. It bracketed out God's Law, as though what people owed to God was a matter of complete indifference. As the law was atheistic, it was no longer possible to be a Gallican, as in the good old days of the Ancien Regime.

For hard-line Catholics, Charles X's policy did not endear the regime to them but merely justified them in standing apart from it and looking instead toward the Holy See. In a state that was no longer Catholic, Gallicanism was redundant. If the state was atheistic, then Catholics could no longer owe it their ultimate allegiance. That allegiance was owed instead to the pope. Lamennais thus came to ultramontanism at about the same moment as the rather older figure of Joseph de Maistre. Their separate but convergent intellectual pilgrimages alike bore witness to the ecclesiological crisis and renewal consequent upon the secularization of the state. As the locus of true authority was no longer to be found in France, neither in its church nor in its state, it resided instead at Rome.

The most illustrious ultramontanes of the nineteenth century were either converts or else cradle Catholics who had, for a while, lost their faith: Lamennais and Veuillot in France, and perhaps Maistre as well; J. J. Görres and George Phillips in Germany; Juan Donoso Cortés in Spain; William George Ward, H. E. Manning, and F. W. Faber in England. Having passed through a period of doubt, they had to reestablish their faith on a new basis, starting from scratch, going back to square one in a world that was no longer that of the Ancien Regime. Their personal doubts were a sort of microcosm of the age in which they lived, which saw the secularization of the state and the questioning of the classical certainties of Catholicism. Doubt kept them in step with their times, and doubt pushed them toward ultramontanism.

The experience of alienation that was so marked in these individuals was felt through much of the Catholic world. As Tocqueville wrote in 1856,

> Do you think it was papal policy that destroyed Gallicanism and caused the bulk of the priests and faithful of France to take up ultramontanism? It was the French Catholics who did this, of their own volition, for reasons that had nothing to do with the curia. It was not a matter of the pope seizing power over the faithful, but of the faithful themselves calling on the pope to become absolute master of the church. And this tendency was, if not universal, then widespread through the Catholic world. The papal position we see today was not so much a *cause* as an *effect*.[32]

Starting in France, ultramontanism spread throughout Europe. It made decisive advances in the 1820s and had secured total victory by 1850.

In a world turned upside down, the papacy stood firm as a symbol of permanence. In a world struggling to find its own organizing principle, it stood at the pinnacle of a hierarchy that embodied stability and order. In a world shaken to its foundations, a world whose lawfully constituted authorities had been systematically dismantled by a Revolution that proclaimed the primacy of the individual conscience, the concept of papal infallibility responded to the craving for solid ground. This concept, of which Joseph de Maistre became the foremost advocate, prevailed at the First Vatican Council, which marked the triumph of ultramontanism in the church. Pope Pius IX convened this council on 8 December 1869, bringing together seven hundred bishops with a view to "finding remedies for the numerous evils which beset the Church." On 18 July 1870 the majority voted in favor of the dogmatic constitution *Pastor Aeternus*, recognizing the infallibility of the bishop of Rome when speaking *ex cathedra*, that is, that "when, in the exercise of his office as shepherd and teacher of all Christians, in virtue of his supreme apostolic authority, he defines a doctrine concerning faith or morals to be held by the whole Church."[33]

Historians are fond of recalling W. G. Ward's remark that he would "like a new papal Bull every morning with my *Times* at breakfast."[34] From the French Revolution to Vatican I, following Maistre's lead, ecclesiology ranged itself under the banner of authority.[35] With the church under siege from hostile forces, Catholics closed ranks around their chief. The magisterium did not content itself with bearing witness to "tradition" but judged between rival versions of tradition. It conceived its doctrinal function more in terms of making decisions than of giving testimony. It aimed not so much to deepen the understanding of revelation in all its richness and fullness as to ensure that, in the final analysis, an authoritative interpretation would prevail against the threat of a chaos in which everyone put forward his own subjective interpretations. Since decisions had to be taken, it was essential that the decision-making authority should itself be clearly defined, otherwise the basis of the church's faith would no longer be clear; and the authority that decided in the final analysis, in an ultimate and sovereign fashion, could be none other than the papacy.

Ultramontanism rapidly developed into a mass movement, for it responded to needs that were keenly felt by large numbers of Catholics, especially by the clergy, who often felt that they had been marginalized and symbolically banished from their nations in the aftermath of the French Revolution. But how could the Gallican tradition be maintained without the clerical estate, without the king and his parlements, on the basis of new dioceses defined to coincide with the Revolution's newfangled administrative "departments"? The clergy was no longer a distinct, wealthy, and privileged corporate body. It was no longer bound to the state by the ties of privilege, nor to the land by proprietorial interests. "The people who stripped the Catholic clergy of all right to real estate, and commuted their revenues into salaries, served only the interests of the Holy See," wrote Tocqueville.[36] Gone were the ties that had once bound the clergy to the interests of wealth and power. The clergy was no longer a power in the land:

> Along with the wealth accumulated from centuries of devotion, they lost their place in political life, which is rooted in property; and with their place in politics, they lost their place in civil society. They were not even, like the township, a corporation, a legal person. Like society itself, they were nothing but individuals.[37]

The wellsprings that fed the nationalist and particularist spirit of the French clergy had dried up. Its members were no longer brought together by the need to defend their privileges nor by their periodic gatherings in national assemblies. The French church was in effect disembodied by the French Revolution. Among the biggest losers were members of the lower clergy, who were stripped of the protection they had once enjoyed under canon law. In the nineteenth century, these clerics looked to the Council of State for protection against their bishops. Had this been forthcoming, it might have purchased their loyalty to the new state.[38] But they looked in vain, and, disillusioned, they turned to the papacy.

By ethos and education, the priests became "strangers in the midst of the new society."[39] Catholics tended to construct their own framework of intellectual reference, cut off from both Revolution and Enlightenment, which they reckoned had led only to disaster. While the Revolution prevailed in harsh reality, Counter-Revolution reigned in their hearts. So the church had *its* novelists, *its* journalists, and *its* philosophers, who either held themselves aloof from the currents of the century or even met them head on. To eighteenth-century classicism they opposed a Christian romanticism that dominated their schools and seminaries, despite its lack of success in the public sphere.

Priests even changed their appearance, abandoning the Gallican collar (which they called the "rabat") in favor of the Roman style.[40] At the intellectual level, Rome took on a new importance. Having long languished, the Roman College (otherwise known as the Gregorian University) was in 1824 restored to the Jesuits. Their teaching soon earned widespread admiration in the clerical world, attracting large numbers of students. The French Seminary established at Rome in 1853 was thronged with students enticed by the prospect of a glittering career.[41] Thus the city of the popes took the place of Paris. The Catholic Faculties of Theology that had been reestablished in France (at Paris, Lyon, Aix, Toulouse, Rouen, and Bordeaux) shared one critical defect: they had all been founded unilaterally by Napoleon, and had never secured canonical authorization from the Holy See. In the wake of the suppression of the great medieval faculties of theology, most notably the Sorbonne, many Catholics felt the need for an authoritative voice to pass judgment on the vital issues of the day—what theologians call the "ordinary magisterium." The teachings of the pope, which had played only a minor part in the lives of Catholics under the Ancien Regime, now took on an unprecedented significance.

When it had sought to enhance its authority, the papacy of the Ancien Regime had faced powerful local churches, often organized on a national basis, fiercely loyal to their liturgical and theological traditions and similarly jealous of their particularity and their autonomy. Modern ultramontanism, a thing of the nineteenth century, was begotten of the weakness of the local churches. Far from resisting Rome, they turned spontaneously toward the papacy as their only hope of freedom and security. Two forces worked upon them: a force of attraction, drawing them to Rome as a focus of authority that could take the place of the Gallican church; and a force of repulsion, alienating them from an apostate regime that had turned its back on "the religion of Reims," the sacred city where the kings of France had for centuries received their anointing.

Against Political Theology

Was the law really atheistic under the regime of the Restoration? Was the theory advanced by Lamennais really justified? Had he not in fact overlooked something? Royer-Collard (1763–1845), a writer who was a liberal as well as a Catholic, remarked that "the Charter is not indifferent; nor, indeed, is it neutral; it is simply irrelevant; law, here below, can take cognizance only of human affairs."[42] According to Royer-Collard, civil law could hardly be "atheistic," since it simply did not exist on the same plane as religion and divine law. The Revolution might have brought enormous changes, but the French had not stopped being Catholics. Their deep-rooted traditions remained vigorous. Church and state were no longer married, but they were still good friends. There was something artificial and needlessly provocative in the thesis of Lamennais. Neither the state nor its law were atheistic under Charles X—one of the most overtly Christian kings in all French history. The ruling elites were still made up of people who had passed their formative years before the Revolution. The accession of Louis XVIII and then of Charles X had brought to power the sort of people who boasted that, since 1789, they had forgotten nothing and had learned nothing. Charles X presented his reign as standing in the immemorial tradition of the Most Christian Kings, and he sought to reforge the links between throne and altar. The secularization of the functions of the registry office had been brought about not by the enemies of the church, but by the non-juror clergy. The so-called law of sacrilege that was passed in April 1825 defined the desecration of consecrated eucharistic wafers as a crime: the state thus acknowledged the Catholic dogma of the real presence.

Lamennais drew his extreme conclusion because he still thought in terms of a state whose foundations had to be essentially religious, in which politics and religion had to be one. The state was either Catholic or atheistic: if it was not Catholic enough, it would inevitably tend toward atheism. Like Maistre, Lamennais espoused a political theology and offered a theological reading of the French Revolution. But these theological positions presented three fundamental difficulties.

In the first place, they implied that every theology would, almost inevitably, have its own corresponding political system. But this was far from clear: one could at most speak of "elective affinities." Plenty of liberal thinkers had seen a relationship between Protestantism and republicanism without coming to the same conclusions as Maistre. Montesquieu had written that "the Catholic religion goes better with monarchy, and the Protestant religion is better suited to a republic," but he did not deduce from this that a change of regime entailed a war of religion.[43] Moreover, Protestantism did not necessarily go with liberal republicanism. It is too easily forgotten that the overthrow of the Catholic system had led, in Calvinism, to the harsh social discipline of the Puritans, and, in Lutheranism, to the absolute state.

Second, "when you venture a detailed interpretation of the intentions of Providence from the course of events, then—recognizing as you must that the choice of means Providence reserves to itself is beyond human ken, and that there is neither any obvious analogy nor any apparent proportion in the divine calculation of cause and effect—then there is one small condition you must meet: you must be inspired."[44] The prophet Lamennais was amply contradicted by events, nor was Maistre invariably inspired. Under their influence, the Catholic Church became a threat to politically moderate regimes. The church marginalized itself in the world of democracy. The ultramontane rewriting of history, which set out to paint the past in the colors of the faith, fed Catholic clerics with illusions, fattening them on false hopes of a "return of the faith" and on equally false regrets for an ever more mythical past.

Third, one must also ask whether the political theologians might not have exaggerated the importance of the religious element in politics in general, and in the history of the French Revolution in particular. The most pressing political issue in eighteenth-century France was not that of church-state relations but of the adaptation of the state bequeathed by Louis XIV to the new needs and circumstances of the age. Louis XIV had bequeathed to his successors an unwieldy and almost uncontrollable system of government. The miscarriage of the great constitutional initiatives that followed his death made the Revolution an almost inevitable, or at least a natural, outcome. Religion had nothing to do with that. To the task of modulating absolute monarchy into a constitutional key the Catholic Church, as such, had nothing to contribute. There was nothing to be gained from relying on a political theory predicated on and dominated by theological considerations. Even the faithful could see that a devout monarch was not necessarily an effective monarch, any more than an ungodly monarch was necessarily ineffective. The revolutionaries did not set out to make kings more Christian (or less Christian for that matter): they wanted to change the political system itself.

As Tocqueville saw it, for example, the construction of the centralized state administration played a more fundamental role than atheism or Protestantism. The absolutist state cut out the aristocracy, stripping its powers and leaving it redundant and parasitic, laden with privileges for which there was no longer any functional social justification. Absolutism undermined the aristocratic pyramid of which it was itself the pinnacle. In *The Ancien Regime and the French Revolution*, Tocqueville showed how absolutism prepared the way for Revolution in taking away the political functions of the nobility and thus taking away also the justification for their privileges. In stripping the nobles of their political functions, absolutism denied them the tasks that their high status required. By thus acquiring a monopoly on political power, the monarchy undermined the feudal order and deprived the nobility of its traditional responsibilities, while leaving its traditional system of rewards in place. An anomaly like this could not last. The Revolution denounced the now unmerited privileges of the aristocracy. In short, the Ancien Regime dug its own grave. But it was the political position of the aristocracy, rather than that of the church, that the Revolution aimed to overthrow. Tocqueville—like Maistre—saw the roots of the Revolution in the reign of Louis XIV. But he focused on the effects of absolutism, where Maistre focused on what he called the "Revolution of 1682," that is, the first article of the Declaration of the Clergy.

It was largely by chance that the French Revolution took on an antireligious character. It was the intimate relationship of church and monarchy in the old society of the three orders that brought down upon the cross, in its turn, some of the hatreds aroused by the fleur-de-lis. If the church had shown itself less ready to make common cause with the Ancien Regime, then as likely as not the revolutionaries would have left it alone. In any case, their religious program did not at first entail opposition to Christianity. As Tocqueville put it, "the ultimate objective of the Revolution was not, as has been thought, the destruction of religious power."

> It was less as a religious doctrine than as a political institution that Christianity provoked such passionate hatred; not because priests purported to regulate matters in the next world, but because in this one they were lords and proprietors, administrators and tithe collectors; not because there could be no place for the church in the new society that was being founded, but because it had held the most powerful and privileged place in the old society that was to be smashed to smithereens.[45]

When Tocqueville maintains that "the ultimate objective of the Revolution was not, as has been thought, the destruction of religious power," this is partly because he reckoned that Christianity and democracy were essentially compatible, but partly also because the Revolution was directed above all at the aristocracy (rather than the church). It was not necessary to see religion in everything. To the extent that the revolutionaries had any issue with the church, it was with the church *qua* political institution.

Tocqueville, of course, was not a political *theologian* but a political *philosopher*. His intellectual approach presupposed a natural order in politics that was not reducible to the supernatural. There is a good illustration of this in the importance that he attached to the "principle of interest rightly understood" in the functioning of society.[46] Self-interest, on its own, could generate social order without any need for the intervention of a church to purify the heart or improve morals. The idea that trade could foster moral improvements implied that a moral order worthy of the name did not necessarily depend on Christianity. There was both a Hobbesian dimension to public life (concern for public order and security) and a Lockean dimension (protection of private property and economic activity) that were not essentially religious. As Montesquieu had observed on the subject of the Ancien Regime,

> In moderate monarchical states, power is limited by that which is its very origin: I mean the concept of honor, which, like a sovereign, rules prince and people alike. There is no need to bring religion into it: a courtier would think that ridiculous. Considerations of honor will do.[47]

When he compiled a list of the principles on which political systems might be based, Montesquieu included honor (in the case of monarchy), fear (in the case of despotism), and virtue (in the case of republicanism). He did not include religion.

Notwithstanding the flashes of insight scattered through the *Considérations sur la France*, Maistre's book furnished at best a one-sided view of the Revolution. He offered a brilliant exposé of the gap between the Revolution's intentions and its outcomes. But in reading it, one loses the sense of what those initial intentions really were. One ends up forgetting that in certain respects it succeeded: it put an end to absolute monarchy and laid the foundations for representative government and democratic politics. Why invoke notions of providential chastisement and satanic intervention when the logic of events makes sense perfectly well in human and political terms? Ockham's razor implies that there is nothing to be gained from seeking supernatural explanations for things that can be explained in natural terms. By insisting on the religious dimension of politics and disregarding the autonomy of the temporal order, Maistre effectively denied himself any chance of understanding the Revolution. He ended up by forgetting what politics was.

In a general way, like the theorists of secularization, the counter-revolutionaries tended to exaggerate both the atheism of the "modern" world and the religious character of the "premodern." These exaggerations are two sides of the same coin, as both presuppose an extravagant sense of the political role of religion. The contrast between the religious heteronomy of the ancient world and the political autonomy of the modern world has become a cliché. Yet this simplistic dichotomy overlooks one simple fact: ever since Socrates founded political philosophy, there have been thinkers capable of analyzing politics in rational terms and of showing that we are not bound to interpret the political life we see around us everyday in theological categories.

In the *Politics*, Aristotle gave an account of the workings of the polities of the ancient world without ever invoking religious considerations. The states of the classical world appear in many respects profoundly superstitious, yet to a remarkable extent religious life was subordinated to narrowly political needs. Politics was a natural phenomenon: it was not necessary to call in the supernatural to make sense of its layout and its workings. In drawing a sharp distinction between divine law and human law, Thomas Aquinas endorsed one of the fundamental principles of the Aristotelian tradition in which he placed himself: "The state is one of the realities which exist naturally, and man is by nature a political animal."[48]

Far from aligning itself with Maistre, the First Vatican Council (1870) emphasized the importance of reason and philosophy.[49] Some years later, in the encyclical *Aeterni Patris* (1879), Leo XIII gave pride of place to scholastic philosophy and to a Thomist rationalism that upheld the positive value of the natural order and therefore *a fortiori* recognized the autonomy of the political sphere:

> Lack of faith is not intrinsically incompatible with political authority. For political authority exists by virtue of the *ius gentium* [law of peoples], which is human law; but the distinction between faithful and infidel, which derives from divine law, does not overrule human law.[50]

Thus, the *corpus mysticum* of the church was distinguished from a *corpus politicum et morale* that was to be analyzed in terms already familiar to pagan antiquity. This was the traditional teaching of the Catholic Church, which the Gallicans had put to the fore in their concern to distinguish the spiritual from the temporal. The teaching was rooted in Paul's epistle to the Romans: "There is no power but from God"—a theory of "divine right" which did not necessarily entail the divine right of *kings*. Indeed, it was precisely this relative indifference to the nature of political regimes which aroused the hostility of such figures as Machiavelli and Rousseau.

Three cases serve to illustrate this relative indifference to forms of government: Pius VI's condemnation of the Civil Constitution; the attitude of the bishops to Louis XVIII; and the condemnation of the law of sacrilege by Royer-Collard.

First, at the very moment that he spoke out against the Civil Constitution of the Clergy, Pius VI took care to specify that he had no intention of "calling for the restoration of the Ancien Regime in France."[51] Politics was not going to be reabsorbed by religion, nor religion by politics.

Again, after the coup of "18 Fructidor Year 5" (1797), Louis XVIII had hopes of regaining the throne and made discreet approaches to various trusted bishops—but in vain. He wrote a letter to two bishops in particular, in which he called upon them to make kingship a sort of Christian ministry or apostolate:

> I would like churchmen to build up monarchical spirit as well as religious spirit among my subjects; to inspire them with a sense of the intimate links between throne and altar, of their absolute indispensability to each other; and to teach them that the Catholic Church, with its discipline and its hierarchy, a wonderful system that has been preserved immune from all error for centuries, is compatible only with monarchy, and cannot long survive without it.

Louis XVIII, in short, wanted a political theology of absolutism. But the bishops were not prepared to follow him onto that ground. They were not so attached to monarchy that they would forget their catechism, and the catechism was clear: the authority of the church was not tied to any single political system. As one of the bishops replied:

> It is not possible to teach the people that the Catholic religion is compatible only with monarchy and cannot long survive without it, for the truth is that the Catholic religion is compatible with any form of legitimate government.

Circumstances compelled even the most absolutist of bishops to distance themselves from absolutism.[52] The divine right of kings had never been acknowledged by the universal church or even maintained by the most learned theologians: the Bossuet who exalted Louis XIV was certainly not Bossuet at his best.

Finally, Royer-Collard measured out the distance between the city of man and the city of God when he mounted fierce opposition to the so-called law of sacrilege. This law, which was debated in 1824–25, concerned itself with core Catholic dogma, introducing a new principle in law by establishing a category of, so to speak, supernatural crimes. Essentially, it confused offenses against God with offenses against society.

> Gentlemen, human societies are born on earth, and live and die here. It is here that they live out their destinies, here that their fallible and imperfect justice begins and ends, for that justice is founded on nothing more than the need for, and the right to, self-preservation. But these societies do not embrace the whole of man. Even after he has committed himself to society, there remain reserved the noblest parts of man, the highest faculties, by which he is raised up to God, to a future life, to the unknown blessings of an unseen world. This is the domain of religious belief, a consolation amid frailty and misfortune, an inalienable recourse against tyranny here below. Bound forever to the things of this world, human law has no purchase on religious belief. In its temporal capacity it can neither acknowledge nor comprehend it. Of things outside this world it has neither knowledge nor jurisdiction.[53]

The problem with the proposed law was that it made not only God but society an object of sacrilege. It thus sacralized society, in contravention of the very spirit of Christianity itself. A law of sacrilege presupposed a theology. Royer-Collard, in contrast, maintained the autonomy of the political order, an autonomy founded upon its essential coarseness, a sort of shortsighted and materialistic incapacity to grapple with the subtleties of religion and the secrets of the soul. The law was not atheistic, for the simple reason that it had no standing in the order of faith. The purpose of the state was primarily to "preserve," to keep the peace. It did not have to be Christian to achieve that.

Reactionary ultramontanism was not rooted in Catholic tradition. Joseph de Maistre broke away from the ideas of the church's leading thinkers, though in his defense it should be said that Bossuet had already stood that tradition on its head in seeking to derive political absolutism from the Bible. Moreover, the revolutionaries had brought an almost religious fervor to their political projects. But there was no good reason for Catholics to imitate them. As I hope to show in the following pages, the ultramontanism that ultimately triumphed in the Catholic Church was not the ultramontanism of the Counter-Revolution, but a liberal ultramontanism that distinguished sharply between the theological and the political domains. Catholics turned toward the papacy because they had come to take it for granted that the modern state could not be a confessional state.

A Papacy Refocused on Its Spiritual Role

Joseph de Maistre's ideal harked back to the great reform undertaken by Gregory VII in the eleventh century: the "liberty of the church" advanced in step with the rise of papal power. To emancipate the church from the constraints under which it had labored for centuries thanks to the rise of lay patronage, Gregory VII had set in motion what became the ultimate affirmation of papal power and of ultramontanism. At the time of the Gregorian Revolution, the church had sought its freedom in the form of political supremacy. The enduring symbol of this was the great scene at Canossa in 1077, when the humbled emperor Henry IV spent three days barefoot, in penitential garb, begging forgiveness from the pope. Under papal leadership, the church worked on detaching its hierarchy and its structures from the structures of temporal power and on establishing its own jurisdictional order.[54] Nineteenth-century ultramontanism followed the same political logic. In each case, the overall aim was the independence of the spiritual power.[55] The stronger the papacy, and the more directly the church hierarchy depended upon it, the less the church depended on kings, princes, barons, and the laity in general.

For Maistre, a new ultramontanism was to bring about a new Gregorian Reform, with the church dominating the state. However, seven or eight hundred years after Gregory VII, that option was wildly unrealistic. Bitterly disputed even in the Middle Ages, the theocratic ideal had lost all relevance in the age of absolutism.[56] In 1801 Portalis observed that "the pope, as a sovereign, can no longer be a threat to any power; he will always have to call upon the support of France."[57] In retrospect, it seems bizarre that the ultramontanes could even for a moment have imagined that the papacy might once more shuffle and deal the political cards in Europe and beyond. The Holy See no longer disposed of political resources adequate to such a role.

Reactionary ultramontanism was something of a paradox. It certainly did not arise from any inherent tendency toward hierocracy in the modern state. The reactionaries turned all the more eagerly toward the papacy because they saw the regimes of Louis XVIII and Charles X fall short of their dreams of a Catholic state. The further they saw the state slip away from the church, the more stridently they called on the state to submit to its supervision. The more the Revolution prevailed in harsh reality, the more the Counter-Revolution took hold of the Catholic imagination. The stronger the current of the age ran against them, the more rigid and cocksure the "ultras" became; the more remote their prospects of success, the more grandiose and messianic their ideology. The deconfessionalization of the state did not depoliticize religion: it merely emancipated religion from the established order. Political messianisms have proliferated over the ensuing two centuries not despite the separation of church from state but because of it.

Reactionary ultramontanism was essentially utopian. Having whipped up a wave of enthusiasm which was not without its dangers to the state, it came back down to earth with a crash. Lamennais was the first to grasp that the reactionary political program was a utopian illusion. Seeing in the Restoration a regime as "Catholic" and "ultra" as any reactionary could reasonably expect, he realized that it could go no further: it would never abolish the secular state, nor would it acknowledge the political authority of the papacy. Lamennais saw that in practice even hard-line Catholics were unlikely to make the papacy the arbiter of European politics.

Disillusioned with Charles X, Lamennais backed away. As he saw it, the Restoration regime was still in hock to the Revolution. Charles X's government was not fundamentally Christian and did not serve the interests of the church. In a book entitled *Des progrès de la révolution et de la guerre contre l'Eglise* (The Progress of the revolution and the war against the church, 1824), he denounced it as "a kind of monstrous civil theocracy." "The annihilation of Christianity in France through the establishment of a national church subordinated in every respect to the government," he wrote, "that is what is being pursued with indefatigable industry."[58]

Lamennais decried the atheism of the state because he hoped for a regime that, in turning toward the church and subordinating itself to the papacy, would rediscover the faith, abandon the Charter, with its essentially contractual character, and entrust the spiritual direction of the people to the church. Yet, by a tortuous path, it was antiliberalism that brought Lamennais to liberalism. The most reactionary government in French history was not enough in his eyes and therefore abdicated its right to intervene in ecclesiastical affairs. How could Catholics stand for government intervention in religion when "one searches in vain for the name of God in our law codes"?[59] Lamennais became a liberal because he came to see that the church no longer had anything to hope for from the powers of this world.

> No advantages that the state might offer her can come anywhere near compensating for the dangers of the perpetual struggle that would have to be fought to preserve her independence. The church will always have more to fear than to hope for from princes.[60]

Having begun in search of a spiritual power worthy of the name, Lamennais realized in the end that the old alliance of throne and altar would no longer answer to the purpose. So he called upon the church to wean itself from temporal power and rely on its own resources. As the state would not be converted, the church simply had to break free of its embrace. Lamennais traded in reactionary ultramontanism for liberal ultramontanism because he saw that it was pointless expecting the state to bow down before the papacy in temporal matters.

Lamennais's thought was dominated by the need for spiritual authority and by the sense that the Revolution had destroyed it. At first, he hoped to recover that authority through an alliance between monarchy and papacy. Then, despairing of monarchy, he threw himself upon the papacy alone, thus adopting the liberal position in separating politics and religion. The denunciation of the atheism of the state, which had initially led him to ultramontanism, led him ultimately to liberalism.

Lamennais urged Catholics not to put their trust in a feeble government that, under a show of patronage, aimed at their enslavement. In 1830 he founded a journal, *L'Avenir* (The future), whose motto was "God and Liberty." Attracted by his newfound liberalism, a constellation of talented young men clustered around him, including Montalembert and Lacordaire. They yearned for a world regenerated by liberty, and a liberty regenerated by God. They struggled against the schism in post-revolutionary Europe which set those who wanted liberty without religion against those who wanted religion without liberty. They asserted the freedom of the spiritual power against the tyranny of the temporal power. Ultramontanism provided a principle of authority which guaranteed order in the spiritual sphere while presupposing that the state had no jurisdiction in spiritual matters. Once that jurisdictional limitation was established, the state would respect the liberty of its citizens.

Gallicanism had no place in a state that was no longer Catholic. Gallican doctrines "sanctioned anarchy in the spiritual sphere, and despotism in politics."[61] One of the regular targets of *L'Avenir* was the divine right of kings, which the reign of Charles X saw some attempts to resuscitate. In an article on the freedom of the press, Lacordaire emphasized that "there is no civil tribunal capable of discerning truth from falsehood in the sphere of politics and religion." He went on:

> Censorship is nothing but the substitution of the prince for the pope. And, given that the prince does not concern himself full-time with matters of the intellect, this means in the end the substitution of a minister of state for the Vicar of Christ. . . . Paganism itself never came up with anything worse. For when the pagans made up their gods, at least those gods were men. What are Catholics asking for when they have nightmares at the thought of freedom of the press? In effect they are asking for ministerial infallibility in place of papal infallibility, preferring the golden calf to Mount Sinai.[62]

That was "divine right": a doctrine of ministerial infallibility in a state that was no longer Christian. The crown had divested itself of its religious character in subordinating itself to the sovereignty of the people rather than that of God. With constitutional monarchy having replaced confessional monarchy, the crown could no longer claim divine right. And if the state no longer had true spiritual authority, then liberty had to prevail.

The First Vatican Council, the answer to the prayers of the counter-revolutionaries, seemed at first a triumph for the most extreme version of papal monarchy. After all, papal infallibility had been upheld by Maistre's followers. Yet Vatican I in fact ensured the ultimate triumph of the ideology of *L'Avenir*. Its blend of ultramontanism and liberalism resurfaced in the shrewd, restrained, and liberal writings of Emile Ollivier (1825–1913).

Although Ollivier was not a Christian himself, he had a certain sympathy for the Catholic Church and a considerable admiration for Lamennais, whom he visited shortly before his death.[63] Addressing the Chamber of Deputies in July 1868, during a debate on the forthcoming council, Ollivier spoke as follows:

> Gentlemen, I am aware of no event since 1789 of such significance as this, namely, the separation of church and state, promoted by the pope himself. The church, for the first time in its history, by means of its own supreme pastor, is giving this message to the secular world, to secular society, to the secular powers: I wish to be myself, I wish to act in my own right; I wish to move myself, to develop myself, to assert myself; I wish to reach out apart from you and without you; I have a life of my own, which I do not owe to any human power, which I hold by virtue of my own divine origin and my own age-old tradition; this life is enough for me, and I ask nothing more of you than the right to govern myself in my own way. Gentlemen, these are momentous and courageous words, and they fill me with respect and admiration. For I admire organizations that trust in themselves, which proclaim in words and deeds, with boldness and vitality, the commitment that drives them and the faith that inspires them. (Hear, hear! Applause.) Yes, this is something new, something momentous: to see the separation of secular society from religious society advanced by the hand of the pope. Thinkers and philosophers have dreamed of such a separation as a distant ideal, a utopian vision obscured in the mists of the future. And now that utopian vision draws near and descends from the realm of dreams: the ideal starts to become a reality. And let history take note that it is the Supreme Pontiff who has taken the initiative.[64]

"The separation of church and state, promoted by the pope himself"! Ollivier's pithy summary was borne out by the unfolding of the council. Why did the leading Catholic states, especially the most powerful of them, France, make no attempt to prevent the declaration of papal infallibility? Because when the council was being planned, Emile Ollivier was one of Napoleon III's most trusted ministers, and he persuaded the emperor not to intervene.[65]

Emile Ollivier's encomium of ultramontanism, like his critique of Gallicanism, was couched in terms reminiscent of *L'Avenir*:

> One must face the fact that there is more liberty and largeness of view, more of dignity and democracy, in ultramontanism than in Gallicanism.[66]

Ollivier wrote this in the context of the debate provoked by Vatican I in the late 1860s and early 1870s. The papacy became the symbol and citadel of the independent church against bureaucratic state churches. The solemn affirmation of the power of the papacy was simply a matter of "balancing the equation after the process of secularization inaugurated by the French Revolution. On the one side, the independence of the state had been secured. On the other, the independence of the church still needed to be established. For without this, the process would be devoid of fairness, equity, and logic."[67]

The Holy See had not entered into negotiations with any Catholic states in advance of issuing the bull convening the First Vatican Council. Nor had it invited any of them to send representatives, although it did not absolutely exclude them if they sought representation. Bavaria sought to be represented, but Spain, Portugal, and Belgium all refrained from doing so, and for a revealing reason: they all concluded that this would be inconsistent with the separation of church and state to which they now subscribed. The states had not been invited precisely because the Council was intended to get to grips with the theological and political changes of the time, which were tending toward the secularization of the state. As Ollivier pointed out, the mere act of not inviting Catholic sovereigns to be represented at the Council "implied a de facto acquiescence in the separation of church and state proclaimed by the French Revolution and recently condemned in the *Syllabus of Errors!*"[68] The church had put an end to a tradition that stretched all the way back to the Council of Nicaea in the early fourth century and had thus freely stepped over the threshold of the post-Constantinian era. Traditionally, princes had been represented at councils for two important reasons: first, because papal bulls could not be implemented without the approval of national political authorities; and, second, because the secular authorities were called upon to punish those who infringed conciliar decrees. Neither of these considerations had any further relevance in the post-revolutionary world.

Though not exactly a papist, Ernest Renan nevertheless wrote in 1868 the following commendation of the papacy: "I have no doubt that in our day a Gallican church, dependent on the state, would press far more heavily on our liberty than a church dependent on Rome. Rather the papacy than the caesaropapism of Constantinople or Moscow." Some years later he added that "there is no longer any place for the state, in the sense of the absolute state as formerly understood by the politicians of France or as now understood by those of Prussia; and I am delighted at this, gratefully acknowledging that Catholicism has done in this case what it has done more than once before—that is, it has prevented the formation of an excessively strong state. A doctrinaire state is always a tyranny."[69] Renan was referring in this instance to the *Kulturkampf*, and the Prussian Protestant conception of the subordination of church to state. Faced with that, he suddenly appreciated the merits of Catholicism, which insisted on its international character and refused to be reduced to the status of a mere state religion.

Vatican I was what the reactionaries had been waiting for. *L'Avenir* had barely survived the thunderous condemnation of liberalism promulgated by Pope Gregory XVI in 1832, and Lamennais had gradually distanced himself from both liberalism and the church. Then, in 1864, came the *Syllabus of Errors*, an uncompromising repudiation of the "modern world." Under the leadership of Louis Veuillot, ultramontanism was once again marching under the reactionary colors it had followed in the days of Maistre. As Vatican I approached, the liberals grew anxious. Lord Acton asked whether a "successor of Alexander VI might distribute the New World over again," and a wave of disquiet rippled through "enlightened" Europe.[70] In the great confrontation that pitted reactionary Catholics against those more favorable to democratic government and the freedom of the individual, it looked as though the reactionaries were gaining the upper hand. To the consternation of many observers, the Catholic Church seemed to be lurching still further to the right, definitively aligning itself with the forces of Counter-Revolution. The papacy seemed to be canonizing the political doctrines of Joseph de Maistre. The autonomy of the temporal sphere was being called into doubt, along with the loyalty of Catholic citizens to their respective states.

In a memorandum written to warn Napoleon III about the dangers of the forthcoming council, one of the remaining Gallican bishops, Monsignor Maret, wrote as follows:

> Will it really be possible to confine the absolute infallibility of the pope to matters of faith? There will be a perfectly natural tendency for Catholics to extend it to everything, or at least to moral and social issues, and then by extension to politics as well, given that politics is so closely bound to them.[71]

At the end of his life, in 1869, shortly before Vatican I, Montalembert, who had long stood for ultramontanism out of loyalty to *L'Avenir*, changed his views because of his disquiet at the illiberalism of the *zelanti*. He wrote that in the end he understood "the salutary reservations and guarantees (however mixed up with discreditable exaggerations) upon which our ancestors always insisted in their efforts to restrain the abuse of ecclesiastical power."[72] For similar reasons, Vatican I still has a slightly sinister reputation today. Historians tend to emphasize the antimodern tendencies that were so marked a feature of it. The definition of papal infallibility was redolent of a yearning for authority, for a hierocratic rather than a democratic way of doing business. The Utopian visions of Maistre gave rise to apparently well-founded fears. However, with the benefit of hindsight, we can say that Maret and Montalembert got it wrong. The council was to signal not a resurgence of the papacy's temporal ambitions but a refocusing on its spiritual role.

In France, Emile Ollivier's position carried the day in 1869–70. Some thirty years later, the advocates of the separation of church and state unconsciously echoed his opinion:

> The promulgation in 1870 of the dogma of papal infallibility, which constituted a clear repudiation of Gallicanism, marked the culmination of the papacy's long struggle to make the church one great strongly centralized society, to concentrate all power in the hands of the bishop of Rome, to exclude from church government any authority independent of his, and to do away with the national churches. In view of this, the separation of the Catholic Church from the French state was a necessary step, one that might have been hastened by events, but which sooner or later must inevitably have occurred anyway.[73]

Ollivier's speech to the National Assembly (which was quoted a little earlier) met with papal disapproval.[74] But it is worth noting that ideas little different from his were expressed by no less authoritative a figure than Cardinal Manning, archbishop of Westminster, one of the most ardent proponents of the decree on papal infallibility. In a pamphlet entitled *Caesarism and Ultramontanism*, he wrote: "Ultramontanism consists in the separation of the two powers and the vesting them in different persons"; and "The natural antagonist of Caesarism is the Christian Church with all its liberties of doctrine and discipline, of faith and jurisdiction; and the vindication of those liberties of the church in their highest and most sacred form is Ultramontanism."[75] Manning saw papal infallibility as the way to escape the danger of "Caesarism," to release the church from the grip of a state which had lost all legitimacy in religious matters.

The spiritual authority of the papacy had thus been asserted with unprecedented vigor, to an extent which was deeply disturbing to states that were anxious about their sovereignty. So the papacy felt obliged to offer some reassurances, emphasizing that it respected the legitimate autonomy of the political sphere. In 1871, it declared

> It is a pernicious error to claim that infallibility reasserts a right to depose sovereigns and to release people from their oaths of allegiance.[76]

This statement was an explicit repudiation of Maistre's agenda, which had sought precisely to equip the pope with the "right to depose sovereigns and to release people from their oaths of allegiance." One of the best theologians of the period, Père Gratry, who had initially opposed the declaration on infallibility, accepted it in the end, explaining

What I was afraid of was a claim to infallibility in the spheres of science, politics, and government. But the actual decree is confined to a doctrinal infallibility in the spheres of faith and morals.[77]

By confining the victory of ultramontanism to the spiritual sphere, the council upheld a separation of the temporal from the spiritual, which they would otherwise have been accused of obliterating. The breach with *ecclesiastical* Gallicanism was thus evident: but there was no such breach with the *political* Gallicanism of the Ancien Regime. When Pius IX and his successor, Leo XIII, dealt explicitly with the relations between the temporal and the spiritual power, they did so in terms that would have been familiar to Gallicans, for they affirmed the sovereignty of the two powers in their respective domains.

Infallibility was thus a prerogative in the dogmatic sphere, which had no implications for papal authority in matters of law or politics. As a perceptive observer wrote in 1868,

> If the council establishes papal infallibility, then it will certainly not ascribe a supernatural character to anything and everything that the Holy Father might say or write. It will hedge around the exercise of this wonderful power with precautions and formalities. The pope will not be declared infallible except under closely defined conditions and in rare and exceptional cases. And what will be the logical outcome of this? That, outside that narrow field, with all due respect, he will be as liable to error as anybody else, so that everybody will feel free to judge and criticize his actions, his speeches, and his writings. So the very victory that strengthens his authority in this one precise point will weaken it in everything else. It may well be that God is inspiring this definition not in order to build up the position of his representative on earth, but rather to set some sort of limit on it, to deflate the virtual apotheosis of the papacy that has been sought in some quarters.[78]

I have already mentioned the ultramontane who wanted to have "a new papal Bull every morning with my *Times* at breakfast." The advocates of infallibility seemed to have won the day, but "infallibility" proved a particularly difficult tool to handle, liable to bring down ridicule upon any pope who risked being seen as abusing it. Would any pope be foolhardy enough to grant Ward's wish for a daily bull? Since 1870, only one papal document has explicitly fulfilled the *ex cathedra* conditions of infallibility—the definition of the assumption of the Blessed Virgin Mary into heaven, promulgated in 1950.

Giving the impression that papal infallibility entailed a kind of papal absolutism, Joseph de Maistre had linked infallibility to the medieval notion of the papal *plenitudo potestatis* (fullness of power). Yet these concepts were in certain respects incompatible. "Infallibility" entails an intrinsic restriction on freedom of action, as it implies that a particular decision may be irrevocable. The papacy itself is bound by an infallible decision and cannot go back on it. Indeed, in the Middle Ages it was the exponents of the papal *plenitudo potestatis* who were opposed to the concept of infallibility.[79] By a curious twist, it was infallibility envisaged as a kind of limitation that the fathers of the council endorsed in 1870. The majority of Catholic theologians subscribed to a very narrow interpretation of the doctrine. Ultimately, it was a matter not of the arbitrary power of the pope and his theological predilections but of the consensus of the universal church. Infallibility was about safeguarding the "deposit of the faith," which was reckoned to have been complete at the death of the last apostle. An infallible definition could neither add to nor take away from the content of revealed truth, nor could it concern any other kind of truth. Papal teaching itself was but a single element in the process of the clarification of revealed truth, a process that involved the whole church. It can be argued that the anti-infallibilist minority had "triumphed in defeat."[80]

In practice, the ultramontanism that triumphed in 1870 respected the sovereignty claimed by the state. It was not a doctrine that aimed at the subordination of the state, for it was not Maistre's program but *L'Avenir's* that had been implemented. This can be clearly seen in the appointment of bishops, in which the pope managed to marginalize the states and secure a free hand for himself. In previous centuries, governments had rarely failed to interest themselves in episcopal appointments. How could they remain indifferent to the filling of posts that often gave their holders immense power? The church had not always been unable to resist government intervention, and for a long time the civil power had played a decisive role in the choice of bishops. This, after all, was precisely the issue at the heart of the quarrel over the Civil Constitution of the Clergy. The members of the Constituent Assembly had sought to put an end to absolutism and indeed to strip the monarch of all power. To rule out any possibility of recourse to the Most Christian King, he was replaced by the people. The Concordat of 1801 solved the problem with a mixture of Caesarism and episcopalianism which got around popular sovereignty: the faithful were under the control of the bishops, and the bishops under that of the emperor, while the emperor had to reach an understanding with the pope. But, as we have seen, this compromise was not without its own difficulties. In a book on *La tradition de l'Eglise sur l'institution des évêques* (The tradition of the church on the appointment of bishops), written between 1810 and 1813, Lamennais set out to defend Roman centralism against Napoleonic pretensions.[81] The fiftieth of the errors that would be condemned by the *Syllabus* of 1864 was the thesis that "the secular power has of itself the right to nominate bishops." Today, the secular authorities hardly ever seek to intervene in episcopal appointments. A canon lawyer was recently able to say something that could scarcely have been dreamed of in 1800 and would still have been far from universally true even in 1900: "The principle of the free choice of bishops by the pope is more firmly established than ever. . . . He freely places his vicars anywhere in the world."[82] The primacy of the pope is directly connected to the liberty of the church.

To the extent that the church cast off the shackles of the state, it regained the power to convene synods or conferences of bishops, and bishops in their turn regained the power to communicate freely with Rome. It was, bizarrely enough, the French Revolution that finally enabled the church to implement the full program of reform envisaged at the Council of Trent, which the Most Christian Kings had refused formally to "receive" by authorizing the promulgation of its decrees.[83]

To sum up: unable to immerse itself in the democratic system without losing its very identity, the church felt the need instead to reassert its character as a distinct entity. It therefore largely abandoned the Gallicanism that had woven it into the fabric of the Ancien Regime. Unable any longer to identify with a state that had cast off its essentially confessional character, Catholics instead identified themselves as never before with the papacy. Joseph de Maistre was in both theory and practice the initiator of this shift, which was officially ratified at Vatican I. "Destroyed in theory by the writings of two great authors, the Comte de Maistre and M. de Lamennais (before he lapsed), Gallican liberties were finished off in practice by a theologian of an altogether different stamp, the First Consul—Napoleon Bonaparte."[84] The ultramontanes turned toward the papacy to protect the church from enslavement to a temporal power that was now entirely alien to it. The church adopted elements of ultramontanism because, jealous of its own independence, it discerned a grain of truth in the thought of the counter-revolutionaries. Although tied up with a stridently antiliberal and counter-revolutionary political movement, ultramontanism had left its mark—not because the church was to be permanently wedded to that kind of antiliberalism, but because ultramontanism responded to one of the most basic concerns of the church in its relationship with the state, the concern for liberty. Confronted with the democratic tendency toward homogenization (as manifested with particular clarity in the Civil Constitution of the Clergy), the church reacted with an attempt to secure a separation of respective spheres by establishing the independence of the spiritual power. Democratic monism needs to be counterbalanced by the liberal separation of church and state. The development of ideas about papal authority reflected wider developments in ecclesiology made necessary by the division of politics and religion consequent upon the French Revolution.

The church now saw the independence of a sovereign papacy, above and beyond the reach of the nation-state, as the only way to safeguard its spiritual autonomy. Of course, ultramontanism was not, in itself, a variety of liberalism. But these two apparently disparate ideologies were able to converge with a disconcerting ease that says a great deal for their underlying kinship. In fact, it was the alliance between ultramontanism and reactionary politics that proved contingent and provisional, because ultramontanism presupposed the very processes of democratization and secularization that reactionary politics sought to undo. Modern ultramontanism came *after* the secularization of the state because it was a result of it. In a sense, the triumph of ultramontanism at Vatican I presupposed the very liberalism that so many ultramontanes despised, and this is, to be sure, why ultramontanism had an influence within the Catholic Church which ought not to be entirely repudiated. If it is true that the laity and clergy are not equally attentive to the words and deeds of the papacy, they are nevertheless far more attached to them than they were before the nineteenth century. The papacy has never had such a central place in Catholic life as it has had since the end of "Christendom" and the coming of "secularization."

First of all, popular devotion to the pope has retained in the twentieth and twenty-first centuries all the vitality that it took on under Pius IX (1792–1878).[85] Catholics go to Rome not, as at one time, to pray at the shrines of the martyrs but to "see the pope."

Second, papal teaching, which had only a limited role in Catholic life under the Ancien Regime, has assumed a new level of importance through the means of papal encyclicals (open letters from the pope to the episcopate) and papal audiences with gatherings of the priests and the faithful. The first-ever encyclical letter was issued in the eighteenth century. Since the pontificate of Leo XIII (1878–1903), the numbers have risen sharply and currently total around three hundred. The genre itself has evolved. The earliest encyclicals were essentially occasional pieces, for example, the manifesto of a newly elected pope or a letter of encouragement to bishops. With the advent of the French Revolution they took on a polemical turn, responding to the tense situation in which the church found itself in modern society. Since the late nineteenth century they have become a means for the papacy to develop and to deepen Catholic doctrine, notably Catholic social teaching. They have thus conferred new importance on the "ordinary magisterium" of the popes.[86]

Third, the jurisdictional primacy of the pope, long disputed within the church but solemnly asserted by Vatican I, is now written into the fabric of canon law. It is this which justifies the role of the papacy in appointing bishops.

> The Roman pontiff, primate in succession to St Peter, has not only a primacy of honor but the full and supreme power of jurisdiction over the universal church, in what concerns faith and morals as much as in what concerns the discipline and government of the church spread throughout the world. This power is genuinely episcopal, ordinary, and immediate; it extends over each and every church and over each and every one of the clergy and the faithful; and it is independent of any human authority.[87]

During the debates over *Pastor Aeternus*, the most lively discussions focused on the terms used to describe papal jurisdiction: *episcopalis, ordinaria, immediata*.[88] These words amounted to an epitaph for the age of absolutism and evoked a different model of relations between church and state, one that had gradually come to prevail since the French Revolution. The primacy of the pope within the universal church, as much in church governance as in the safeguarding of doctrine, "no longer causes problems in Catholicism today," as a well-informed observer has remarked.[89]

Notwithstanding both the hopes of reactionaries and the fears of liberals, the definition of papal infallibility did not upset the new relationship between church and state established in the wake of the French Revolution. In order to respond to the democratic tendency toward the homogenization and politicization of society, it was necessary to separate the two spheres, as the liberal ultramontanes wanted, but it was also necessary to deepen the Gallican conception of a Christian politics. The local rootedness of the Catholic Church, if it was not balanced by central authority, could give rise to a violent theological polarization that precluded any moderation or middle way. But the central authority of the pope, if it was not balanced by a Catholicism with deep local roots, could degenerate into hypercentralism and spiritual despotism.

Alexis de Tocqueville and the Preservation of Gallicanism

Lamennais's liberal phase is of especial importance because it shows how the process that led from the secularization of the state to ultramontanism took for granted the separation of church and state which the liberals demanded. However, this phase of his life was short. The papal encyclical *Mirari vos*, which appeared on 15 August 1832, condemned *L'Avenir,* along with the "erroneous or, rather, insane thesis that freedom of conscience should be accorded to anyone who demands it," and denounced "the execrable and detestable freedom of the press." But in any case, ultramontane liberalism was a tender plant.

Lamennais had become an ultramontane in the hope of preserving the Catholic character of the state: the superior authority of the papacy would somehow keep within the confines of Christendom states that were no longer explicitly confessional. In the end, anxious to protect the church against a state that refused to put itself under the tutelage of the Holy See, he became a liberal, denying the state any right whatsoever to intervene in religious affairs. But the initial problem remained: how to ensure that the state remained within or reentered the orbit of Christendom? Reactionary ultramontanes were chasing a utopian will-o'-the-wisp, but their fantasy was at least theoretically coherent. Liberal ultramontanes renounced the utopianism, but in doing so they forfeited what gave ultramontanism its political vitality: the capacity to evangelize, to energize collective life thanks to the political authority of the papacy.

It was not enough to show how the church could be protected against the ill-timed or ill-judged interventions of an apostate regime: it was also necessary to show how the church could maintain its spiritual authority over the state. The church aimed to defend its freedom of worship, its internal autonomy, its very existence. But it also aspired to spread its message, to christianize social life, and to shed its light upon the temporal world. Freedom had two dimensions: one negative, the absence of constraint; and the other positive, the opportunity to participate in the good. Once he had become a liberal, Lamennais's priority was the freedom of the church understood as the absence of constraint. But what did he have to say about the formulation of legislation or government policy? If such matters were not to be decided under the supervision of the papacy, as the reactionaries wanted, how were they to be decided? Lamennais had no answer to these questions, at least not in the *L'Avenir* period.

After *Mirari vos*, in 1832, Lamennais renounced Catholicism, though not Christianity. He became a democrat, substituting the infallibility of a people come of age for that of the kings and the church which had not heeded him. He had relied upon kings, acting under the aegis of popes, to infuse political life with a Christian character. But kings had proved unwilling to accept papal guidance, so it was necessary to seek some other authority capable of conferring that Christian character upon the state, its laws, and everyday life. In *Le Livre du peuple* (The book of the people, 1837), *La Religion* (1841), and *L'Esquisse d'une philosophie* (Outline of a philosophy, 1840–46), Lamennais vested his hopes in the people. This new direction in his thinking provides a telling illustration of the problem that liberal ultramontanism posed: how to infuse a Christian spirit into the social and political world created by the Revolution? Squeezed between his reactionary phase and his democratic phase, Lamennais's liberal phase was short, because it ran up against the question of the ends that the state ought to pursue. In entrusting the political hopes of Christianity to the people, Lamennais blazed a trail that the church would eventually follow. It was a new path, the path of Christian democracy and Christian political parties. But by abandoning the church for a form of anti-institutional Christianity, Lamennais deprived himself of any further opportunity of exercising a direct influence on Catholicism.

Lamennais had turned toward the people because it seemed to him that the people were genuinely Christian. This intellectual and political move showed that, despite the Revolution, Christianity had not been exorcised from France. The law might be atheistic, but the people were still Christian. It was no longer necessary to look to the papacy to keep the nation within the ambit of Christendom. It was still possible to be Gallican! And, indeed, there were still some Gallicans in France who refused to dismiss the Revolution as a satanic enterprise.

I have already mentioned Portalis, the author of the Civil Code, one of the greatest jurists in French history. He maintained that Gallicanism was indispensable, observing that the crucial tenets proposed in the Declaration of the Clergy in 1682 "cannot be ignored by any good citizen."[90] He defended Gallican principles for several reasons. For one thing, a close connection between church and state was good for the state, because "law and discipline are not enough.

The law regulates only specific fields of action: religion embraces everything. The law reaches only the body: religion touches the heart. The law binds only the citizen: religion binds the person."[91] Portalis reckoned that atheistic skepticism made people "not tolerant, but unruly."[92] Yet a close connection between church and state was also good for the church: "When a religious leader clashes with the secular power, he compromises his religion in the opinion of the people."[93] The union of church and state was entirely symbiotic.

Notwithstanding the French Revolution, many right-minded men remained attached to the old certitudes of the French monarchy. Portalis felt no need to look to Rome. He was happy to remain a Gallican, and he was not alone. Royer-Collard, Monsignor Henry Maret (1805–84, dean of the Sorbonne), and Monsignor Darboy (1813–71, archbishop of Paris) all shared his views.

Gallicans such as these were sensitive to the Christian currents that still ran in French society, and indeed the French state, and thought them worth maintaining, renewing, and fostering. They had no intention of entrusting the hopes of French Catholicism to any power outside France itself, such as the Holy See. They relied on the still vigorous traditions of centuries of Christianity. Nineteenth-century France remained profoundly Catholic. True, not all the French were devout: but had they ever been? Art and literature, the framework of intellectual life, social institutions, and national identity—all remained as Catholic as ever, if not more so. Religious vocations were rising, and there was an unprecedented fervor for missionary work overseas.

Monsignor Darboy laid particular emphasis on the embeddedness of Catholicism in France, invoking the classic distinction between "missionary territory" and "countries with established churches." The latter were characterized by their "bishops, the duly established ordinaries, who, subject to the Holy See and within the limits of the law, wield full authority and exercise full responsibility." In missionary territory, however, the Holy See had a more direct role. For Darboy, French Catholicism continued to flourish and the French church remained "established." It had its own customs, its own organization, and its own resources—hence his opposition to Vatican I. For him, the Vatican Council was surreptitiously imposing on France "a regime appropriate to missionary territory."[94] His aim was to stop post-revolutionary dechristianization being used as a pretext for treating France as though it were China or India. He was determined to make sure that French ecclesiastical institutions were not stripped of their relative autonomy and distinctive identity by being brought systematically under Roman control. There was no reason for Catholics to feel alienated, strangers in a country that remained as profoundly Catholic as France.

This point can be further developed with reference to issues of geography and sociology. Taking geographical considerations first, it should be noted that the attitudes of the minority and of the majority at Vatican I reflected remarkably closely the extent to which they felt rooted in, or alienated from, the cultures of their home countries. Ultramontanism triumphed in France and Spain, where the impact of the Revolution was greatest. But it remained weaker in those places which the Revolution had almost passed by, where the ordinary course of things was barely affected by events. Who were the members of the minority that was defeated with the definition of papal infallibility? They came for the most part from the most conservative regions of Catholic Europe, where the church was still firmly integrated, where the impact of the French Revolution was barely felt, and where there was little sense that the world had changed or that the church therefore needed to adapt: Austria, Bavaria, and Switzerland.[95] Ultramontanism was an opposition phenomenon—but in these countries Catholics were not in opposition. The schism of the "Old Catholics," who rejected the definition of papal infallibility, was a decidedly conservative schism.

From the sociological point of view, it is worth noting that, within France, the divisions over infallibility reflected class structure and social background.[96] The ultramontanes were for the most part either from humble or from aristocratic backgrounds. Those of humble origins had no illustrious past to hark back to: Louis Veuillot, for example, was the son of a cooper. As for the aristocrats, they had borne the brunt of the Revolution, which overthrew their class. The great prelates of noble birth, who felt an almost feudal attachment to their dioceses, had been brutally detached from them by the experience of exile. The new episcopate was no longer woven into the social order by noble birth and ancient landed endowment. The nineteenth-century Gallicans, on the other hand, tended to have neither aristocratic nor humble origins. They came from the bourgeoisie, mostly from its upper reaches. They were very much at home in the new world, which embodied the political victory of their class and was, in effect, created in their image. They did not see their Catholic faith standing in any kind of opposition to the world that had emerged from the bourgeois revolution.

Gallicans therefore strove to maintain close links between church and government in order to preserve and reinvigorate the Christian character of the state. During the Second Empire, Monsignor Maret and Monsignor Darboy collaborated closely with Napoleon III's ministers.[97] This connection secured the appointment of a series of Gallican bishops who identified more closely with the nation than with their ultramontane counterparts. These latter, in contrast, were politically out of step with the nation and were seen as too eager to subordinate the French church to Rome.

Moreover, Maret also worked hard to strengthen the Catholic theology faculties, which had been reestablished in 1808, hoping to see them become pillars of both church and government. To prevent the clergy from becoming strangers in the new society, he devoted himself to building up these institutions, despite the misgivings of the Holy See. In the interests of tightening the bonds between the state and the religious elites, and of integrating Catholic intellectual life with that of the nation, he was happy to see Catholic higher education carried out within the interdisciplinary context of the University of France.[98]

As long as they were good patriots (i.e., Gallicans), Catholics took an active part in political life. Thus, they sought to give the state a Christian character that would render state intervention in religious matters more acceptable. The nineteenth-century Gallicans saw themselves as continuing the Gallican traditions of the eighteenth century. However, their Gallicanism was different in one crucial respect from that of the Ancien Regime, which yoked the church to political absolutism. Gallicans such as Royer-Collard and Maret were not absolutists in the mold of Bossuet, and for that reason it is better to describe them as "neo-Gallicans."[99] Royer-Collard was an especially energetic opponent of the sacrilege law, and Maret had once been a disciple of Lamennais. They did not seek to deny the relative secularization of the state, and they were as committed as the ultramontanes to the defense of the freedom of the church. They protested against the Organic Articles, and they insisted on the freedom of the press. The keynotes of *L'Avenir* had left their mark on the neo-Gallicans, who shared its liberalism, though not its ultramontanism.

The policy of the neo-Gallicans was to pursue close collaboration between church and government, while accepting that an important underlying change had taken place. Maret explained that the separation of church and state "was a simple fact, and had been for half a century."

> From the moment that freedom of conscience and worship were established in our laws, there was no longer a state religion or an official system of doctrine. As there was no longer any uniformity in doctrine, there had to be a legal and political separation. The arrangement embodied in the Concordat is a pragmatic alliance, an administrative and financial understanding that prescinds from the question of the truth of Catholicism, which it regards simply as a social fact, a social utility, a national belief.[100]

To say that church and state were already separate was to imply that there was nothing to be gained from any further separation and thus to justify the Concordat's pragmatic collaboration between church and government, even if the latter regarded Catholicism merely as a "social fact" rather than as the true religion.

The Gallican ideal was of a harmony between religious and political life. In the age of absolutism, this committed the church to absolute monarchy. But in the democratic era it committed the church to democracy and thus to a political role for the Catholic laity.[101] What was the best way of ensuring the proper separation of church and state, of maintaining the proper distinction between God and Caesar? It was to entrust political authority to lay believers, to *convert Caesar*—the "Caesar" that was the sovereign people. Before aligning himself with the regime of Napoleon III, Maret had been one of the pioneers of

Christian democracy.[102] For the neo-Gallicans, the more Christian the sovereign people, the more Christian the law. If, as it said in the Concordat, Catholicism was "the religion of the majority of the French people," and if democracy was a form of government that ensured the rule of the majority, then the church ought to lend its weight to that form of government, so that neither the state nor the law would be atheistic. Differentiating between the spheres of religion and politics did not necessarily entail the privatization of religion.

Portalis, Royer-Collard, and Maret were astute figures who sought to reconcile Gallicanism with the spirit of 1789, but they lacked the breadth of vision of a Maistre or a Lamennais in political theology. Does this mean that the finest minds of the age were ultramontanes rather than Gallicans? Only if one leaves out the greatest political thinker of the nineteenth century, one whom we have already had cause to mention: Alexis de Tocqueville (1805–59).

Brought up a Catholic, Tocqueville had lost his faith in adolescence. However, unlike some of his contemporaries, he made no public issue of his religious doubts. In one aside in *Democracy in America*, for example, he wrote that as "a member of the Roman Catholic Church I was more particularly brought into contact with several of its priests."[103] In the acceptance speech he made on admission to the Académie Française, obliged to say something about the late Tocqueville, whose place he was taking, Lacordaire was able to say, "if his faith was at times lacking, there was never any impiety in his heart, nor did blasphemy ever pass his lips."[104] Tocqueville was a great admirer of Pascal and took Christianity extremely seriously. His lack of faith was more a matter of regret to him than of pride. Lacordaire may have exaggerated in declaring that "there was never any impiety in his heart," but he was right in emphasizing that Tocqueville never lapsed into blasphemy.

In a letter to his brother, Tocqueville once wrote:

> My highest aim in entering political life was to play some part in reconciling the spirit of freedom with the spirit of religion, and the clergy with the new social order![105]

From the social and political point of view, Tocqueville was not so much opposed to the Catholic Church as inclined to support it. He wanted to be French and Catholic: he was a Gallican, and he admired the clergy of the Ancien Regime:

> I do not know whether, all in all, notwithstanding the extraordinary vices of some of their members, there has ever in all the world been a body of clergy more outstanding than the Catholic priests of France at the moment the Revolution overtook them—more enlightened, more patriotic, less preoccupied with purely private virtues, more abundant in public virtues, yet at the same time of more faith. The persecution proved it.[106]

There is more than an echo here of Bossuet's boast that "the Gallican church has produced the most learned, the most holy, and the most illustrious bishops

there have ever been." But Tocqueville adds special praise for the political qualities of the clergy as "patriotic" and "abounding in public virtues." As a Gallican,
he was committed to the separation of the temporal and the spiritual orders,
but he saw the political spirit of the clergy as crucial to the smooth functioning
of that separation. He contrasted such a clergy with the ultramontanes, who, he
concluded, had become "foreign to the passions and interests of their own
country."[107]

Joseph de Maistre had remarked with some bitterness that "Louis XIV found
no difficulty whatsoever in establishing it as a fundamental law that a *General
Council is superior to a pope*; yet that is as much to say, by clear, direct, and ir-
refutable logic, that the *Estates-General is superior to the king*."[108] Tocqueville's
position was the converse of Maistre's: he was in favor of ecclesiastical councils
precisely because they embodied the same spirit as representative political institutions. Commitment to parliamentary government led him to defend conciliarism against ultramontanism.

> What! You are living in a recalcitrant century that denies or challenges
> authority wherever it finds it; you are living in the midst of a skeptical
> nation that only just tolerates the rule of laws it has made itself and which
> has no respect for any power, not even for those it has itself raised up;
> and yet among all the forms that Catholicism might take on, you choose
> the one in which authority flaunts itself in its most absolute and arbi-
> trary colors, and you want to impose that upon the faithful. You have
> the amazing good fortune to find in our country a sort of ready-made
> doctrine of representative government in religion [i.e., conciliarism], a
> doctrine that puts constitutional limits, so to speak, on papal authority,
> and yet you turn your back on that French Catholicism, so thoroughly in
> harmony with the contemporary spirit and institutions of our nation, and
> rush instead to embrace doctrines and principles [i.e., ultramontanism]
> that are foreign to our history and our traditions, and which even the
> Ancien Regime rejected.[109]

At the level of political theory, the conciliarist tradition was the most reasonable and the most balanced system, and not simply because it furnished practical juridical solutions for the problem of a pope who became heretic. Throughout the Middle Ages, Christians had debated the political merits of conciliarism,
and in hindsight those debates were among the wellsprings of parliamentary
and constitutional government—not just in the eyes of Joseph de Maistre but
also in those of many historians who in no way shared his political and theological predilections.[110]

Tocqueville explained to his Catholic friends that the march of democracy
was unstoppable. Indeed, he was so struck with society's steady progress toward
equality that he spoke of it in religious terms, as a "providential" movement,
almost as if there were some new kind of "divine right," a divine right of peoples
rather than of kings. He warned reactionaries that it was futile trying to turn

the clock back. The work of the French Revolution was irreversible. Moreover, it was absolute monarchy itself which, in denuding the aristocracy of its traditional power, had prepared the ground for the Revolution by beginning a process of social leveling. Those who hankered after the Ancien Regime were indulging in nostalgia for the system that had actually engendered the very developments they deplored! For Tocqueville and other neo-Gallicans, Catholics simply had to become, to some extent, democrats.

There were two complementary elements to Tocqueville's argument. On the one hand, he argued that the appropriate mode of political operation for religion, above all in a democracy, was indirect—hence his disagreement with Maistre. On the other hand, he argued that it was democracy above all that needed religion's indirect power, and that this would strengthen the authority of the church.

Tocqueville supported the separation of church and state because it protected the church against corruption and enhanced its spiritual authority. The great discovery of liberal philosophers was that the beneficial social effects of Christianity need not depend on its formal establishment in a confessional state, as under the Ancien Regime. The state could do without an established or official religion, and it was within such a context that religion could best fulfill its true political destiny, namely the exercise of indirect influence.

The post-revolutionary liberal tradition to which Tocqueville belonged was keenly aware of the vulnerability of true liberty, and of the dangers in a liberty without limits. Therefore, in his view, liberty had to be not only protected but restrained. Yet was not restraint the opposite of liberty? It was here that Tocqueville saw a political role for religion, as he explains in this passage:

> Religion in America takes no direct part in the government of society, but it must nevertheless be regarded as the foremost of the political institutions of that country; for if it does not impart a taste for freedom, it facilitates the use of free institutions.[111]

Only religion could restrain liberty without destroying it, precisely because its action was indirect. Religion had a central role because it alone could be "the foremost of political institutions" without having "a direct part in the government of society." Under democracy, the individual was liable to experience serious deracination and a sort of intellectual paralysis. Liberty needed to be regulated, but this should not be done directly. This was why "free peoples have always acknowledged that they find it harder than others to do without religious beliefs."[112] The paradox lurking here is that it is religious authority that can stave off authoritarian politics. The advantage of moral or spiritual authority lies precisely in the fact that it is moral or spiritual, rather than physical.

One of the most important chapters of *Democracy in America* is devoted to the "Indirect influence of religious opinions upon political society in the United States." Every word in that title is carefully weighed, and attention is drawn to four key points: it is a matter of "influence," rather than of power or some political or legal prerogative; that influence in turn is "indirect," and not direct; it is an influence exerted by religious "beliefs," rather than the political activity of a clergy whose position is officially recognized by the state; and finally, this influence is exerted upon "political society," rather than on the state or on the government as such. Christianity does not organize or manage social life; it inspires or informs it.

Tocqueville insists on the inevitability of progress toward democracy all the more willingly because democracy is capable of being evangelized. Revelation fosters the practice of the virtues that society needs. It imposes limits on the state that serve as guarantees for its citizens. In constantly calling attention to the Gospel message, the church reins in, impedes, and counteracts wicked designs and policies that fall short of the basic demands of justice.

> Nature and circumstances concurred to make the inhabitants of the United States bold men, as is sufficiently attested by the enterprising spirit with which they seek for fortune. If the minds of the Americans were free from all trammels, they would very shortly become the most daring innovators and the most implacable disputants in the world. But the revolutionists of America are obliged to profess an ostensible respect for Christian morality and equity, which does not easily permit them to violate the laws that oppose their designs; nor would they find it easy to surmount the scruples of their partisans, even if they were able get over their own. Hitherto no one, in the United States, has dared to advance the maxim, that everything is permissible with a view to the interests of society; an impious adage, which seems to have been invented in an age of freedom, to shelter all the tyrants of future ages. Thus, while the law permits the Americans to do what they please, religion prevents them from conceiving, and forbids them to commit, what is rash or unjust.[113]

For Tocqueville, "the American, in professing his religion, forbids *himself* from envisaging everything, forbids *himself* from daring everything. He recoils, through fear or prudence, from the idea of absolute autonomy at the heart of the democratic idea." Thanks to religion, "democracy voluntarily stops this side of the untrammeled human sovereignty that its own principles postulate."[114] Christianity furnishes a moral framework and a background of fundamental laws from which a Christian society, to the extent that it is Christian, can neither easily nor entirely detach itself.

A liberal society does not have so great a need for virtue as an ancient democracy, in which each citizen was expected at all times to put the common interest of the state above his own private interest. For liberal societies exist in the context of a state that looks after the common good and thus fulfills the tasks that in the ancient republics were demanded of civic virtue. Nevertheless, a liberal society still has need of virtue. Some disposition to obey the law is essential. One can hardly have a police officer watching over each and every citizen, or indeed over each and every police officer. Some sense of the identity and worth of the state is also necessary. For some citizens must devote themselves to the common good as judges, civil servants, or politicians. In the absence of virtue, democracies tend toward Caesarism.

Norbert Elias has described the birth of modernity as a "process of civilization," focusing attention on the rise of self-restraint in individual behavior.[115] In doing so he has returned to a theme which has fascinated political thinkers from Montesquieu to Tocqueville, namely the sociological preconditions of liberty, and in particular the place of religion among them. "The less repressive the religion, the more repressive the civil laws have to be," wrote Montesquieu.[116] In a similar fashion, Tocqueville explained that religion facilitated the practice of liberty. Indeed, he went so far as to say, "I doubt whether man can ever support at the same time complete religious independence and entire public freedom."[117] A people that is master of itself needs to be subject to God. For if it is not subject to God, it will not be master of itself. Religion had the capacity to regulate social customs: "Liberty is begotten not so much of institutions as of social customs, and social customs are begotten of beliefs."[118]

The advent of modern democracy was accompanied by the emergence of two languages: the language of interest and the language of individual rights. These two languages relate to the two extremes that threaten modern democracy: complete materialism, when "interest" dominates; and absolute individualism, when individual rights are idolized. Tocqueville observed that Christianity afforded democracy some level of protection against these extremes. Although the progress of equality "lays open the soul to an inordinate love of material gratification" and tends to isolate people "from each other, to concentrate every man's attention upon himself," the "greatest advantage of religion is to inspire diametrically contrary principles."[119]

The ultramontanes harbored two related aims: to guard the liberty of the church from a state that had become alien to it, and yet to retain that state within the orbit of Christendom. They looked to Rome for the realization of these aims. Catholics of the school of Tocqueville shared their aspirations but not their trust in Rome. They thought it more prudent to campaign for a liberal regime that would respect the freedom of its subjects and therefore also of the church. Even in a liberal democratic regime, Christianity could play the restraining role that it was thought to play in confessional states. The error of the ultramontanes was to imagine that democracy could be neither evangelized nor restrained except *from the outside*, by the pope. The American example allowed Tocqueville to argue that democracy could be both evangelized and restrained *from the inside*, by Christianity. Christianity was able to impose certain beneficial restraints upon democracy. It limited the sphere of the politically imaginable. It reined in democratic hubris, which could not be restrained by any legacy of aristocracy. And it could do this all the more effectively in that it acted indirectly.

Tocqueville criticized the ultramontanes' preference for absolutism in ecclesiastical government and was scornful of the political recklessness and stupidity that they displayed. Thus, in the context of the debates over freedom of education, in which he thought the church had an excellent case and ought to prevail, Tocqueville suffered agonies at the way the ultramontanes prejudiced their chances by an extremism that ended up alienating everyone whose support they needed. In December 1843 he offered the following opinion in a letter:

> They claim that the church has an intrinsic right to control education, and with this precious nonsense they arouse fears of an authoritarianism to which, in fact, they do not aspire. They have set out principles that would enable them not only to teach freely in their own schools but even to control the education offered in other schools: principles that they have neither any real intention nor the remotest chance of applying in contemporary society. This is simply to reawaken all the old fears and hatreds of the *philosophes*, without the slightest necessity.[120]

In the wake of the Revolution, Catholics could not expect, as Catholics, to set the agenda for the whole of society. Moreover, most of them had no real ambition to exercise the kind of authority that they liked to invoke in their more extravagant rhetoric. With this sort of contempt for compromise, the ultramontanes managed to provoke the liberals even when they themselves were merely demanding liberty. Such counter-revolutionary posturing was simply counterproductive.

In the same letter Tocqueville identified the culprit behind this misplaced zeal:

> When I reflect on the roots of this problem, I find that the principal, though not the sole, source is a journalist by the name of Veuillot. This one-time Saint-Simonian and republican has turned fanatical Catholic and become editor of *L'Univers religieux* [The religious universe]. But he has taken with him all the extremism and bitterness of his old affiliations, and he has done more than any other person to bring about the deplorable turn that events have taken. For the past two years I have been warning influential religious figures of the danger of what has now happened. I have spoken to all those who might have had some influence over *L'Univers*, but to no avail. I have also done my best to soothe the irritation of their opponents, at times with some success. But there is nothing more I can do, and this business, like so many other weighty matters, is now in the hands of fools and knaves.

After the condemnation of *L'Avenir*, *L'Univers* had been set up to give the ultramontane party a new mouthpiece. Veuillot joined it in 1839 and soon became its figurehead. For forty years he was to shape the conscience of the French clergy in both religion and politics, calling for wholehearted obedience to the teachings and the very wishes of the pope. In the Veuillot of 1843 Tocqueville could already discern the Veuillot of the Second Empire, a lay bishop whose intemperate rhetoric and savage irony brought joy to the hearts of rural parish priests who despaired of bishops who were often advocates of moderation and compromise.[121]

At bottom, Tocqueville criticized the ultramontanes as inept politicians. In Gallican fashion, he deplored their lack of patriotism:

> With regard to those entrusted to them for education, or over whom they have influence, I do not ask priests to make it a matter of conscience whether to support republicanism or monarchy. But I certainly do want them to emphasize to their flocks that, at the same time as being Christians, they belong to one of those great human societies that God has established in order, no doubt, to make more visible and tangible the ties that ought to bind individuals to one another. These societies we call "peoples," and their territory we call their "fatherland." I would like them to drum it into people's heads that everyone has a debt to this collective entity which takes priority over their individual autonomy, and that with regard to this collective entity, indifference is simply not an option.[122]

For all that religion can pose a danger to the state, this risk arises not only when religion is too political, as is generally imagined, but also when it is too apolitical, when believers develop a tendency to see nothing beyond their own religious group and become oblivious of the civic community to which they also belong. People are not just co-religionists but also fellow citizens.

Tocqueville's ideas had little immediate influence on the Catholic Church. Yet they would be vindicated at the Second Vatican Council, which reconnected with certain aspects of the liberal Gallican tradition: a commitment to religious liberty and to the role of the laity, and a more favorable outlook on democracy.

II

A New Role for the Laity

THE ORIGINS OF VATICAN II

3

Intolerant Secularism and Liberal Secularism

After a particularly lengthy and stormy debate, article 10 of the Declaration of the Rights of Man was formulated with a certain ambiguity. The statement that "no one shall be troubled over their opinions, not even in religion" was hardly a ringing endorsement of religious freedom. And the second part of the article, which read "provided that their expression does not disturb the public order established by law," was heavy with menace. One assembly member proposed an alternative formulation: "Everyone has freedom of opinion; every citizen has the right to profess his religion freely, and no one shall be troubled on account of his religion."[1] In fact, many revolutionaries were worried that the relegation of religion to the strictly private sphere might weaken social ties, undermining social cohesion and public morality. They were much taken with the idea of a new religion which could wean people off superstition while at the same time inculcating in them the revolutionary spirit.

Just as Catholics found it difficult to shed the habits of a lifetime spent under absolutism and ended up simply substituting papal absolutism for the royal version, so too the Revolutionary party found it difficult to divest itself of the absolutist notion that there had to be a state religion, even if it was no longer to be Roman Catholicism. The revolutionaries felt it imperative to find a substitute for Catholicism. After the setback over the Civil Constitution of the Clergy, they excogitated various cults (the cult of reason, theophilanthropy, the religion of the Supreme Being) in an attempt to anchor the Revolution in popular culture and to capture the imagination with civic pomp and ceremony.[2] "The revolutionaries, notwithstanding the popular view to the contrary, were not really secular, were not really emancipated from ideas of religion and worship. The vast majority of them did not believe that a nation could survive without religion and worship."[3]

The revolutionaries hoped to exorcise the church's power over souls by establishing a new spiritual power. But they failed. They bequeathed the problem to the nineteenth century, which sought to establish a *lay spiritual power*. Jules Michelet, for example, was hostile to the churches. However, the reason for this was not hatred of religion but the fact that, in his eyes, the true church, the true religion, was the Revolution itself. For him, the sight of a crowd gathered to mark the feast of the Federation, entering into communion with all humanity in the hope of a new world, represented the dawn of a new era. Transcending both space and time, the Revolution had celebrated the marriage of France with humanity.

Many republicans felt that the destiny of France had to be divorced from the destiny of the Catholic Church. The Gallican synthesis struck them as illusory or simply outmoded. At the Collège de France, in the 1840s, Edgar Quinet dedicated a course of lectures to the subject of ultramontanism, which he bizarrely presented as a constant feature of the Catholic Church through the previous few centuries; at the same time his colleague, Michelet, gave a course that, no less bizarrely, portrayed French national identity as essentially non-Catholic.[4] Having abandoned the monarchy of the "Most Christian King," they were searching for substitutes, divinizing liberty, equality, and fraternity, and trying to find a new religious truth in revolutionary democracy. The modern world was fulfilling the promise of Christianity, rendering the Catholic Church itself redundant. Prophets arose to elaborate political eschatologies and proclaim the new dawn.[5] Quinet, Michelet, Saint-Simon, and Leroux all felt that society could not do without spiritual power. But the Catholic Church's claim to this power was, by default, to be transferred to other churches. They would found their own churches and thus, at a stroke, set all humanity free from confusion, oppression, and imperfection.

Auguste Comte: From Papal Infallibility to the Infallibility of Science

Among the philosophers who were inspired by Joseph de Maistre one must include another founder of a religion, Auguste Comte (1798–1857). Neither a papist nor even a Catholic, Comte was essentially a radical agnostic. But he thought that Maistre was right on one key issue. Like Maistre, Comte saw the achievement of the Revolution as essentially negative and destructive. Individualism left people to their own devices, without guidance. In the absence of any organizing force, the post-revolutionary world was characterized by intellectual anarchy, a cacophony of individual opinions. Maistre and Comte agreed on one fundamental point: society was held together by spiritual bonds. To the extent that its individual members did not subscribe to a set of general principles capable of constructing a common social philosophy, society itself was essentially brittle.[6]

"Dogmatism is the default setting of the human mind."[7] Society exists only so far as its members share common beliefs. Comte had little sympathy with the concept of toleration, in which he saw only a metaphysical delusion:

> Systematic toleration cannot exist and really never has existed, except with regard to opinions regarded as unimportant or doubtful. This is evi-

dent from the actual proceedings of revolutionary politics, for all their talk of freedom of conscience.[8]

Unrestricted freedom of conscience left minds wandering and lost. Like Maistre, Comte had a profound contempt for the "purportedly constitutional regime," which demoralized citizens and degraded character. The Revolution had left society in a state of anarchy because it had failed to establish any spiritual power capable of generating a degree of intellectual consensus. Comte had real admiration for the Catholic system of the Middle Ages, and he was keen to emulate the success of the papacy in the twelfth and thirteenth centuries. In 1856 he even approached the Jesuits' superior general with a proposal for an alliance!

Comte saw the need for spiritual power in order to guide opinions and to impose some restraint on temporal power. Spiritual power reminded the powerful that they were in power only to carry out a socially useful function. It disciplined the pursuit of purely material interests. It moderated the rule of force, which it rendered less necessary and therefore less dangerous. It also guided people's interior lives. By disseminating a common pattern of thought, it secured the conditions of possibility for a just and stable organization of society and the state. In the absence of such spiritual power, temporal power would lack legitimacy, the sense of duty would evaporate, and egoism and brute force would prevail.

According to Comte, each stage in human history was marked by a distinct pattern of thought. But between these stages were times of transition in which society experienced difficulties as it found itself faced with inconsistent patterns of thought, which drew on ideas from incompatible philosophies. Such was the situation consequent upon the Revolution. In Comte's view, Maistre had at least understood that some unity in belief was imperative; he had simply failed to appreciate that the unity offered by Catholicism no longer spoke to the spirit of the age. Comte reckoned that Maistre's treatise *Du Pape* (On the pope) "had set out the most methodical, most penetrating, and most exact analysis of the ancient spiritual organization."[9] But it was here that Comte's path diverged from that of his predecessor. For Maistre had, precisely, described the *ancient* spiritual organization, not the *new* one. In fighting to preserve a bygone age, Maistre could offer no solution to the problems of the present: indeed, he was part of the problem. Unlike Maistre, Comte did not place the blame for intellectual anarchy on Gallicanism. As he saw it, the anarchy bequeathed by the Revolution arose from the contradiction between a social order founded on theology, which was passing away, and a social order based on science, which was coming into being.

The pattern of thought that for Comte characterized the modern world was that of the scientists, and it was superseding the pattern characteristic of former times, that of the theologians. Science was moving into the space previously occupied by theology. Scientists were replacing priests as the custodians of the intellectual and moral basis of the new social order. For Comte, the age of theology was past, because reflection on first causes and final ends had proved illusory. The ancient ideal of knowing God and knowing oneself had collapsed. Christian theology had received a fatal blow from the progress of the human spirit manifested in scientific discoveries. Christian theology was preventing society from organizing itself rationally, for it made society dependent on imaginary external forces, on fictitious anthropomorphic wills that served only to disrupt and to disturb. Comte was influenced not only by Maistre but also by the rationalist philosopher Condorcet.

In analyzing the French Revolution, Comte and Maistre were alike struck by the apparently irresistible course of the changes they witnessed, as well as by the sheer chaos to which they gave rise. Both reckoned that religion was at the heart of these changes and that religion, properly understood, could bring order to bear upon them. The recognition of the right to religious freedom, the assertion of the sovereignty of the people, and a particular conception of science had profoundly shaken the theologico-political underpinnings of the Ancien Regime, facing both men with the same set of questions. What was to be the character of the new order in political theology? Where would spiritual power reside? How would it be exercised? Maistre turned to the papacy. In his eyes, you could not rely on reason alone, as it could provide no lasting foundation. Comte also betook himself to an external authority, but for him it was the authority of science. Mistrustful of representative democracy, he wanted to forge a religion predicated on science and industry.

Once the church had been stripped of its prerogatives, where would one find a spiritual authority competent to define the ends of social life and to indicate the means of attaining them? Comte saw the answer not in the Christian religion but in a new religion. After the *Cours de philosophie positive* (Course of positivist philosophy), which introduced the "science of humanity," he wrote his *Système de politique positive* (System of positivist politics) to introduce the "religion of humanity." The religion of humanity was to facilitate the transition from the age of theology to the age of positivism while responding to the lasting human need to love something greater than self. In the absence of the supreme being, God, that something was humanity itself. A religion without transcendence or the supernatural, the religion of humanity had for its object the very best that the human race had brought forth, its highest achievements and examples. It was a sort of Maistrean Catholicism with the Christianity left out. Its vision of a united humanity was a secularized version of Catholic concerns for uniting the visible with the invisible and for sustaining the visible unity of a universal church (in contrast to the invisible church of the Protestants).

The somewhat eccentric ideas of Auguste Comte might seem of little consequence. Yet they were not without appeal in their time and ended up as in effect the official dogma of the founders of the Third Republic (who put up a statue to Comte in the heart of the Université Française, the Place de la Sorbonne). These republicans saw in positivism an alternative to the reactionary Catholicism that they loathed. It was "Science against Religion," as Comte had seen it—but it was promoted in order to establish bourgeois, liberal representative government, for which Comte had had little sympathy. In political terms, Catholics were effectively marginalized for the duration of the Third Republic, right down to 1940.

Republicans attributed the failures of the republic in 1848 and 1851 to the lack of mass education. For them, the church's stranglehold on education was responsible for the essential conservatism evident in universal suffrage under Napoleon III. If the people were to be sovereign, then they had to be educated in a republican fashion so as to train them for the political role that Catholic anti-republicanism had prevented them from assuming. Positivist anticlericalism therefore became the key to republican ascendancy. Schooling would put an end to the axis of throne and altar, ensuring the triumph of republican principles. Schooling would strike simultaneously at political and religious obscurantism. Science, the foundation and guarantee of democracy, would rescue universal suffrage from the byways of ill-informed liberty. Science would guide a free people. This was in effect to set up "rational" infallibility in place of the papal kind.

The founders of the Third Republic, Gambetta, Ferry, and Littré, were all Comteans, advocates of Science against the church. Educational policy was their flagship issue, and that policy was shaped by positivism. Their republic set out to explode the hierocratic fantasies of their counter-revolutionary opponents. Gambetta, Ferry, and Littré took from Comte the notion of a transition from the age of theology to the age of positivism, along with his distinctive conceptions of science and education, which they put at the top of their agenda.[10]

Church and state struggled for control of the formation of citizens or believers. In the secular logic of the republicans, school was a microcosm of republican society and also a kind of sanctuary. It was at school that children would learn to be enlightened citizens. As the forum for the transmission of "Science," school became a battleground: the state, "Progress," and the schoolteacher against the church. Under the Third Republic, the schoolteacher was the "modernized" version of the parish priest, and a republican catechism was the "enlightened" version of the old Catholic catechism. The "écoles normales" that trained the teachers were the seminaries of this new clergy. People even spoke of the "secular faith."[11] State schooling was the tool that would shape a national unity on a basis that was no longer Catholic: it was the nearest thing to the positivist church of which Comte had dreamed.

The majority of leading republicans avowed an explicit atheism based on a scientistic rationalism. Many of them were members of the Masonic Order of the Grand Orient of France, which in 1877 eliminated the ritual invocation of the "Grand Architect of the Universe." The state's schools were not neutral institutions; they were weapons. State schooling, republican schooling, was not based on the liberal principle that tended to regard school as an extension of the family. For the republicans, families—Catholic families—were simply not enlightened enough for the state to rely on.[12] Republican policy took up the Napoleonic conception of high school and university as state institutions. It was for the state, in particular, to define the standards of excellence. But republicanism was marked by a tension between respect for freedom of conscience and the desire to promote science. Republicans wanted to compel citizens to become free and rational. Schooling had a vital role in this endeavor because it enabled some uncomfortable contradictions to be avoided: one could not *force* an adult to be free, but one could *educate* children for autonomy. Hence the special importance of the year in the curriculum that was devoted to philosophy.[13]

The laicist tradition is not really liberal. Where liberals tend to regard the state with a certain suspicion, laicists see it as a force for emancipation. In their eyes, the state ensures the promotion of individual autonomy. The state frees people from the tyranny of outmoded intermediate institutions, in particular from religious bodies. "The stronger and more active the state, the freer the individual," wrote Durkheim around this time.[14] In restricting the power of everything other than itself, the state sets the individual free from ties and constraints. For the laicists, the state is not the enemy of individual freedom, but its strongest guarantee.

Laicism as Statism

The Third Republic had two births. The first was in 1875, when a parliamentary regime was established in accordance with the relatively conservative ideals of the Orléanists. The second was the crisis of 16 May 1877, which saw the republicans unite against and triumph over parliamentary rights. The crisis of 16 May was provoked by a papal statement that called on the faithful to lobby their governments for the preservation of papal independence. In newly unified Italy, the papacy had lost the Papal States, and felt hunted, harried, and exposed. The response of the republican government was to warn against dreams of a "return to an impossible past" and against a reckless foreign policy in support of papal temporal power that could lead to war with Italy and perhaps even Germany. The crisis unfolded against the background of a conflict of ideas over the place of the church in society, a conflict that was to define the fundamental character of the republican regime.

Having long called for the separation of church and state, the ultra-republican Gambetta had a change of heart. In a speech of May 1877, he announced himself an "advocate of a system that binds the church to the state once more," before finishing with the famous parting shot, "Clericalism? That's the enemy." Far from demanding the separation of church and state, anticlericalism now called for them to be kept together, for only thus could the civil government keep a firm grip on the ecclesiastical hierarchy. So Gambetta called for a return to the Concordat, in which he explicitly included the Organic Articles unilaterally added by Napoleon. In making his case, Gambetta alluded to Vatican I:

> The triumph of ultramontanism in 1870 has had the effect of reducing to obedience or silence all those who once featured in what one could legitimately call the national clergy. Gentlemen, that is the new situation against which we protest.[15]

His comments had obvious resonances in French history. He was making capital out of old Gallican bugbears: ultramontanism, clericalism, and the detachment of the clergy from the national interest. At the same time, he was keen to exploit the prerogatives that had been bequeathed to the republic by the Ancien Regime and the empire. The Concordat was to be implemented "to the letter," as would soon be said. The initial impulse of the republicans had been to separate church and state. But their actual move was rather different. Now that they had come to power, they saw the value of the legal tools Napoleon had left them, and they thought them worth preserving.

The law on freedom of association promulgated on 1 July 1901 is a perfect illustration of this. It is notable first and foremost for what it excluded: religious activities. Liberal with regard to associations in general, the law was anything but liberal for religious orders. The creation of any new religious order had to be approved by parliament, and the opening of any new house of that order required a mandate from the Council of State. The law made it a criminal offense, punishable by imprisonment, to establish a religious order without authorization. A well-informed commentator remarked that "it would be puerile to deny that the objective of the legislature was not so much to grant freedom of association in general as to submit specific associations, namely religious orders, to a rigorous system of control."[16] Loyal to the position of Gambetta, Waldeck-Rousseau, the man behind this law, was opposed to the separation of church and state. In his eyes, "a free church in a free state" meant in effect "Catholic anarchy in an impotent state."[17]

The 1902 elections returned a Chamber with a center of gravity to the left of Waldeck-Rousseau. So, having named Combes as his successor, Waldeck-Rousseau stood down. Combes applied the new law with the utmost severity. Official authorization was systematically refused to the four hundred congregations that petitioned for it. Under Combes, a law passed to secure control became an instrument of prohibition. The old *compelle intrare* (compel them to come in) had been replaced by *compelle exire* (compel them to get out). Not long afterward, a law of 7 July 1904 forbade religious orders to have anything to do with education, and they were also subject to systematic discrimination in comparison with other common-law associations. There was no recourse for appeal against these extraordinarily restrictive measures. More than two thousand schools closed. Many members of religious orders went into exile. It was as though the French cult of national unity had to be pursued at the terrible price of periodic expulsions: the Huguenots in 1685, the émigrés at the time of the Revolution, and the Jews under Pétain.[18]

The law of 9 December 1905, which brought to a close the era of the Concordat by separating church and state, was initially conceived in a Gallican spirit. The minister for worship in Combes's government is credited with this telling observation: "We are working to lay the foundations of a national church."[19] The idea of such a church had been seriously canvassed in the latter stages of the French Revolution, but Napoleon had not endorsed the option to which Combes was now returning. Combes sought tighter state control over the church and, in particular, over the appointment of bishops. The intention was not to give more latitude to Rome in this matter—which would have been in line with a real and growing separation of church and state—but, on the contrary, to recover the rights conceded to the state under articles 4 and 5 of the Concordat. In 1903 Combes had already revoked the practice of the "preliminary understanding" between Rome and the government, which Emile Ollivier had introduced in place of state nomination when he was in power thirty years before.

Combes raised the specter of separation of church and state not because that was what he wanted but in order to cow the church into submission. What he envisaged was only a "sham separation,"[20] an instrument of blackmail to regain control over the ecclesiastical establishment in the interests of republican self-defense. This Gallican policy of republican control over the church raised two questions. Was it legitimate? And was it necessary? In the wake of the Dreyfus case, republican circles were rife with rumors of a possible military coup, although the archives furnish no evidence that these had any basis.[21]

The separation itself, which ought to have put an end both to state intervention in religious matters and to Combes's blackmail, was simply another form of interventionism. For many anticlericals it was not about leveling the playing field but about undermining the church. That is why a substantial part of the Catholic community opposed it. Article 4 of the proposed law envisaged the establishment of *associations cultuelles* (worship associations), which would hold legal title to the property and goods of public religious bodies. As originally drafted, this article made no reference at all to the internal organization of the church. On the pretext that faith was a private matter, the draft measure afforded no recognition to the Catholic Church as an organized body. On the pretext of the principle of separation, the laicist party maintained that the state had no competence to acknowledge the Catholic hierarchy, especially the bishops, as having any official role. Catholics feared that the *associations cultuelles* would foster the proliferation of schismatical groups, and that was indeed the secret hope of some anticlericals.[22]

The *associations cultuelles* would have been associations of laypeople within the parish structure, and nothing more. The draft law ignored the existence of the church as a "social fact," proposing to recognize only individuals. As such, the state would recognize individuals performing acts of worship but not churches. The new legislation was predicated on a sort of legal blindness or detachment. In a conflict among Catholics, the state would accord no preference to Catholics in communion with their bishops or with the pope, because the prevailing opinion was that to do so would be tantamount to giving legal recognition to a distinction between heresy and orthodoxy. For the Catholic Church, the whole project was utterly unacceptable. It was sheer fantasy to pretend that the state could remain entirely oblivious to religious questions, whether in disputes between believers and non-believers or in disputes among co-religionists. Lawcourts could not treat a priest in conflict with his bishop and a priest obedient to his bishop in exactly the same way. Portalis, the author of the Organic Articles appended to the Concordat, was hardly solicitous for the liberties of the church, but even he had stated that "when one acknowledges a religion, one necessarily acknowledges it along with its doctrines and its discipline."[23]

An absolute separation was not liberal because an institution could not enjoy the protection of the law under laws that ignored its existence. Churches are among those social institutions whose existence public authorities simply must acknowledge. The separation of church and state comes down to two issues: freedom of worship and the nonestablishment of any church. The discussion over article 4 raised a fundamental problem, for it showed that these two issues could be contradictory. The refusal of any recognition to churches could prove incompatible with freedom of worship, because refusal to recognize a church could amount to an injustice against it. What Catholics termed "laicism," to distinguish it from what they saw as acceptable "laicity," was the reduction of faith to a purely private option. From the church's point of view, its own internal structure had to be taken into account by the law; otherwise, the law would be imposing upon it, against its will, a congregationalist structure. It would be the Civil Constitution of the Clergy turned upside down, with the church's constitution being henceforth entirely a matter of private law.

At this point it is worth returning to the debates of 1790. In his speech in favor of the Civil Constitution of the Clergy, Treilhard spoke as a "liberal," classifying religion as an entirely spiritual matter, outside the sphere of political life:

> No two things are further apart in their objects than temporal authority and that which is called spiritual jurisdiction. Temporal authority is established to keep peace and order in society and to promote the welfare, through the course of this life, of all its members. That is an incontestable truth. The object of religion is entirely different, and however much it may contribute to the welfare of people in this world, that is nevertheless not its primary purpose. Its true object is the salvation of the faithful, and it is entirely spiritual both in its end and in the means which it employs to achieve that end.

However, if Treilhard spoke as a liberal, it was not in order to pursue liberal policies, but to impose on the church a complete change in its organization. In effect, because religion was entirely spiritual, every aspect of its temporal organization—such as the number and size of its dioceses, the method of appointing bishops—was to become a matter for the state: "The demarcation of ecclesiastical districts is not intimately related to doctrine or faith, and no more is the method of filling benefices." The civil power, therefore, had the right to legislate in this area. The spiritual jurisdiction of the church did not extend to its own governance. "This is the full scope of the power bequeathed to the apostles: teaching, and the administration of the sacraments."[24] The "exterior" organization of the church was not of divine institution. It was therefore a matter for the legitimate authority, the state. Significantly, some advocates of the separation of church and state were delighted with the Civil Constitution of the Clergy—which was not, of course, supposed to separate them![25]

Once the Civil Constitution had been passed, priests were required to subscribe to it on oath. The geography of subscription to the oath is highly significant. In those areas where priests took the oath to the Civil Constitution, religious observance declined the most, whereas in those areas where priests refused the oath, religious observance remained strongest. The division between republicans and Catholics that was etched into the first decades of the Third Republic can thus be traced back to 1791.[26] The extreme Gallicanism that emerged at the time of the Revolution shaped the long-term geopolitics of French laicism. In his *Histoire de l'idée laïque en France au XIXème siècle* (History of laicist thought in nineteenth-century France, 1929), Georges Weill observed that, along with evangelical Protestantism, deism, and freethinking, Gallicanism was one of the four sources of laicism. Aggressive laicism presented itself as the continuation of absolutist political Gallicanism. Combes himself described his anticlerical policy as "the implementation of secular principles whose only defect is that they have been set aside for too long."[27]

Paradoxically, the state which purported to ignore the church completely was in fact seeking to take its place. Under the law that Combes proposed, if two rival *associations cultuelles* quarreled over a particular district, it was not for the bishop to adjudicate, but for the Council of State. This quasi-regal pretension was greeted with savage irony by Emile Ollivier, who, though over eighty at the time, followed the debates with interest: "A secular Council of State pronouncing *ex cathedra* on what is or is not in accordance with the constitution of the church: it would be funny were it not pitiful."[28] The concept of faith as an essentially private matter went hand in hand with the notion of the "external" organization of the church as a matter for the state.

At first sight, the concept of religious faith as an essentially private matter would not seem to pose many problems. Yet in reality it was deeply ambiguous, for it could be taken in two very different ways. It might mean that the church was free to organize itself as it saw fit. But it might also mean that, because faith was a purely "internal" matter, the "external" sphere belonged to the state, which could legitimately impose its will on the spiritual power. Thus, everything that the state could separate from the content of the faith as such would fall within the public domain and under civil jurisdiction.

If there were advocates of the separation of church and state among the liberals in the first half of the Third Republic, there were also exceptions. The advocates of separation mostly belonged to a radical tradition of ultimately Jacobin inspiration. Since the first half of the nineteenth century, looking back on the Civil Constitution of the Clergy, many liberals had seen the dangers in a state-sponsored individualism that gave legal recognition only to individuals, threatening all intermediate bodies, as well as the church. For this reason, some Catholics had been very quick to defend freedom of association against revolutionary and Napoleonic Jacobinism.[29] Catholics insisted on the church's exclusive right to determine its own discipline and governance. As Henry Maret put it,

> Since the authority of the church is exercised only over the soul and only in the order of liberty, the parliamentarians want to confine it to the invisible sanctuary of the conscience. They want it to have no external or tangible expression, so that the church will have no real power in the world, and so that the world will know only one power—civil and political power. As soon, they argue, as religion descends from the heights of the divine and the level of the conscience to manifest itself by external actions, to come into contact with the world, to move, act, and live in the world—as soon as it does this, it falls, as an external matter, under the jurisdiction of the civil powers. It is therefore for them to regulate with sovereign power both the organization and the discipline of worship; for them to administer all discipline, not only in matters that impinge upon public order but in anything else that has any exterior aspect. Armed with the principle that everything external falls under civil jurisdiction, the temporal power can restrict the free exercise of church authority to as narrow a sphere as it likes.[30]

It was this political Gallicanism, thus described and denounced by Maret, that the advocates of separation between church and state aimed to implement. As Combes explained, "all that we ask of religion . . . is that it shut itself up inside its churches."[31] The advocates of separation thus showed the same tendency as the advocates of the Civil Constitution of the Clergy, namely to separate what was "religious"—private, and graciously conceded to canonical authority—from the "civil," over which they claimed legislative sovereignty and from which they rigorously excluded a church that they harried from pillar to post.

The restriction of faith to a mere private conviction implied a denial of the Catholic concept of the church. It also implied a wholesale reorganization of that church and a weakening of the episcopate to the advantage of the state, which would be able to intervene all the more effectively in the internal life of the church as it ceased to conceive of itself as Catholic. The National Assembly was subjecting Catholics to a kind of despotism even as it proclaimed freedom.[32]

In the nineteenth century, the Catholic critique of liberalism was above all founded on the fear that liberalism was a form of regalism. The church wanted more than freedom for Catholics: it wanted freedom for the church, which in turn meant some acknowledgment of the existence of the church as an organized body, with its own traditions, canon law, and hierarchy. The spiritual had also to be corporal, had to manifest itself in action and as institution. As soon as thought emerged from the sanctuary of conscience, it made itself "external" and took on a social character.

Countering the concept of the church as purely spiritual, and theories of public law that gave secular authorities complete control over the external organization of its life, Catholics insisted on the status of the church as a "society." Originally worked out by Cardinal Bellarmine in the context of the struggle against absolutist Gallicanism, the concept of the church as a "perfect society" was retrieved in the 1850s and 1860s after a long period in obscurity. The phrase "perfect society"—a technical term meaning that a society is self-sufficient in terms of the ends it pursues, not that it is without sin or blemish—neatly sums up the church's self-image. State and church are alike perfect societies, possessed of all the means required to achieve their respective ends. The freedom of the church is not a gracious concession on the part of the state: it is part of God's order, enshrined in canon law. The church claims to govern itself by its own laws and conceives of itself as existing by inherent right. The notion of the church as a perfect society had polemical overtones, for it emphasized, in contrast to Protestantism, that there were social and juridical dimensions that were integral to the existence of the church, in short, that the church was *visible*. Jesus Christ had founded a "religion" in the literal sense of the term: an institution that has binding power (from the Latin *religare*, to tie or fasten). Religion is not simply a matter of individual ethics; it is communion.

The French bishops invoked the concept of the perfect society to challenge the Civil Constitution of the Clergy,[33] and the concept returned to prominence in the context of the "Roman Question" after 1848. Faced by the threat of Italian unification, the Holy See sought to preserve the Papal States and thus its political autonomy. The phrase "perfect society" was deployed in the *Syllabus of Errors* of 1864 (articles 5, 19, and 20), which cited a number of texts written against the background of Italian unification. The great treatises on ecclesiastical public law written at that time—for example, those of Tarquini (1862) and Cavagnis (1882)—reprised Bellarmine's views on the nature of the church. At the First Vatican Council, chapter 3 of the draft decree *Supremi Pastoris* was entitled "The Church is a true, perfect, spiritual, and supernatural society."[34] That decree was never officially promulgated, but it still had a real influence on subsequent ecclesiology, notably through the encyclicals of Leo XIII. It was the church's response to the homogenizing drift of democracy, which tended to understand politics solely in terms of the relationship between the state and individuals, to the grave disadvantage of religious organizations. The debate on article 4 of the law of December 1905 was in a sense the fundamental debate, for it summed up the unease of religions in the democratic era, the difficulty they now had in finding their place on the chessboard of social and political life. Catholicism fought against the democratic urge toward homogeneity and the erasure of difference, the quasi pantheism that Tocqueville had feared.

The representatives of the City of God were not always scrupulous about keeping within its bounds, and the keepers of the earthly city were not always wrong in calling them to order. However, on occasion the latter were no more careful to stay within the bounds of their own city and ended up advancing their own theology and their own notions of immortality, trespassing way outside their legitimate domain. Then the church had a perfect right to call them to order. Moreover, in these circumstances, it was the church that showed the most energy in defending true liberty against creeping totalitarianism.

Two Kinds of Laicity

It is important to distinguish between two kinds of laicity. On the one hand, republicans sometimes took on the church by means of an anti-Catholicism that had little regard for religious freedom. This kind of laicity slid easily into "laicism"—a fanatical and discriminatory ideology based on the false idea that science could take the place of religion.[35] On the other hand, republicans could be legitimately concerned to limit the political power of an anti-republican church. It was not necessarily an injustice to take robust measures in defense of liberty itself. Faced with Catholics who could not envisage their church without the monarchy, republicans often had little choice. In 1883 Ferry wrote that "we have reduced the religious orders and the clergy to obedience, and we are imposing obedience upon the magistracy. Now we can follow a moderate policy" ("moderate" was as much as to say "liberal").[36]

Thus, it is possible to distinguish two types of laicity: one reasonable, the other sectarian. It is not altogether clear that Ferry was justified in expelling the Jesuits even in the interests of the Republic. Littré, for one, disapproved of this step. A genuine liberal, he approved of punitive measures for crimes committed, but not of preventive measures that restricted liberty in anticipation of crime.[37] A controversy between Jules Ferry and Paul Bert brings out the contrast between the two kinds of laicity. Ferry wanted school buildings to be made available for clergymen to use for religious instruction outside school hours. In his view, it was not appropriate to impose the task of religious instruction upon schoolteachers, but there was no reason why religion should not be taught within school buildings. Ferry secured the provision of chaplaincies in secondary schools but not in primary schools, because this latter proposal was defeated by an unholy alliance between the Far Left (led by Paul Bert) and a group of diehard Catholics determined to cut off their nose to spite their face. Under the law of 28 March 1882, religious instruction had to be given outside primary school. Three years later, with the benefit of hindsight, Ferry regretted the "sectarian spirit that swept us all into political blunders" which "a little wisdom and foresight could have avoided: for example, denying the use of school premises for teaching the catechism, which seemed pointless and petty even to the least clericalist of our peasants."[38]

Despite the expulsion of the Jesuits, Jules Ferry was for the most part prudent and cautious in his educational policy. He tried not to alienate Catholics as a whole. Genuinely committed to freedom of conscience, he thought it a waste of time to attack religion, which he believed would wither away of itself. He insisted that political emancipation from the church did not entail the persecution of Catholics. His policy was intended to be anticlerical, not antireligious. In comparison with Germany and Italy at that time, where the Catholic Church was mercilessly harassed, the situation in France seemed moderate, and Ferry stood out as a spokesman of the liberal state, a man with whom it was possible to do business—that was certainly Leo XIII's opinion.[39]

In the long term, it has become apparent that the Third Republic was a great success. On the one hand, it reconciled liberalism with universal suffrage. On the other, it reconciled republicans with the propertied middle classes, from whom they had hitherto been distanced by their dreams of fraternity with the workers. A republic that has been described as "opportunist" (the "gradual" or "step-by step" Republic) provided a forum in which Left and Right could reach some understanding. In the 1880s and 1890s, the regime flourished by eschewing divisiveness. After a century of political turmoil, France had established a certain equilibrium. In 1892 Leo XIII made his call for *ralliement*, urging Catholics to unite behind the republic (before the policy of Combes once more soured relations). This gesture is the best testimony to the liberal character of one kind of laicity.[40]

Whereas in the United States the separation of church and state was driven primarily by the need to protect the churches from the state, in France it was driven by the need to protect the state from the church. The French state's fearfulness of religion was grounded in two great historical facts. First, France's thousand-year history of Catholicism, a massively dominant religion whose hierarchy seemed all too often to have prevailed at the expense of the civil power. Second, the recent history of post-revolutionary France, when that majority religion was turned against the principles of the Revolution by the will of its hierarchy. The political Gallicanism of the Ancien Regime had been the French state's response to the first of those facts. Republican laicity was its response to the second. That laicity saw itself in continuity with the Gallican tradition, notwithstanding the crucial modification that precluded the state from intervening in religious matters. The rights of the state stopped at the threshold of the individual conscience.

Republicans found themselves facing a dilemma. On the one hand, they wanted to draw the teeth of a church that was both powerful and, often, bitterly opposed to the republican regime. On the other, they were setting up a liberal regime, the first genuine and lasting liberal regime that France had known, the first to bring about a satisfactory reconciliation between the revolutionary ideals of liberty and equality and the political realities of the nation. Between 1880 and 1884, a series of major laws had been passed relating to municipal liberty, freedom of association, trade-union rights, and the freedom of the press. How could the power of the church be restricted without trespassing upon a package of liberties that applied to Catholics as much as to any other citizens? In 1905 the Catholic Church would achieve a satisfactory outcome in the diocesan controversy because those republicans who were committed to liberalism (notably Aristide Briand) appreciated that the church's claims were reasonable, being founded on that very principle of liberty for which the republicans had been fighting since the Revolution.[41] Under a republican regime established by a pragmatic party loyal to the principles of 1789, the political Gallicanism of Combes could not prevail without calling into question the whole nature of the constitutional settlement.

As discussion of the proposed law unfolded in 1904 and in 1905, it became apparent that only genuine liberty could defuse the tensions between Catholics and laicists and silence the "doctrines of hate" that were plunging France into something close to a war of religion: anticlericalism, anti-Semitism, anti-Protestantism.[42] The virtual despotism of Combes was not to have the last word. In the end, the Catholic Church secured a tolerable compromise. In its final form, article 4 of the law of 1905 allowed *associations cultuelles* to be constituted "in conformity with the rules of that organized body of worship which they propose to practice." This formulation had a significant influence on the jurisprudence of the Supreme Court of Appeal (*Cour de cassation*) and the Council of State. When it was faced with such questions as what was meant by "worship" or by "an act of worship," or who could lawfully claim the title of "priest," the Council of State referred itself to what the canon law of the church itself said on the subject. Up to a point, public law therefore recognized canon law as such.[43] Religions were no longer "recognized," in the technical sense of the term as used in the Concordat, but that did not mean that the state took no cognizance whatsoever of religion. It guaranteed the free exercise of religion, and it even afforded religions a degree of protection. Article 2 of the law, according to which "the Republic neither recognizes, subsidizes, nor supports any religion," took on its full meaning only in the context of article 1, which "guarantees freedom of conscience and the free exercise of religion."

The democratic urge toward homogeneity evoked by reaction a dissociation of the political and the religious spheres, which in turn helped fend off totalitarian monism: a free church in a free state. The separation of church and state in 1905 freed the church from the yoke of the Organic Articles, which it had ceaselessly protested against. The government would no longer meddle in the recruitment of the church hierarchy—cardinals, bishops, and the major parishes. The church now had a free hand in appointing bishops, who recovered their freedom of action.

In *L'Orme du mail* (1897), a novel published some years before the separation of church and state, Anatole France summed up the current situation in the words of a Jewish mayor to a priest who was hoping for promotion to the episcopate: "My wife is for you, and Noémie is strong enough to make a bishop"—a statement all the more disturbing because Noémie is presented as a pretentious and superficial woman devoid of any sense of the sacred.[44] When the separation came, in 1905, one of its supporters, the Abbé Hemmer, remarked of the members of the government that "they come from Jewish, Protestant, indifferent, or atheist families, they were educated in secular schools, and they have seduced the electorate with the glamour of their anticlericalism." He added, indignantly, that "they have taken it upon themselves to say which priests are suitable to become judges in matters of faith, guardians of the church, and pastors of souls."[45] Hemmer thus called for a Catholic liberalism in much the same terms as Lamennais. How could Catholics denounce the influence of Freemasons on the French state while accepting the right of that same state to nominate their bishops?

In renouncing any claim to intervene in episcopal appointments, the French state was setting a precedent of some jurisprudential consequence: for the first time, a great Catholic state was abdicating direct concern with such matters. The new code of canon law promulgated by the Catholic Church in 1917 set down a new general principle that was derived directly from the Separation of 1905: "The Supreme Pontiff *freely* appoints bishops."[46] Governments had traditionally asserted their right to put forward objections on civil or political grounds, challenging candidates on account of family background, personal history, education, or social attitudes.

The church henceforth allowed only a strictly and increasingly limited scope for governmental objections to episcopal candidates.[47] Thus a curial memo of 1921, setting out the relevant procedure in the case of France, stipulated that it was for the Holy See "to decide on the appointment of bishops in France, and it is for the Cardinal Secretary of State to enquire of His Excellency the French Ambassador [to the Holy See] if the government has any objections *on political grounds* to any given candidate."[48] Over the past century, case by case and country by country, the Holy See has gradually extended its freedom of action in episcopal appointments. In the course of the twentieth century, all over the world, the civil power gradually lost its influence in such matters. In 1965, at the end of the Second Vatican Council, the church voiced the hope that civil authorities would renounce "all rights or privileges" in this area.[49] Today, the principle of the pope's freedom of choice in episcopal appointments is well established, with most governments having lost their prerogatives in the matter.[50]

The liberal character of the Separation can be appreciated from the regrets about it that were voiced by those laicists who remained attached to the Gallicanism of the Organic Articles.

> From the point of view of jurists . . . the Separation, unilateral to boot [imposed on the church without negotiation, it required no reciprocal undertakings on the part of the church], was a catastrophe, which has deprived the state of many of its powers and of an important potential influence over the dioceses.[51]

There are plenty of examples of nostalgia for the Organic Articles and the Concordat among hardened laicists, but two will suffice: the excommunicated theologian Alfred Loisy (1857–1940), and the Protestant François Méjan (1908–93), head of the *Bureau du service des Cultes* at the start of the 1950s. Méjan denounced what he saw as the self-mutilation of the state in 1905:

> Plenty of laicists were against the Concordat out of some collective aberration or mystical conviction—at any rate, the Concordat puzzled them. I knew old freethinkers who sincerely believed that, by ignoring the church, the state would succeed in harming the church and promoting the laicity of the state, but the history of the past fifty years amply demonstrates the falsity of that irrational belief.[52]

Significantly, these words were in an article advocating a new concordat. Loisy, for his part, was astonished at Catholic protests:

> One was faced with the most bizarre spectacle . . . the indignant protest of the pope (the encyclical *Vehementer*, 11 February 1906) and, following his lead, a furious clamor from the Catholic press, all against a law whose principal defect was to hand over complete control of French Catholicism to the papacy, without any reservation or limitation.[53]

Thus, the arguments over the separation of church and state in 1905 seem to some extent to have been back to front. The anticlerical republicans discarded a Concordat that had given them a degree of control over the church, while the Catholics fought to defend a Concordat for which they had never much cared and against whose exploitation by anticlerical governments they had often protested.

Emile Littré's "Catholicism of Universal Suffrage"

The founding fathers of the Third Republic found themselves in a very delicate situation. Their hearts and minds were set upon a liberal and democratic regime that would embody the ideals of the Revolution. But they faced hostility from the upper levels of the Catholic Church, which were sympathetic to Napoleon III, mistrustful of democracy, and ready to give a hearing to the ideologists of Counter-Revolution. In the *Syllabus of Errors* of 1864, Pope Pius IX seemed to have issued a categorical condemnation of liberalism. But the majority of the French people were Catholics. What was to be done? A good number of the bishops were more favorably disposed to the world that had arisen out of the French Revolution, but not enough to set the tone.[54] It was out of the question to try to impose republicanism by a sort of war of religion, not only because wars of religion were terrible but also because there was no hope of basing the republic on anti-Catholicism when Catholicism was the majority religion. If the republic wanted to establish itself securely, it could not afford to make acceptance of the new regime contingent on the rejection of a religion that was grafted onto the body of the nation. The republic could not win by reviving the old project of dechristianization. It had to avoid the mistake that the Revolution had made in requiring parish priests to swear allegiance to the republic, for this had simply driven a large part of the church into outright opposition.

The Third Republic had no future if Catholicism was intrinsically and inseparably linked with anti-republican politics, as Joseph de Maistre had insisted it should be. So the republicans had to establish that Catholicism did not entail Counter-Revolution. That is why they took care to distinguish two types of Catholicism: a majority Catholicism, compatible with republicanism; and a minority strain of counter-revolutionary Catholicism, which they fought relentlessly.

The key text here is an article by Emile Littré (1801–81) opposing the expulsion of the Jesuits, in which he drew a sharp distinction between the "Catholicism of the clericalists" and the "Catholicism of universal suffrage." For Littré, it was the Catholicism of the clericalists that was responsible for the Revocation of the Edict of Nantes and, in the nineteenth century, for the condemnations of liberalism.[55] In contrast to that, there was a kind of Catholicism which, while loyal to the faith, was nevertheless tolerant and moderate, and could be seen at work in general elections:

> On this ground, the Catholicism of universal suffrage puts on one side differences of belief and religion among candidates and focuses on their political opinions alone. It does not care whether they are Catholics, Protestants, Jews, or freethinkers, provided that they meet specific requirements that, of course, vary according to the circumstances, but which nevertheless have a common basis, namely respect for the essential characteristics of modern society as shaped by the Revolution.

On this common ground of citizenship it was possible to forge consensus among those who differed in religion. The Catholicism of universal suffrage was "essentially political and, as such, had definite ideas over which it did not want priests to stand in judgment, however much it might respect them in other matters." Littré was therefore hopeful about the future: "Clericalism has fallen from its position of dominance and is trying to clamber back up; the sociologist who considers this phenomenon concludes that its efforts will come to nothing."[56] Littré relied on the integrative powers of liberal democracy. He opposed political theology of any kind and repudiated the yoking of political creeds to religious creeds.[57] Political life had its own dynamic which would ensure that in political matters Catholics would think and act for political reasons rather than on account of irrelevant religious considerations.

Those Catholics and republicans who clashed head on had one thing in common: they agreed that throne and altar were inseparable. Edgar Quinet thought so, quite as much as Joseph de Maistre. Catholics defended the throne out of love for the altar; republicans attacked the altar out of hatred for the throne. But they were both wrong: Catholicism was not a political theology. In fact, the Third Republic could not function without the active participation of Catholics. Although the leading thinkers of the new regime often gave the impression that it was an anti-Catholic cabal, the system was successful only thanks to the active goodwill of a population that, for the most part, remained faithful to Rome. Revolutionary France had been predominantly Catholic in 1789 and 1793; republican France was little less so in 1880. Littré's thesis, which Ferry openly adopted, is one of the keys for understanding the Third Republic. It explains what laicity was at the most fundamental and most legitimate level: a critique of political theology, to which Catholics could subscribe as easily as republican liberals.[58]

In 1903 it was not only Catholics who were disturbed by the policies of Combes. Good republicans shared some of their concerns: "To get rid of the religious orders, we are turning France into one vast religious order," a "State-Pope."[59] Combes was trying to set up a sort of antichurch. His anticlerical politics was inspired not by liberalism but by a sort of dark mirror image of political theology.

After having mobilized strongly against the proposed law of 1905, the Catholics ended up appreciating the liberty which separation conferred on them. Three things played a part in improving relations between Catholics and anticlerical republicans.

First, the intrinsic logic of the Separation satisfied republicans by making the prospect of a reactionary clerical regime more remote, while it ensured real liberty for Catholics. After the Separation of 1905, the government no longer interfered in appointments within the church hierarchy. The church could choose its leading clergymen for itself.[60] The church was free, and its internal laws were recognized by the state to the extent necessary for the exercise of that freedom.

Second, Catholics now realized that Catholicism would remain part of French society. French laicity did not exclude a certain level of Catholicism. It did not exclude financial assistance to private educational institutions that were 90 percent Catholic, nor did it exclude chaplaincies in schools, colleges, hospitals, asylums, prisons, and the armed forces. It was, in the end, Littré's beloved "Catholicism of universal suffrage" that had triumphed. In the Republic's schools, the great Christian authors were not banished from the bookshelves: Pascal, Racine, and Chateaubriand remained central to the curriculum. The republic did not challenge Christian morality and happily left the direction of the inner life of its citizens to the church. The separation of church and state did not mean the toppling of wayside crosses or the introduction of a republican calendar or the complete separation of public holidays from religious holy days. The burdens of attendance at school weighed more heavily on Jews than on Christians—Sunday, not Saturday, was the day off. Republicans had rejected the Catholic Church but not Catholic or Christian culture. One of their leading lights, Ernest Renan, a lapsed former pupil of priests, explained in his *Souvenirs d'enfance et de jeunesse* (Memoirs of childhood and youth) that he had remained faithful to their moral teaching: "In terms of character I am still a pupil of my old teachers," he stated proudly.[61] That sums up the compromise of the Third Republic.

Finally, the two sides found reason to be grateful to each other in the context of the First World War, in the shared task of national defense. The struggle for survival against Germany put an end to all strife over religion. For the old republican, the priest became a comrade whose rights were to be fought for, while even the most anti-republican Catholics had to admit that the republic did indeed defend the nation, even if they had thought until then that it would never have the stomach for such a task.[62] The war brought men together in the trenches: party divisions were no longer spoken of, and old foes discovered in the common struggle that, even if they were not of the same religion, they lived in the same country. The war put political unity in the foreground, and relegated religious divisions to the background. During a debate in the Chamber of Deputies in 1921, one member summed up the change in these terms:

> It was the war that changed all our attitudes. It was the war that took all our children to the battlefield, that brought them together with a single common purpose—I might almost say in a single religion, but for the fact that some of them had a personal faith that helped them grasp and practice that other faith, the religion of patriotism.[63]

Catholics and republicans found themselves united against a common enemy in a "religion of patriotism," in a union that was readily defined as "sacred."

At the very moment when the French Revolution put an end to absolutism, nationalism (whose birth is often dated to Valmy, 1792) in effect took possession of the political theology of the defunct regime, adopting the absolutist era's sacralization of the state and thus of the body politic. The extraordinary sacrifices of the Great War can only be understood, if at all, in terms of a mystical dedication to the body politic. Modern nationalism draws its energy from what it has inherited: the confusion, in the divine right of kings, between the sacred and the profane, nature and grace. "There's such divinity doth hedge a king," wrote Shakespeare. "There's such divinity doth hedge a nation," is how this was rewritten by nationalists.[64]

Charles Péguy: The Eternal Dwelling in the Temporal

The "sacred union" of 1914 reintegrated the histories of Catholic and republican France. Charles Péguy (1873–1914) used to laugh at those who thought France had undergone some total transformation between 31 December 1788 and 1 January 1789. He never stopped celebrating the republic in the monarchy and the monarchy in the republic, ascribing a mystical vocation to republican France, taking issue with the Maistrean historiography that saw in the Revolution a satanic irruption. At the time of the Dreyfus affair, he was wholeheartedly engaged on Dreyfus's side, in the name of revolutionary values, but this did not stop him valuing pre-revolutionary France. An anticlerical and socialist republican who became a Catholic around 1907, and was then killed early in the First World War, Péguy wrote that "The Revolution is eminently the work, the operation of the old France."[65] Better than anyone else, he showed how Catholics and laicists could find common ground.

Reactionary Catholics and anticlerical republicans were not as far apart as they had imagined. Clericals and anticlericals alike recognized the atheism of the state, even if the former regretted it while the latter rejoiced in it. The clericalists took the church's side, though they rejected the political tradition of Gallicanism and tended to undervalue political life. They sneered at democracy. The anticlericals stood on the side of political life, in which they saw no room for religion. They sneered at the political irresponsibility of Catholics. But both sides agreed that political life lacked any sacred dimension. Neither side envisaged that the eternal might dwell in the temporal.

Péguy observed that "we are constantly steering . . . between two kinds of clergy: the ecclesiastical clergy and the laicist clergy . . . ; the laicist clergy deny the eternal aspects of the temporal; . . . and the ecclesiastical clergy deny the temporal aspects of the eternal."[66] Catholic clericalism had no time for nature, while republican anticlericalism had no time for grace. Each was oblivious of the fact that human life involves nature and grace. Their mutual animosity fed on equal and opposite misapprehensions.

The temporal is the location of choice for the spiritual. The city of God is at work in the earthly city, conferring on it substance, depth, and worth. "The greatest temporal powers, the greatest bodies within the state stand, exist, only by virtue of interior spiritual powers."[67] At bottom, that is what neither the laicists nor the clericalists appreciated, as both refused to acknowledge the presence of spiritual powers at work in the "greatest bodies within the state." One group sided with the state, and the other with the spiritual power, but each regarded them as entirely separate realities, with no intrinsic relationship, as if the city of God was absolutely foreign to the earthly city.

As Saint Augustine explained, even apart from religion, the desire for peace and tranquillity which forms the foundation of the state already has something of the nature of desire for peace in God. Temporal peace is deceptive but is nevertheless a reflection of divine peace. Even the bare minimum of order found in a society that is not actually in the throes of civil war is related to order of a higher level. Even the devil, who chose "not to remain in the tranquillity of order, nevertheless has not eluded the power of the Creator of order."[68] The more one deepens the demands of the *pax temporalis* (earthly peace), the more one is drawn toward a more divine peace. For his part, Péguy observes that the ancients were right in believing that

> the foundation of a city was no ordinary act or operation; it was an extraordinary, a religious thing . . . In a sense, it is literally a human participation in the act of creation.[69]

Péguy draws a parallel between the creation of the world and the creation of a body politic, as also between obedience to the mystical body of the church and obedience to the body politic. There is a touch of the sacred at the heart of civic life. Péguy speaks of a "coincidence," a "collusion," a "consubstantiality," a "co-essentiality" between the temporal and the spiritual.

Politically, Péguy stood with Alexis de Tocqueville against Joseph de Maistre. The church did not need to have direct control of society in order to christianize the world. Christianity could be at work in the heart of society even when the church was not directly recognized by the state. Péguy was far from unhappy with the separation of church and state, for which his *Cahiers de la quinzaine* had lobbied since 1901. In his view, the temporal power as such ought not to meddle in the spiritual: its "hoisting gear" was too crude.[70] "Under the new regime, we shall never again get bishops quite as bad as the bishops of the Concordat period," he wrote.[71] But the indisputable merits of the Separation need not stop one from insisting all the more on the essential interweaving of the temporal and the spiritual, of the City of God and the earthly city. For this interweaving meant that one did not have to accord the Separation a religious significance it did not really have: it did not entail the complete displacement of Catholicism from public life.

It is worth comparing the clericalists and the anticlericals with each other. The anticlerical party has to be censured for its intolerance: "One should not vex people who are saying their prayers." They can also be criticized for their narrow, dogmatic rationalism, their contempt for eternity, their positivism. But the Catholics too were open to criticism, notably on account of the contempt they showed for nature and the temporal. They had no more idea than the anticlericals of how far the temporal and the eternal were bound up with each other. Many of them seemed to have forgotten that God took flesh, that the present world was an integral part of creation, and that the trials of this life had a place in the economy of salvation.

> In that sense, as you can see, growing old, aging, and age, are an integral part of creation. Otherwise it would not be worthwhile. The earthly trial, the labor would be pointless and vain: it would be just too much, superfluous; not just a part that has gone wrong but, what is worse, a part that does nothing, redundant, mere vanity. Otherwise, it would not be worthwhile. The *kingdom of God* would follow at once, and not the *city of God*. You can feel the difference here, not as between the monarchical and the democratic, but as between the monarchical and the civic, the strictly monarchical and the strictly civic. That is what our clerks, both those who live under the Rule and even those who live in the world, too often lose sight of and forget. There is downright impiety in the way they ignore the temporal world.[72]

Against the Christian tendency to subordinate this life to the next too readily and too radically, Péguy emphasizes the meaningfulness of the temporal condition: the trials of this life, and thus political life (the "essentially civic"), have a value all of their own. Given that it is not all in vain, not devoid of all significance, it simply must be taken absolutely seriously. When God created the world, he did not fire a blank. Péguy denounced the "failure to appreciate what creation is, what constitutes creation as such, what it tastes of, that taste all of its own, that flavor on the tongue." Jesus is the founder "in *time* and in eternity."[73] Jesus did not only distinguish God from Caesar; he also took flesh.

Reflecting on the dechristianization of the modern world, Péguy refused to interpret it in terms of the causes generally invoked—historical, political, economic, sociological—because they seemed to him inadequate. Such causes were just not of the same order as their effects. "To explain such a disaster, a mystical disaster, a disaster in the order of mystique, it must be the case that some mistake has been made in the order of mystique."[74] The mistake of "mystique," in his view, was disregard of the temporal.

> The eternal has been temporally suspended, because those charged with power, those in whom eternal power has been vested, have failed to recognize, have ignored, forgotten, despised, the temporal.[75]

Here Péguy alludes to something he denounced more directly elsewhere: the growing identification of the Catholics with the bourgeoisie, their increasing avarice and the weakening of their attachment to the more concrete, the more everyday forms of solidarity. It is the socialist in him that says things like this: "What remains of the Christian world socially is today profoundly lacking in charity. It is not arguments that are lacking. It is charity."[76] This disregard or even contempt for the temporal was a function of the loss of the Gallican tradition of respect for the political order. Secularization was not a process of "disenchantment" but the reinvesting of spiritual energy outside the church, in the political life that the church had ended up neglecting.

From the point of view of republican anticlericalism, Christians looked like bad citizens because they preferred the city of God to the earthly city and put holiness above heroism. Rousseau went so far as to describe "good polity" as "impossible in Christian states."[77] Péguy both accepted and repudiated this critique of Catholicism. He accepted it insofar as he too reproached the "ecclesiastical clergy" for denying "the temporal dimension of the eternal." But he rejected it on the grounds that this apolitical stance was not intrinsic to Catholicism.

> You Christians, the most civic of people, who are commonly said not to be civic, but who are if anything too much so, to an almost insane degree, and are thus, so to speak, civic Christians, people of a new civics, who have introduced a new civics, an eternal Christian civics.[78]

The Christian is committed to the earthly city precisely because he discerns there the underlying and abiding presence of the city of God.

The stark contrast between republicanism and Christianity harks back to a tradition that, from Machiavelli to Rousseau, rebuked Christianity for its lack of civic commitment, contrasting the religious principle of radical self-denial with the political principle of self-assertion, and setting holiness against heroism, Christian humility against pagan magnanimity. Yet self-denial and self-assertion were not incompatible. As a Christian, Péguy upheld an ethic of humility; as a Frenchman, he upheld an ethic of due self-assertion and legitimate pride:

> I loathe a humiliation, a humility that can never be a Christian humility, *the* Christian humility, but would be a kind of civil humility, civic, lay, an ersatz, counterfeit humility. In civil and civic matters, in the lay or profane sphere, I want to be bursting with pride.[79]

Christians were well able to demonstrate their civic virtue. The humble believer could be a proud citizen. Legitimate pride alone could be the foundation of Christian humility, for that humility presupposed that the temporal order would be taken up and valued. Civic humility was part of that contempt for the temporal that Péguy deplored.

Despite their mystical error, the Catholics had not in fact completely abandoned political life, and anticlerical polemic against them was therefore something of an exaggeration. In the wake of Vatican I, Catholics became more nationalistic than ever, excessively so if we are to judge by the Dreyfus affair, during which they often sacrificed justice to a blind love of country. There was something odd in the way the anti-Catholic newspapers of the republicans and the socialists denounced Catholics for lack of commitment to the nation-state.

> Like everyone, wrote Péguy, I am sick and tired of reading the same ar-
> ticle in *L'Aurore* every morning, where all the arguments, so brilliant, boil
> down to identifying French Catholics as Romans; as if it were not the
> worst bet in historical and social analysis to write off as "Roman" an en-
> tire system of worship, an entire religion, which is so old, so much at
> home, so much a part of our land, so deeply rooted.[80]

Rousseau worried that Christians would make at best poor soldiers: "They
know better how to die than how to conquer."[81] Faced with the same criticism,
Augustine had emphasized that Christians were not pacifists and developed the
theory of the just war.[82] Péguy was no more a pacifist than Augustine. Faced
with the threat of Germany, he joined up at once.

Once one renounced the false opposition between spiritual and temporal
power, and took account of the presence of the eternal within the heart of the
temporal, the division between the parties lost much of its importance and significance. Once one took into consideration "the mysterious subjection of the
eternal itself to the temporal," the war between the two Frances was reduced to
more manageable proportions.[83] To make sense of the war between the two
Frances, Péguy contrasted "politics" (in the pejorative sense of the term, that of
partisan maneuvering) with "mystique" (referring to the presence of the eternal
within the temporal). In the final analysis, the war between schoolmasters and
parish priests was entirely superficial. "It is simple enough to be a good Christian and a good citizen, *as long as one does not go in for politics*."[84] Christian
mystique and republican mystique were in a communion that transcended political differences. They were not contradictory, because each saw the presence
of the eternal in the temporal. Imbued by the Third Republic's educational system with a religious admiration for the Revolution, Péguy was determined to
remain faithful to his republican training as well as to his Christian faith.
Strictly speaking, the dispute was not between the laicist republic and Christian
monarchy. Each side was loyal to the same eternal reality: France, "the Republic, our kingdom of France," the France of Valmy and of Joan of Arc.

Long before he became a Catholic, Péguy had become fascinated by Joan of
Arc. A martyr for God and France, she symbolized for him the intimate union
between Christianity and patriotism. Joan of Arc proclaimed that "those who
wage war against the holy realm of France, wage war against King Jesus."[85] At
once a saint and a heroine, Joan combined in her own person both forms of
greatness: greatness in the church's terms—holiness; and greatness in the state's
terms—heroism.[86] "The contest is not between heroes and saints; the fight is
against the intellectuals, against those who despise heroes and saints alike. The
argument is not between these two orders of greatness. The fight is against
those who hate greatness itself."[87] Here, "intellectual" is used to denote those
who feel that they belong neither to the nation nor to the church, those who, for
that reason, do not share the ideals of greatness pursued by either institution.

Péguy proposed a synthesis of contrasting politico-religious sensibilities: an attachment to what was best in the Ancien Regime combined with a profound commitment to individual freedom; a passionate sense of justice and of the worth of political life combined with an acute awareness of the finitude, the limitations of the human condition. Péguy insisted on the continuity between the old and the new, as the old awareness of the sacredness of civic life remained indispensable in the age of modern democracy. A society cannot be free and just unless the political community is founded on religious respect. Faith in what is best in the community is indispensable if the community is to act with all the dignity of which it is capable. Freedom cannot endure except insofar as the citizens have a real confidence in the use they can make of it. That is the nexus at which Christian life and civic life come if not to merge, then at least to stand shoulder to shoulder.

The modern world evoked in Charles Péguy a degree of pessimism. But, by a sort of dialectical reflux, this pessimism could lead to a most fundamental Christian optimism:

> The misery of mankind or rather the distress of mankind, and above all a certain sort, a certain taste, of the distress is the mark itself and even the articulation of Christianity. When a certain distress, when a certain taste of a certain distress, when a certain degree or rather when a certain tone of a certain distress, appears in the history of the world, it is then that Christianity returns.

Insofar as Christianity is true, then that which is true participates in Christianity, whether or not there are Christians to see it, understand it, or proclaim it.

> Yes, the modern world has done everything to proscribe Christianity, to eliminate from itself all substance, every atom, every last trace of Christianity. But if I see an invincible, an unsinkable, an irrepressible Christianity springing up once more from below, breaking in once more from outside, am I going to disavow it just because I, feeble as I am, have been unable to work out precisely where it comes from?[88]

The Christian mystique has no need of the state's support. The truth does not need to be defended by force, for it has a force all of its own. The church does not need to call upon the state to defend the truth, if it is the truth that it is defending. Péguy is the author of a famous saying that "everything starts in mystique and ends in politics." But he tempered this pessimism with his more fundamental sense of the truth: "Politics makes fun of mystique, but it is still mystique that feeds even politics."[89]

4

The Political Virtues of Moderation

Neither Maurras nor Marx

The French Revolution broke with long tradition by accepting freedom of opinion in religion. For the foes of the Revolution, separating religion from politics in this way represented a tendentious relegation of Christianity to the private sphere. How far could such a separation survive? Could the state actually do without an established religion? Tocqueville, ever the liberal, thought so, for in the United States he had seen a regime that brooked no establishment and took little heed of religion. The counter-revolutionaries thought otherwise. For them, the privatization of religion jeopardized the social fabric and called into doubt the very existence of the nation. Accepting a right to religious freedom struck at the very heart of society.

Catholic counter-revolutionaries emphasized the need for harmonious collaboration between church and state. As we have seen, their analysis was followed by those political philosophers who, while not themselves believers, reckoned religion integral to the social fabric. Auguste Comte, author of the *Catéchisme positiviste* (Positivist catechism), is a case in point. For him, the lack of shared beliefs left a social vacuum that made a new spirituality imperative. However, his "religion of humanity" did not quite make the instant impact he had expected. Some of his successors, above all Charles Maurras (1868–1952), therefore looked to reach some accommodation with the Catholic Church. Atheist disciples of Comte made common cause with Bonald's school of believers. Maurras, a convinced monarchist and the ideologue of Action Française, was not a man of faith. His ideology, *empirisme organisateur* (organized empiricism), did not avail itself of any theological underpinnings. He viewed the church from the outside. Nevertheless, he found the church's spiritual life appealing, as it furnished the sort of civic theology he required: a catholicism without Christianity. So he forged an alliance with Catholics for purely tactical reasons. His *nationalisme intégrale* (integral nationalism) could never give much scope to the universality, the catholicity, of the Church of Rome. What he saw in the church was an essentially conservative force, a force for order, the buttress of monarchy rather than the mystical body of Christ.

In spite of this, Maurras struck a chord with many Catholic reactionaries. Anti-Dreyfusard, anti-republican, antidemocratic, antiliberal, they saw in Action Française a new hope. As the nineteenth century had worn on, old-fashioned royalism had seen its vitality gradually seep away. Maurras's new approach gave it a blood transfusion. From the other side, the way in which the republicans lumped together Catholicism and the Ancien Regime under a blanket condemnation forced Maurras and the Catholics into each other's arms. So this unnatural union was consummated, assuring "to Action Française the preservation of the social order and the transformation of politics; and to Thomism the preservation of the religious order. . . . Within their respective domains, both Thomism and Maurrassism laid claim to rationality: the former to reason in theology and the latter to reason in politics."[1] Was there not a real affinity between the system of Thomas Aquinas, a doctrine of order in metaphysics, and the system of Maurras, a doctrine of order in politics?

This union was to bear some remarkable fruit: the Marxist Christianity that flourished in France in the 1950s and 1960s was, if not quite the spiritual heir, then at least the prodigal son of the Counter-Revolution. The condemnation of liberalism promulgated in the *Syllabus of Errors* of 1864 had paradoxically favored the extreme Left. The "worker-priests" had been brought up in the traditions of Action Française, and they were all the more to the liking of the Communists for their hostility to representative democracy, which, as good monarchists, they had learned to hate a generation before. The shift can be followed in the pages of the journal *Jeunesse de l'Eglise* (Church youth). The earliest numbers, in 1942, still had overtones of conservative Thomism, but the final issues, a decade later, had come to regard Marxism as the "immanent philosophy" of the working class.[2] Before they learned from the Communist Party to contrast "real democracy" with "formal democracy," many of the faithful had invoked the distinction between the "real nation" and the "legal nation" deployed by Maurras against the Third Republic. On the rebound from royalism, the postwar generation was all the more easily seduced by Marxism through having already been persuaded that the Catholic faith could be held alongside a political philosophy apparently alien to its principles. Some of the "red" Dominicans of the 1950s and 1960s were the pupils of the royalist Dominicans of the early twentieth century.[3] Postwar Marxist Christians sought to "baptize" Marx in the way that Thomas Aquinas had "baptized" Aristotle. And a Catholicism that had made an accommodation with Maurras was no less ready to come to an arrangement with Marx. However, the papacy condemned the worker-priests in 1954 just as it had condemned Action Française in 1926.

Committed opponents of such "modernists" as Tyrell and Loisy, who sought to "contextualize" the Gospel, the early twentieth-century Thomists were essentially ahistorical in their intellectual approach. It was not until the 1930s, and by no means without difficulty, that M.-D. Chenu taught them to consider Thomas Aquinas in his own social and intellectual context. For them, nature trumped history—in principle if not always in fact. Driven by hatred for both the Revolution and the Republic, the neo-Thomists of the turn of the century heeded Leo XIII's call for a return to the *Summa theologiae*. They were all the more biddable in that they thought to distil from the *Summa* a sort of quintessence of the Ancien Regime, "all Chartres and Christendom."[4] It is easy to forget today the fog of nostalgia that hung over the Counter-Revolution, and the way its exponents rewrote history, enlisting the past under the banner of the faith and almost purposefully glossing over the chicanery of the kings they canonized so indiscreetly. In keeping with the spirit of the 1920s, Thomism played its part in the *Défense de l'Occident* (Defense of the West, to borrow the title of a book by Henri Massis). Dominican accounts of Thomist metaphysics were scholarly and exact: unfortunately, one cannot say the same for their accounts of Thomas's political thought. They took advantage of the relative vagueness of his comments about the state (a subject that did not detain him long) to put forward reinterpretations that at times bordered on the bizarre. They devoted far too much attention to what he had to say about monarchy, ignoring the fact that it was marginal to his political philosophy (the author of the *Summa theologiae* was, above all, a theorist of the eternal law). Their Thomas Aquinas was dressed up from a motley political wardrobe—corporatist, anti-individualist, anti-Rousseauian, anticapitalist, counter-revolutionary, and traditionalist: not so much a medieval figure as a neo-Gothic gargoyle. Driven by ideological rather than intellectual considerations, the Dominicans of Action Française were, in political terms, the Viollet-le-Duc or Pugin of Thomist Aristotelianism.

Did this reading of Aquinas prepare the ground for Marxism? Very probably. Thomism was all the more readily dismissed in that it could easily be seen as integral to a bygone age. In yoking medieval theology and metaphysics so tightly to the Ancien Regime, that school of neo-Thomism could easily give rise to the idea that political transformation had rendered the theology and metaphysics of Saint Thomas redundant and that a revolutionary Christianity was now called for. In the postwar years, the church seemed in poor shape. Was it not bound up at one and the same time with peasant culture, reactionary politics, and Aristotelian philosophy, as Louis Althusser wrote, when he was still a Catholic, in *Jeunesse de l'Eglise*?[5] His article provides a perfect illustration of the perception of the general malaise. It was at one and the same time that he would soon reject the church, its sociology, its politics, and its philosophy, to become part of the vanguard of Parisian Marxism. There was a fashionable slogan in those days to the effect that it was a vital to break out of the Catholic "ghetto," even going so far as to privilege unbelievers at the expense of believers (the "bourgeois").[6] The new-style Marxists set out to make a reality of Messianism and (why not?) to bring about a "hyper-Christianity," a mirror image of sacral Christendom. This was "salvation for the proletariat."

The same body of doctrine could be pulled in two different directions. Leninist political romanticism undoubtedly owed a great deal to the "improved" and "purified" Christianity of Dostoyevsky and Tolstoy: they disagreed about God, but they were at one in their hatred for the contemporary world and in their yearning for social transparency and universal love. They were at one also in their loathing for 1789, either out of nostalgia for the Ancien Regime or out of hope for a declaration of rights along the lines of 1793. In many cases, the revolutionaries of 1917 and 1945 were the children of the reactionaries of 1880 and 1910. Inheriting their parents' hatred for the bourgeoisie, liberalism, and the West, and their refusal to come to terms with the present, they simply stood their politics on its head. Why look back to the past when the future held the abolition of the class struggle and the triumph of the proletariat? Why try to turn the clock back when the forward march of History was inevitable? Thus, the Pan-Slavists evolved into Leninists and the Thomists of Action Française into Christian Marxists: "Reaction" mutated into Revolution, and the most hidebound Christianity into mystical Communism. Unable to come to terms with the bourgeois world, Catholics found themselves singing from Lenin's hymn sheet.

Having sung the praises of the world as it was before the rise of bourgeois commercialism and individualism, the Maurrassians were primed to hear the gospel of a society reconciled with itself, collectivist and socialist. Monarchists recoiled not only from the French Revolution but also from the individualism of the *nouveaux riches*. Individualism, in their view, could coexist only with the most lukewarm faith. The Christian Marxists, and after them their disciples, the liberation theologians, climbed up onto this antibourgeois platform to proclaim that, in the final analysis, only the working class could be truly Christian.[7]

A century beforehand, Lamennais had already blazed this trail. Once an associate of Maistre and Bonald, a traditionalist Catholic, royalist, and ultramontane, he transferred his allegiance to a messianic humanitarianism and a church-free Christianity. Once a devotee of throne and altar, a rebellious Breton royalist in love with the faith as the basis of hierarchy, he came in time to uphold liberty against authority, and he replaced the infallibility of popes and princes with that of a people now come of age. When Charles X's government did not take up his extremism, he turned libertarian. The old society had had its day, and kings no longer embodied the will of the people. Anticapitalism took the place of the old Catholic "antichrematistic" ethic of suspicion toward the pursuit of riches. The most reactionary form of Catholicism became radically progressive. Lamennais turned to the working classes, setting off down a path that many would follow. To reconcile Christianity with a world that was apparently being built in opposition to it, he declared that the world itself was the product of the will of God, a will progressively revealed in the course of human history.

To its contemporaries, the French Revolution was an overwhelming force, far beyond the control or comprehension of adherents and opponents alike. It seemed to have a logic of its own, sweeping everything before it and reducing individuals to insignificance. Given the way that it overshadowed the intentions of political agents, it could only be the work of Providence. After the French

Revolution, people had the sense that they were living with the inevitable. It was all so new, so extraordinary, that Chateaubriand, Tocqueville, and Michelet felt obliged to interpret it in religious terms, as though Christianity itself were on the brink of its own full and final realization. A new society had arisen at a stroke. An irresistible force was on the march and would produce a just, a better world. The counter-revolutionaries, including the young Lamennais, saw the Revolution as a satanic irruption permitted by Providence as a punishment for the godlessness of France. But "Providence" was quickly given a new name: as an undirected, impersonal force, it came to be called "History" or "Progress." Lamennais's volte-face was an expression of this shift. It was also the prelude to another key moment: no longer the separation of politics and religion, but their conflation. Politics and religion exchanged their attributes: politics founded itself anew on metapolitics, while the faith was reduced to a voluntary "commitment." A century later, the Catholic followers of Maurras retraced the steps of Lamennais.[8]

This political messianism might have involved a revival of the Joachimite heresy, according to which a Third Age, the Age of the Holy Spirit, was destined to succeed the First Age, the Judaic Age of the Father, and the Second Age, the Christian Age of the Son, heralding radical popular upheavals.[9] Such political messianism can also be viewed in the context of the pantheism to which I alluded in the introduction, and which Monsignor Maret described as follows:

> Isn't humanity inspired, infallible? Isn't the human spirit the unique and necessary revelation of God? Whence else come all truth, all religion, all philosophy? Isn't it the human spirit that has fashioned the past and will create the future? What is God? No matter. What is man? A progressive being, shaper of his own destiny, bound to *progress* at all costs. Isn't this the sum total of this century's wisdom? Isn't this the substance of all the philosophy taught in Europe these last fifty years?[10]

To the extent that democracy takes root, people feel more and more that sovereignty is theirs. Judges of everything, masters of everything, they end up mistaking themselves for God. The course of history seems filled with immanent significance. The ultimate consummation of the spirit will be achieved not after the end of human history but within its heart, not in eternity but within time itself.

Toward the end of the nineteenth century, the Catholic Church began to develop its own social teaching, according to which economics should be at the service of man, not vice versa. Catholic teaching emphasized that economic organization ought to take account of considerations of social justice.[11] This social teaching was directed not only against the exploitation and injustice to which capitalism can give rise but also against revolutionary socialism and communism. Marxist materialism was no more attractive than capitalist materialism, especially not if it was accompanied by militant atheism and a philosophy of history that purported to supplant the Christian understanding of time—as if it were possible to make a reality of the ideal, to bring about heaven on earth, and, leaving original sin out of the reckoning, to abolish evil by the mere modification of social and economic arrangements. Péguy had remarked that "what remains of the Christian world socially is today profoundly lacking in charity." The Christian Marxists took this to heart, but, paradoxically, they gave charity only a secondary role, because they took on board Marx's radical subordination of the individual to the collective. The charity they preached had lost its distinctively Christian character.

If historicism amounts to putting oneself in the place of God, the Christians under consideration here adopted political positions that were all the more extreme because they believed that they ought to exercise the proper responsibility of God, and to rely on their own efforts to sustain the faith. They felt that without political backing the faith would tend to lose its hold, and that the separation of church and state urged by liberals would lead to the collapse of Catholicism. If they felt obliged to act as substitutes for a God who was so hidden, so absent from the public sphere, as to seem enfeebled, then they were not far from thinking that the destiny of the world lay in their hands rather than in those of the Providence they thought to serve. Thus, they felt they could combine two contradictory positions: a Maurrassian or Marxist politics and a reduction of politics to the service of the supposed dictates of theology, as if politics could not be good unless allied to religion, nor religion strong unless allied to politics.

The reactionaries turned back to the past, to a "world we have lost," in which church and state were firm allies. They denounced freedom of religion on the grounds that "error has no rights," that no one had a right to be wrong—in other words, a right not to be Catholic. Freedom was to be sacrificed to truth. Because they set freedom against truth, because they did not think that free human beings could freely and willingly find or recognize truth, they actually found it helpful to locate truth in the past. The best way to divorce truth from freedom was to fossilize it. The revolutionaries went the other way. Overwhelmed by a sense of the inadequacy of the truth that had been passed down to them, they looked to a future in which history or liberty would uncover the real truth. They looked to the future because they were convinced that the old "truth" was too deeply implicated in the old injustices to be politically credible. For them, it was liberty that would work out salvation through history. In sacrificing tradition on the altar of liberty, they would in the end attain the fullness of truth—hence the urge to a complete break, to a future with roots in neither the present nor the past.

The Thomists of Action Française meant to defend the Catholic Church, but they bound the church to a type of politics from which, in retrospect, it was in fact separable. They focused so intently on the *defense* of the truth that they separated it from the *search* for the truth. They brutally sacrificed the rights of conscience to the rights they attributed to revelation, invoking monarchy as the last bulwark against freedom of religion. The Christian Marxists went in the opposite direction, abandoning the preservation and transmission of the truth in favor of the search for it. They subordinated concern for revealed truth to the often erratic demands of their conscience. They replaced a flight to the past with a dash for the future and ended up strangling the faith they had set out to resuscitate.

Cardinal Henri de Lubac (1896–1991), Father Gaston Fessard (1897–1978), and Jacques Maritain (1882–1973) warned systematically against this kind of theological and political opportunism. All three launched vigorous denunciations of Maurrassian, Nazi, and communist ideologies.[12] During the German occupation of France between 1940 and 1945, they emphasized the importance of "spiritual resistance" to Nazism. They repudiated the Pétainist political theology according to which French defeat in the war was a providential punishment for the sins and moral corruption of the nation. This thesis sought to justify the loss of political independence, the German occupation, and the politics of collaboration in essentially theological terms. For Lubac, Fessard, and Maritain, this was to confuse two separate spheres. In the spiritual sphere the French may not have had much to be proud of, but this did not in any way entail resignation to defeat, which was a fact in an entirely separate sphere.

It was under the influence of theologians such as Fessard, Lubac, and Maritain that the Second Vatican Council extricated the church from an impasse. It took the intervention of a general council to impose a middle way on Catholics (or most of them). In order to reconcile or at least escape the two extremes, Vatican II reaffirmed the given and revealed character of the truth at the same time as it recognized religious freedom, that is, the freedom to search for the truth. The council struck a new balance between the needs of the political order and the transcendent status of the faith, recovering a sense of tradition as something that combined the acceptance of revelation with its reinterpretation.

The condemnation of Action Française in 1926 was not therefore a stray event but a key moment in the development of the Catholic Church. The Maurrassian or Leninist allure of the slogan *politique d'abord* (politics above all) was resolutely resisted in the name of the "primacy of the spiritual" in harmony with Catholic tradition, a primacy that Jacques Maritain had defended forcefully in a book justifying the condemnation of Maurras's party.[13] Notwithstanding the aspirations of the Thomists of Action Française and of the Christian Marxists, the church was not prepared to accept its own subordination to the interests of ideologies that were so definitely *of this world*.

Political philosophers often define the "bourgeois" in terms of the fear of violent death. Immersed in the delights of private life, the "bourgeois" strives to build a world of personal comfort from which the prospect of death, and even more of the City of God, is as far as possible excluded. The Far Right and the Far Left, however, yearn to tear off the blinkers and break the silences that comfort the "capitalist" and the "liberal," and to make them face up to death and recognize it for what it is. A noble and praiseworthy desire, one might well say! But it is worth noting that these ideologies, which culminated respectively in Hitler's Germany and Stalin's Russia, finished up not by putting death back into perspective as one of the Four Last Things, but by glorifying atheism and the absolute power of assassination.

From the French Revolution to Vatican II, France played a decisive part in shaping the response of the Catholic Church to liberal democracy. For much of that time, republican anticlericalism drove the religious authorities into the arms of the monarchists and the reactionaries. In the nineteenth century, the air rang with thunderous condemnations of rationalism and individualism. Yet at Vatican II the Catholic Church officially recognized religious freedom and came to terms with some of the key features of liberal democracy. How come? It was in fact the totalitarian moment that proved decisive.[14] Totalitarianism was the dead-end destination of all French antiliberalisms, from that of Maistre to that of the Christian Marxists.

It is revealing on the one hand that Vatican II's *Declaration on Religious Freedom* was condemned by one of the last French disciples of Joseph de Maistre, Monsignor Marcel Lefebvre (1905–91), and on the other that one of its foremost advocates was an American theologian, John Courtney Murray (1904–67).[15] It was familiarity with American political life, gained while a refugee there during World War II, that converted Jacques Maritain to wholehearted support of democratic government. He had been sympathetic to Action Française before its condemnation, but he ended up advancing a democratic interpretation of Thomas Aquinas, in contrast to that of his Dominican teachers.[16] He became one of the theorists of the "Christian democracy" that spread so widely after the war, notably in Latin America, and that helped stabilize Western Europe and stave off communism.[17] For Maritain, the Thomist affirmation of the intellectual life and of the value of the natural order served to justify the relative autonomy of the temporal order.

The American model had long been considered in exclusively negative terms, or at least as an essentially marginal curiosity. Leo XIII wrote that, if the church in the United States enjoyed great liberty, it was not necessary "to conclude that the best situation for the church is that which prevails in America."[18] For many decades it had been held that, in the United States, "the Catholic Church is still in the process of formation: it will still be a long time before a definitive judgment can be passed upon its organization."[19] Through Maritain and others, the church came to realize, nearly 150 years after Tocqueville's visit to America, that democracy and pluralism could deliver real benefits. In *Democracy in America*, Tocqueville proposed two ideas. On the one hand, Catholicism was adjusting to democracy and managing perfectly well without monarchy or aristocracy. And on the other, Catholicism did not necessarily benefit from official recognition as the sole religion of a state. Indeed, it could positively flourish in a society, such as the United States, that accorded it no special privileges.[20] More than a century later, the church effectively deferred to Tocqueville, whose ideas were so flatly contrary to those of the counter-revolutionaries. Having initially responded with the utmost suspicion to the political changes that followed the Revolution, to the affirmation of the rights and freedoms of the individual, the church eventually realized that it could actually benefit from them.

In a former time, the church had tended to see in totalitarian movements nothing but a reaction against liberalism, a reaction akin to its own: since 1789, the church had often had the uneasy feeling that liberal democracy was gaining ground at its expense. Having had to suffer at the hands of liberalism, the church had not at first appreciated that it might itself come to regret the loss of the freedoms that had been invoked against it. Catholics did not at first recognize the new foe, and did not grasp the kinship between their views and liberal democracy until the last moment. In the end it was totalitarianism that led the church to turn its back upon political antiliberalism. It was at last possible to understand that, in condemning spiritual tepidity, Jesus was not condemning political moderation.

The Political Role of the Laity

The Second Vatican Council seemed to adopt a relatively indifferent stance toward politics. The draft constitution on the church, prepared by the Theological Commission before the council opened, included a chapter entitled "Relations between church and state," which brought together papal teaching and made a few general comments.[21] But this chapter was omitted from the final text, and the council offered no other statement on the subject in its place. However, this apparent indifference toward politics was not the full picture. If Vatican II had nothing of a formal nature to say about church and state, this was for a reason that the Gallicans of the Ancien Regime would have applauded: namely, that it no longer saw the ecclesiastical order as a political rival to the civil order. From now on, the ecclesiastical order would back away from the political limelight.

At Vatican II, the church took up the old Gallican conception of the political primacy of the laity. As an actual political tradition, Gallicanism had died at Vatican I. But Gallican ideas survived the death of Gallicanism as such. *Lumen Gentium* emphasized the *consecratio mundi* (consecration of the world), the notion of specifically Christian service in the temporal sphere. The council emphasized the importance of lay activity:

> A secular quality is proper and special to laymen. It is true that those in holy orders can at times engage in secular activities, and even have a secular profession. But by reason of their particular vocation, they are chiefly and professedly ordained to the sacred ministry. . . . But the laity,

by their very vocation, seek the kingdom of God by engaging in temporal affairs and by ordering them according to the plan of God.[22]

With these solemn declarations, the church officially renounced clericalism. The church no longer exercised "power" in the temporal sphere, but "influence"—and this by means of the laity. The hierarchy could no longer regard the laity as foot soldiers to be given their orders at elections.[23] In the Code of Canon Law issued in 1983, it was laid down that the clergy no longer had the right to wield direct political authority.[24]

The laity was still bound to obey the bishops in their capacity as leaders in the church, but this obligation did not extend into the political sphere. The bishops could draw attention to general moral and spiritual principles, but it was for the laity, especially that element involved in politics, to give those principles practical application in public life according to the dictates of conscience.[25] It was, significantly enough, in his open letter in defense of papal infallibility that Cardinal Newman delivered the following eulogy of the autonomy of the conscience:

> It is a messenger from Him, who, both in nature and in grace, speaks to us behind a veil, and teaches and rules us by His representatives. Conscience is the aboriginal Vicar of Christ.[26]

Cited word for word in the *Catechism of the Catholic Church*, this text subordinates even the pope (one of whose titles is "Vicar of Christ") to the individual conscience, "the aboriginal Vicar of Christ." In the church's eyes, human beings have two paramount moral obligations: to inform their conscience; and to follow their conscience, *even if it is in error*. The church's mission is to enlighten the conscience, not to overshadow it.

At the height of their power in the Middle Ages, the popes had sometimes claimed a direct supremacy in the temporal sphere. Boniface VIII (1235–1303) and the curial theologians maintained that, as Christ had all power, the pope, as his vicar, had the right to set up and bring down princes. The spiritual power embraced the temporal: the temporal power depended on the spiritual. The theory of the direct temporal power presupposed a hierocratic world in which priests would take upon themselves the guidance of the state. Other theologians developed a theory of indirect temporal power, in which the church could affect politics only at arm's length. In this theory, the temporal power was credited with its own sphere of action. Papal power extended into this sphere only, as it were, at second hand, and this indirect power was to be used only in exceptional circumstances, in cases of heresy or other grave offenses on the part of princes, necessitating their excommunication and deposition.

Gallicans had always rejected the idea that the pope had any direct political power, and had long opposed the idea of indirect power as well, on the grounds that such indirect power in the end came down to direct power.[27] The pope's jurisdictional competence with regard to kings might be indirect, in that it arose only when spiritual issues were at stake. But once that jurisdiction was established, then the pope could act directly on the temporal sphere, for it was the pope who would depose the king, without any intermediary. The Gallican view of this question was that the papacy had at most a "power of influence." The pope and the church possessed true wisdom, but they had no specific competence in political matters. Reflecting on the classical distinction between direct and indirect power, Henri de Lubac concluded that it was inadequate. He preferred instead the concept of a "directive power." In his view, the theory of indirect power was nothing but an "untenable bastard compromise between the theory of a direct temporal power and the theory of a directive power."[28] His comment in effect reprises the classical Gallican critique of the indirect power as a direct power that dare not speak its name. In reality the church had only one power, and that was spiritual.

There is a tendency today to look back on Gallicanism as a political theology that ineptly mixed up religion and politics. Nothing could be further from the truth. Gallicans were emphatic on the autonomy of the state and the lay monopoly of politics. The Gallican theory of the divine right of kings ascribed to the king a legitimacy derived directly from God without any clerical mediation: it was an anticlerical theory.[29] Gallicans reserved temporal matters for the laity—the Catholic laity—to the exclusion of the clergy, whose sphere was strictly confined to the spiritual. Political Gallicanism was intimately connected with what was once called, in the title of a famous book, "the birth of the lay spirit in the later Middle Ages."[30]

The founders of modern political philosophy, Marsilius of Padua, Hobbes, Spinoza, and Locke, posited the juridical and political supremacy of the civil hierarchy over the ecclesiastical hierarchy, because they felt that the clergy tended to subordinate nature to grace, the temporal to the spiritual, too readily and too radically, at the cost of those basic goods that society could and should protect first: in particular, security, property, and liberty.[31] These thinkers took as their starting point the existence of a natural order which was not reducible to the order of grace. Although the clergy might see all nature in relation to God, the laity dwelled rather longer on nature as such. Although the clergy might consider the world as a means to know and serve its Creator, the laity considered it as deserving of interest in its own right. Although the clergy might use nature simply as an arsenal of examples to illustrate the sovereignty of the Creator, the laity took engagement with the temporal order more seriously. Although it was the clerical vocation to regard the world in an instrumental light, the lay vocation was to honor the world for what it was in itself.

In the tradition of Marsilius and Spinoza in particular, the best way to circumvent the quasi-political power claimed by the clergy was democracy. Democracy subordinated the civil and ecclesiastical hierarchies alike to popular sovereignty. It got around the tension between the two hierarchies by making the people the ultimate authority—and the people, in theory, would not ignore the political imperatives that were liable to be overlooked by the clergy. For Marsilius, clerical power was neither jurisdictional nor political: the mission of the clergy was not to govern but to teach.

Without subscribing to the anti-Catholic elements in the theories of Marsilius, Hobbes, Spinoza, and Locke, the majority of Gallicans agreed with them in their critique of clericalism. The aim of the revolutionaries who had drafted the Civil Constitution of the Clergy was to achieve a radical transformation in the balance of power between clergy and laity, to the advantage of the latter. This was distinctly reminiscent of Marsilius.[32] Unlike Joseph de Maistre, the Gallicans viewed the Revolution without great alarm, for they had begotten the Revolution, and it promised to achieve their aim—the assertion of the primacy of the civil power, the laity, in its own sphere. The exponents of political Gallicanism were magistrates in the parlements, lawyers, and pamphleteers. They had no qualms about reducing the political influence of the clergy if they could, feeling as they did that the clergy had no business in politics, which was their affair. Pioneers of national unity, the lawyers had long before taken up Roman law and turned the *Corpus iuris civilis* into the first great secular text, to rival the Bible.[33]

It is worth returning to the first article of the Declaration of the Clergy of 1682, which we have already cited:

> Popes have received from God only a spiritual power. Kings and princes are not subject in temporal affairs to any ecclesiastical power.

No ecclesiastical authority (pope, bishop, or council) had any power, direct or indirect, in temporal matters. No such authority could depose a prince or release subjects from their due allegiance. In his *Défense de la déclaration de 1682* (Defense of the declaration of 1682), Bossuet advanced a strikingly nonreligious theory of political legitimacy. Though often depicted as the most obscurantist of classical thinkers, Bossuet was nevertheless the author of statements that in hindsight look liberal. For example, in the *Défense de la déclaration* he wrote that:

> On the one hand, the church and true religion can survive perfectly well without being united to the temporal power; and on the other hand, temporal power and political government can also exist self-sufficiently, without the true church and true religion.[34]

A subject insofar as he was a Christian, the monarch was nevertheless aware that he need not be a subject insofar as he was a sovereign. Thus, the power of the laity was upheld.

That Bossuet's statements were to a certain extent liberalism *avant la lettre* was self-evident to the ultramontanes. Maistre drew a parallel between the "revolution of 1682" and that of 1789. In his eyes, Gallicanism was the "depths of the abyss" whence, in the eighteenth century, emerged the prejudice that worked the destruction "of the religious system and of political religion." The Gallicanism of the Ancien Regime was the first whisper of the Revolution. The secularization of 1682 (i.e., the proclamation of the autonomy of the secular power in the first article of the Declaration of the Clergy of France on Ecclesiastical Power) was the prelude to the secularization of 1789. Maistre opposed Gallicanism not only because of the French Revolution but also because he saw in Gallicanism, quite rightly, the opposite of the political theology and clericalism for which he stood. When they reflected on the origins of the French Revolution, the ultramontanes saw its political deification of the laity as the culmination of centuries of Gallicanism.

For Lamennais in his counter-revolutionary phase, before *L'Avenir*, Louis XIV had solemnly enacted the separation of religious society from civil society:

> In 1682, servile bishops made a religious dogma of what, until then, had been nothing but the craven flattery of the sovereign courts [i.e., political Gallicanism], namely, that sovereignty among Christian peoples is independent of Christ and his law. . . . Gallicanism states that, *by God's command, kings and sovereigns are not subject to any ecclesiastical power in temporal matters* [article 1 of the declaration of 1682]; with the result that, in the temporal order, that is to say in all that concerns the proper exercise of sovereignty, sovereigns have no superior—neither temporal (for otherwise they would not be sovereigns), nor spiritual (for otherwise they would not be independent, as sovereigns, from ecclesiastical or spiritual power).

Lamennais related these themes directly to the question of liberalism (the term, in its modern sense, was then entirely new):

> Liberalism refuses to recognize not only divine law but also the only authority by which one can know it with certainty, and Gallicanism frees the sovereign, as sovereign, from both.[35]

In similar vein, the ultramontane author of *Histoire critique du catholicisme libéral jusqu'au pontificat de Léon XIII* (A critical history of liberal catholicism down to the pontificate of Leo XIII, 1897), Monsignor Fèvre, saw connections between liberalism and Gallicanism. Having learnedly explained that "liberalism has existed as an idea since the revolt of Lucifer," and that "liberalism is, in itself, a mortal sin," he linked it to Gallicanism. He traced the "heretical origins of liberalism" to Philip the Fair, the hero of political Gallicanism, and emphasized the continuity between the age of absolutism (or Gallicanism) and that of liberalism. "It is easy to set these two eras in opposition to one another," he wrote, "and they are indeed diametrically opposed in terms of organization; yet in their principles they are *identical*."[36]

The counter-revolutionaries were not the only ones who thought this. Edgar Quinet, who devoted his life to defending the Revolution and denouncing the evils of ultramontanism, agreed with Maistre as to the laicist character of Gallicanism. Like Maistre, Fèvre, and Lamennais, Quinet saw Gallicanism as a prelude to Revolution.

> One thing alone served to limit the monarchy of Louis XIV, and that was the authority of the church, which soared high above the king. Its distant shadow became intolerable: the demigod of Versailles could not bear to be outdone by the demigod of the Vatican. The French clergy, by the declaration of 1682, set the monarch free from this spiritual dependence. The political state was set free from the religious state. The Gordian knot had been cut: the throne was detached from the altar, and now reckoned itself strong enough to rely upon its own resources. Everyone at Versailles at the time thought that, once freed from Roman supervision, absolute monarchy had nothing more to fear. Yet as it turned out, this apparent emancipation was the downfall of unlimited monarchy. The liberties of the Gallican church, proclaimed for the benefit of Louis XIV, proved to be the first act of the French Revolution. . . . The absolute monarchy of Roman Catholicism was a necessary condition of the absolute monarchy of Louis XIV: the two were inseparable. In reality, emancipation from Rome meant, for Louis XIV and his successors, contradicting their own first principles and undermining their own foundations.[37]

Quinet approved of "the separation of the spiritual and the temporal, which is the basis of the Gallican church," but to him it seemed incompatible with Catholicism. Indeed, in his view, it was closer to Protestantism. Quinet was thus at one with Maistre in seeing Catholicism as essentially ultramontane and absolutist, the sort of religion an absolute monarch such as Louis XIV needed in order to bolster his power. Like Maistre, he saw the declaration of 1682 as the "first act of the French Revolution."

The Gallican ideal was of a close association between church and state, in which the temporal and spiritual powers accorded each other due recognition in their respective spheres. The state conferred privileges on the church in return for an acknowledgment of its own autonomy in politics. The union of church and state was not a conflation of religion with politics but a contract formulated precisely to preclude such an outcome. Through Gallicanism, the confessional state was made to serve the purposes of a kind of secularism. That was why the neo-Gallicans saw an affinity between Gallicanism and liberalism. Referring to the first article of the 1682 declaration, Maret remarked that "when it restricted itself to proclaiming the independence of peoples and their magistrates in the civil and political sphere, when it restricted itself to confining ecclesiastical power within its proper limits, this doctrine appears to us as one of the greatest claims to fame of Bossuet and the French clergy."[38] This is what Maret thought he could preserve from the declaration of 1682, in the form of his own version of the four articles:

While, in my opinion, the substance of the doctrines of 1682 is solid, the language in which those doctrines are formulated is fraught with difficulties. Everything changes with time. Just as the Gallicanism of Bossuet was not that of Gerson, so the Gallicanism of the nineteenth century cannot be that of the seventeenth. In my opinion, our Gallicanism can be summed up under four headings: 1, the independence of the secular power with regard to all political jurisdiction ascribed to the church; 2, the legitimacy of the principles of 1789 and of the constitution of modern society; 3, the vesting of spiritual sovereignty in the body of the episcopate united to the Supreme Pontiff; and 4, the limited nature of papal monarchy.[39]

It is obvious that the first two headings here are closely related and mutually reinforcing; this is the essence of liberal Gallicanism. The state cannot be liberal if it is not first sovereign. It is also obvious that the last two articles seek to add to the representative principle in the state a representative principle in the church. Though an admirer of Bossuet, Maret entirely transformed his political teaching. In effect, under the Ancien Regime, there had been "a state religion that sought complete and exclusive predominance. In the modern state, everything has changed; and the grand and noble liberties for which there was hardly room in the vocabulary of the old state are counted among the principal aims of the modern state."[40]

The consensus among the neo-Gallicans and ultramontanes on the Gallican origins of liberalism did not, of course, stop them disagreeing radically about the merits of liberalism itself. For the ultramontanes, it was the task of the clergy, and in particular of the pope, to keep states within the ambit of Christendom by their political action and authority. For the Gallicans, it was the task of lay Catholics, by virtue of their political role and competence, to confer a Christian character on liberal and democratic states.

In absolutist Gallicanism, the king was sovereign, autonomous in temporal affairs, because he was the Most Christian King, the monarch by divine right, consecrated at Reims. The king, standing at the head of the civil order, could govern temporal affairs without clerical intervention, because he occupied such a prominent place in the church that he protected. In liberal and democratic neo-Gallicanism, Catholic citizens took the place of the king. Through participation in the machinery of government and parliament, through the ballot box, through their civic and political activity, they brought Christianity into politics without the mediation of the clergy. Clerical interventionism could only impair the relative autonomy to which the temporal order laid claim. In nominating bishops, the state retained "under a representative form some element of lay intervention in the choice of pastors."[41] The task of illuminating the temporal order was henceforth to be entrusted to the laity. "The church respects the legitimate autonomy of the democratic order."[42] In the political order of worldly affairs, the church benefited by admitting that it had no special competence. The church "does not hesitate to obey the laws of the earthly city by which are administered those things that promote the sustenance of mortal life," as Saint Augustine had written long before.[43]

The spirit of liberal Gallicanism is found today at the heart of the work of Pierre Manent (born 1949). A Catholic and a liberal, Manent does not hesitate to write in an almost anticlerical vein that "the church governs badly," or that, "more precisely, she gets in the way of good governance."[44] His liberalism, in the tradition of Marsilius of Padua (one of the great points of reference for Gallicanism), consists in calling for a distinction between teaching and commanding. The church should teach, not give orders. For a Catholic, Manent pays unusual heed to the most fiercely anti-Catholic of political thinkers: Machiavelli and Rousseau. In showing that "the church governs badly," these two philosophers paradoxically offer a better understanding of the distinction between temporal and spiritual power. In his *Histoire intellectuelle du liberalisme* (An intellectual history of liberalism, 1987), Manent does not start, as one might have expected, with Constant or Tocqueville, both of whom were writing at the time when the word "liberal" became current in its modern connotation. On the contrary, he ends with them! His story begins with Marsilius of Padua and Machiavelli. His thesis, which would not have disconcerted the classical Gallican authors, is that the roots of liberalism lay in critical reflection on the political power of the papacy.

Liberalism has often been associated with a critique of politics, a sort of politics of antipolitics.[45] Manent lays bare the shortcomings of this approach by emphasizing the close link between liberalism and the defense of politics against theocracies of all kinds. He defines liberalism not as a doctrine that gives pride of place to the private sphere or to human rights but as the assertion of the autonomy of the temporal sphere. He demonstrates that liberal democracy presupposes a particular political framework, the nation-state: the nation delimits the body of those who, as equal citizens, constitute a people. United in their common citizenship, a people can accept religious difference.

Manent sees a close connection between political life and legitimate pride. Like Péguy, he could write that "in civil and civic matters, in the lay or profane sphere, I want to be bursting with pride." This does not prevent him, any more than it prevented Péguy, from thinking humility in other contexts a virtue, and by no means the least of them. Manent sees the tension between civic pride and Christian humility as the dynamic of Western history. It is that sense of legitimate pride that makes citizens aspire to govern themselves rather than to be governed by others. There can be no autonomous temporal power unless citizens are ready to fight in defense of liberty. It is only "within the framework of the political community that this sense of pride in being free can unbend to acknowledge the Christian law and to yield to it," notes Manent, adding that "this was the basic truth in Gallicanism; in this it had hold of something authentic."[46]

The testimonies of Maistre, Lamennais, Quinet, Maret, and Manent are united in seeing the great tradition of Gallicanism as the first truly secular tradition. This tradition was born in the Middle Ages as a reaction against the political extremism of certain popes, and it deserves a more distinguished place than has generally been accorded to it in histories of the foundations of modern political thought, of democracy and liberalism.

Why has this tradition been so widely overlooked? Undoubtedly because it had the double misfortune of being distorted first by the absolutism of Louis XIV, and then by the hyper-Gallicanism of the Civil Constitution of the Clergy, which between them gave it an essentially illiberal appearance. The lay and liberal character of Gallicanism was obscured by both absolutist and revolutionary illiberalism. In hindsight, the revolutionary paradox can be better understood. The Catholic Church lost its secular tradition at the very moment that saw the triumph of the laicity on which so many of its members had always insisted. The Catholic Church felt itself powerfully drawn toward political theology at the very moment when the secular power was redefining itself against such a theology. Conversely, there is something to be said for seeing Vatican II as marking the reconciliation of the Catholic Church with liberal Gallicanism. The council emphasized the political role of the laity, and showed that the church could be at ease with democracy and liberalism. It represented the long-delayed victory of Christian democrats such as Maret.

Between Vatican I and Vatican II, the church devoted itself to establishing a parallel world of Catholic social structures and institutions: schools, universities, hospitals, sports clubs, charities, cinemas, unions, political parties, newspapers, magazines, and so on.[47] Alienated by the secularization of the state, Catholics turned not only toward the papacy but away from the world, establishing a counterculture, an alternative world of religiously polarized sociability. In the wake of Vatican II, Catholics questioned this approach. It was the era of *aggiornamento*. The church at last found itself at home in the world begotten of the democratic revolutions, just as it had once been at home in the pre-revolutionary world. The divine right of peoples could almost be said to have replaced the divine right of kings. The counter-revolutionary interlude seemed definitively closed.

The church had become ultramontane because it had felt alienated by the course of history. As society was reconstructing itself without the church, the church reconstructed itself without society. At Vatican II, the church found itself once more in step with the world. Politically, this enabled it to reconnect with the forces of "progress": with democracy, the "Left," and a certain kind of radicalism. The church abandoned Reaction. It reconnected, almost, with the Catholicism of the revolutionaries, who were often simultaneously Catholic and "modern."[48] The church became less clericalist because it no longer felt the need to contrast clerical Catholicism with laicist corruption.

Vatican II is often said to have brought to a close an era in ecclesiastical history that began with the Council of Trent, as though Vatican I still belonged essentially to the premodern world.[49] Vatican I and Vatican II are set in sharp contradistinction as, respectively, "reactionary" and "progressive." However, as is well known, even the "reaction" was itself something profoundly new, simply in reacting against change. The council that marked the end of the Ancien Regime for the Catholic Church was Vatican I. In sweeping away the relics of Gallicanism, ultramontanism put an end to absolutism and even to what had been called Christendom. Paradoxically, Vatican II reconnected with an older Catholic political tradition, which, since the thirteenth century, had asserted the importance of the role of the laity and the autonomy of the political sphere. Counter-revolutionary ultramontanism sent the church up a blind alley, cut off from the main path of political development. The Catholic Church boxed itself in with a sweeping repudiation of the world that emerged from the Revolution and thus threw away the influence it had hoped to preserve or even reinvigorate. It was Tocqueville who saw the danger most clearly. And it was he who showed that the church could blend up to a point into the democratic world, as it finally set out to do at Vatican II.

Vatican I and Vatican II, taken together, constitute the twin poles between which the Catholic Church still oscillates. Roman centralization has the defects of all forms of centralization. It saps life at the roots, curbing initiative and constricting the imagination. The ultramontane tendency can thus result in a disciplined church, "orthodox" on the doctrinal level yet lacking vitality—an empty shell, reactionary and sectarian. The lay tendency and the trust in freedom associated with Vatican II have the capacity to redress the balance.[50] The ecclesiology of *Lumen Gentium* is a counterweight to that of *Pastor Aeternus*. Vatican II established the synod of bishops and the national episcopal conferences that the ultramontanes of an earlier era had looked on with deep distrust.[51] Although the episcopal conferences wielded rather less power than some people thought or hoped they would, and although one has scarcely seen any steps toward setting up national ecclesiastical administrations along the lines of the Roman Curia, Vatican II has put fresh emphasis on local churches.[52] Alongside the figures of the pope and the layperson, there is now another central figure: the bishop, who was at the heart of Gallican ecclesiology, and whose importance was restated at Vatican II.[53]

Vatican II saw the Catholic Church reappropriate some elements of the Gallican tradition. But this Gallicanism was no longer tied to the existence of an essentially Catholic state and a Most Christian King. In that sense, the absolutism of Bossuet belonged to another world. The Catholic Church abandoned the notion that the state had special obligations toward the church. Henceforward, freedom of religion would stand at the heart of its political teaching. Acknowledging the autonomy of the temporal sphere induced the church to underline the fact that fellow citizens did not necessarily have to be fellow believers.

Freedom of Religion as the Cornerstone of Catholic Political Thought

As the church had a duty to lead heretics back to the right path, it had long felt that it was justified in using force to achieve this. It had never thought it had a right to compel Jews or Muslims to become Christians, as it claimed authority only from the moment when, by baptismal consent, the baptized placed themselves under its jurisdiction.[54] The baptized granted the church a power over themselves, just as the married traditionally granted the state power over their marriage: the undertaking was free but, once made, binding. When the church felt the use of force justified, it looked to the state, its "secular arm," to apply it. The church, as such, had neither the will nor the capacity to deploy force. It could not bring compulsion to bear upon heretics or schismatics without the aid of the state, to which it was closely tied. The spiritual power did not aspire to displace the temporal power.

However, the gradual separation of church and state changed the terms of the problem. From the moment that the church was detached from the state, when the state no longer considered itself the church's "secular arm," the idea of using force to bring errant believers back to the faith lost all purchase. Catholics now drew a clear distinction between loyalty to the church and loyalty to the state. The end of the absolutist confessional state therefore entailed a transformation of the church's teaching on freedom of religion. In practice, the church effectively recognized pluralism and freedom of religion in the nineteenth century. It tended to defend liberty for want of anything better, because once it had lost its hold on the state, it would itself rather be free than subject to domination. It adjusted itself to schisms, heresies, and other religions because it no longer had the means to persecute them. It defended liberty merely as a *modus vivendi*. But in theory it continued to condemn it, maintaining that the civil power had "the right and the duty to inflict penal sanctions upon those who violate the Catholic religion."[55]

Since the *Declaration on Religious Freedom* (1965), however, the church has upheld religious liberty not as the least worst solution but in principle. It now insists that freedom of religion should be recognized and guaranteed by the state as of right for each and every person and for every community of believers. The *Declaration on Religious Freedom* thus constitutes, if not a complete break with the past, then at least a major modification of Catholic tradition, without doubt the most significant change in its political history.

At Vatican I, the church had defended its own liberty *ad intra*, by reference to its own structure and to papal infallibility, in the context of a doctrine maintaining that the church could of itself deduce and define the principles that ought to govern its relations with the state. But the church did not defend its liberty *ad extra*, by reference to a constitutional principle limiting the power of the state. Still less did it defend religious liberty in general. That would have to await the *Declaration on Religious Freedom*. That declaration was based not simply on the nature of the church as such but also on human rights and on the constitutional provisions necessary to guarantee those rights. The church relied for the defense of its own freedom upon the universal right to freedom of religion. It claimed "freedom for herself in her character as a society of men who have the right to live in society in accordance with the precepts of Christian faith."[56] The church was concerned to defend its freedom of action—for example, freedom of internal communication, freedom of association, freedom to define its own territorial organization, freedom in the choice of bishops, freedom to teach, and the autonomy of the canon law of marriage.

Traditionally, the church had tended to condemn religious liberty in the name of the rights of truth: "Error has no rights." The "Free Church in a Free State" that liberals called for was tantamount, in their eyes, to "free error in the state." At Vatican II, the church did not stop believing that it was the Truth. But henceforth it emphasized the *search* for truth. The freedom that it recognized was the freedom to search for and discover the truth. At Vatican II, the church also emphasized the value of ecumenism and interconfessional dialogue, on the grounds that even if they were strictly outside the Catholic Church, anyone who was searching for truth was making a worthwhile use of their liberty. In the *Declaration on Religious Freedom* we read:

> It is in accordance with their dignity as persons—that is, beings endowed with reason and free will and therefore privileged to bear personal responsibility—that all men should be at once impelled by nature and also bound by a moral obligation to seek the truth, especially religious truth. They are also bound to adhere to the truth, once it is known, and to order their whole lives in accord with the demands of truth.
>
> However, men cannot discharge these obligations in a manner in keeping with their own nature unless they enjoy immunity from external coercion as well as psychological freedom. Therefore, the right to religious freedom has its foundation, not in the subjective disposition of the person, but in his very nature.[57]

For as much as there was freedom of conscience and a duty to follow that conscience, even if erroneous, that freedom itself was ordained toward the search for truth. The church repudiated the use of the state as its "secular arm," but it did not repudiate its traditional teaching: the freedom to choose between good and evil (*liberum arbitrium*, or negative liberty) was subordinate to the freedom to do good (*libertas*, or positive freedom), that is, the proper use of free will.[58]

The freedom to perfect oneself (freedom to do good) is of a higher order than the freedom of indifference.

In the nineteenth century, following Lamennais, liberal Catholics mounted an eloquent defense of religious freedom. They cherished a real confidence in human nature and in the direction of history. As Montalembert (a disciple of Lamennais) wrote in 1852:

> By a marvelous secret of divine mercy, everywhere today free inquiry benefits nothing more than the truth. . . . Today, to fear freedom or to fear science in the purported interests of religion, is to doubt the truth.[59]

But at that time neither counter-revolutionary Catholics nor curial officials were prepared to follow liberal Catholics onto such ground. Where the liberals trusted in human nature and the course of history, the counter-revolutionaries evinced a profound mistrust both of human nature (as grievously wounded by original sin) and of the course of history (as headed in the wrong direction). No good could come of liberty, only corruption and atheism! At Vatican II, the church rediscovered a degree of confidence in human nature and in the power of truth, a confidence evidently more in tune with its tradition. The church rallied all the more willingly to religious liberty because it was in keeping with the nature of the act of faith, which theologians had always held to be necessarily free. "The truth cannot impose itself except by virtue of its own truth, as it makes its entrance into the mind at once quietly and with power."[60]

However, the liberalism with which the church aligned itself in the *Declaration on Religious Freedom* was not exactly the same as the liberalism that it had previously condemned. We must be careful not to set Pius IX's condemnation of liberalism in too sharp a contrast with Vatican II's recognition of religious liberty, as if the church had performed some abrupt volte-face and thrown in its lot with the "progressives." The *Syllabus* of 1864 was directed against a liberalism that made the state neutral, as though theology could be rigorously set apart from politics. The liberalism of the *Declaration on Religious Freedom* supposed nothing of the sort. Religious freedom was not founded on the neutrality of the state but on a religious obligation prior to all human customs and positive law.

In the protracted debates that led to the *Declaration on Religious Freedom*, it was the French theologians (suspicious of liberty since the time of the Revolution) who, above all, insisted on the importance of truth, clashing head-on with the Americans, who insisted above all on liberty.[61] The French secured a partial victory, in that the freedom endorsed by the church at Vatican II was not just any liberty. The right to religious liberty was interpreted in terms of a concept of conscience seen in relation to God. The *Declaration on Religious Freedom* was not predicated on "freedom of conscience." The council fathers avoided saying that individuals had an objective right to do something objectively wrong. Freedom did not mean the freedom to do absolutely anything; it was not the freedom to choose one's religion, or no religion, just as one pleased. Freedom of religion was not so much the right to "do" anything (*jus agendi*) as the right to demand (*jus exigendi*) something from the state.[62]

The theological and the political understandings of the *libertas ecclesiae* (freedom of the church) were not identical, because the state could take cognizance of the autonomy of the church only in its outward manifestation, not in its essence. But the recognition of freedom of religion had the advantage of bringing together two perspectives that reinforced each other. From the political perspective, the state was limited by political constraints, in the interests of individual liberty; from the religious perspective, the state was limited by its inability to substitute itself for God in legislating for matters of religion. In short, the Catholic Church aligned itself with liberal democracy because it offered its own interpretation of what liberal democracy ought to be. The separation of church and state was accepted because it imposed an unprecedented limitation on the power the state, which could no longer intervene in the highest matters or substitute itself for the individual conscience.

The church no longer called upon society to establish the public worship of God. In the church's eyes, the state no longer had a positive religious mission with regard to society and could not offer worship to God by virtue of a corporate act of faith of its own. The church thus aligned itself with the sort of liberalism that Royer-Collard had advocated in 1825:

> We, individual and identical persons, true beings, made in the image of God and endowed with immortality, we have religious discernment among our glorious gifts; but God has not bestowed that gift upon states, which do not have the same destiny as us. And not only has he not given it to them, but, one might say, he has positively withheld it from them, for he has permitted, he has willed, in his inscrutable providence, that false religions should confer on societies the same benefits as the true religion in terms of stability and splendor.[63]

The state no longer has to guarantee the true faith, to make an act of faith in its own right. The state should serve God in its own way, in making laws in accordance with justice for the sake of the common good, and in protecting the inviolable rights of the person. But it should never again be reckoned competent to decide on the truth claims of a religion. The legitimacy of the state is no longer contingent upon its officially recognizing the truth of Catholicism. There would never be a "League of Christian Nations" akin to the "Organization of the Islamic Conference." Henceforth Catholics would accept the legitimacy of the state provided it respected natural law and freedom of religion. The state could stand before its subjects devoid of any legitimation or justification beyond the purely human. It could demand obedience without appealing to any divine power over and above the power of law. Thus, a long tradition came to an end. The Catholic character of the nation and the king was no longer, as for Bossuet and Maistre, a precondition of temporal autonomy. The question that had been left hanging for so long had at last been settled in the clearest possible terms. The *Declaration on Religious Freedom* ended the long struggle between the antiliberal faction and the "liberal" faction that, since the time of *L'Avenir*, had raised the cry "God and liberty."

In 1864 the *Syllabus of Errors* had repudiated one of the anti-Christian wings of the Enlightenment, whereas the council integrated a theory of liberty that takes account of the evils sparked off or fueled by modern political voluntarism: *after* Nazism, which brought opprobrium on the excesses of the "Right"; *after* Stalinism, which discredited the excesses of the "Left." The liberalism that the church maintained owed less to an anticlerical model of laicity than to an assertion of the limits of state authority in religious matters. After the Enlightenment had been duly humiliated, stripped of its pride by the ideological folly and warmongering that it had done so much to engender, the church recovered the natural law tradition that it had itself fashioned. In recognizing freedom of religion, the church certainly did not stop hoping that society might become as Christian as possible. It rallied to the cause of liberty all the more readily because it saw in liberty an opportunity to evangelize more effectively. It had no hesitation in reaffirming that justice and peace would result from "men's faithfulness to God and to His holy will."[64] It had no hesitation in maintaining that "there can be no genuine solution to the social question outside the Gospel."[65]

The church had ended up embracing a liberal modesty concerning the aims and objectives of political life, chiefly because it had recovered a forgotten strand of its own political tradition. In book 19 of the *City of God*, Augustine had shown that the earthly city could, despite (or because of) the egoism on which it was based, tend toward a relative harmony. Even in the absence of the church, even in the absence of love, the earthly city was capable of achieving certain objectives within its own sphere. As thieves had to have some mutual understanding in order to split the proceeds, so too the citizens of a godless city could reach a level of understanding adequate to the avoidance of civil war and the enjoyment of a relative tranquillity. "Even that which is disordered must needs be to some degree at peace."[66] Augustine had drawn attention to the limits of that order and to its deceptive character. He had shown that Christian harmony went very much further. Yet even in the absence of an explicit acknowledgment of the truth of revelation, some civic order was possible. Augustine has not been widely regarded as a liberal, yet he wrote: "As for this mortal life (whose span is so brief and whose end is so soon), what difference does it make, to those who have to die, under what authority their life is lived, as long as those in command do not constrain them to perform unholy or wicked acts?"[67] Above all, the church requires liberty. It was possible for the church to accept the turn taken by modern political philosophy because it harked back to intuitions it shared all the more because it had previously put them forward itself!

In retrospect, it appears that the denial of freedom of religion owes less to Christianity as such than to a particular political history. The Catholic Church can secure its own place in liberal democracy by relying on the principles of democracy and liberalism. In accepting the modern idea of liberty, it can co-opt and baptize that new source of energy and dignity. It can thus do justice to the legitimate pride of citizens as well as to their legitimate desire for individual autonomy.

A Degree of Disenchantment since Vatican II

During the Cold War, the church was firmly on the side of liberty against communist tyranny. The Polish pope, John Paul II, embodied the alliance of the church with the lay center-left against totalitarianism. Here is what was written in 1977 by one of the key intellectuals of Solidarity, Adam Michnik, an agnostic of Jewish background: "All people of goodwill oppose the ongoing process of Sovietization. . . . But it is the church that puts up the most systematic resistance." These lines come from a book that Michnik wrote for his secularist comrades, to prevent them from being confused as to the real enemy. The church was not an inveterate enemy of individual liberty. For all its reactionary aspects, the church defended its own freedom and therefore the cause of freedom as such. "Religious liberty is the most obvious sign that civil rights are healthy. The encroachment of power upon this liberty is always a sign of the totalitarianization of intellectual life. There is no exception to this rule, because it is only totalitarianism that is unable to accept the apostolic injunction "to obey God rather than man."[68]

The political development of the secular center-left for which Michnik was a spokesman had its parallels within the Catholic Church. In practice, the church had adapted well to democratic and liberal regimes since the later nineteenth century. In 1892 the Holy See had called on French Catholics to "rally" to the Republic. Yet at the same time the church long remained suspicious of the human rights agenda, seeing in it a unilateral assertion of individual liberty at the expense of truth. So the church for a long time favored more conservative and authoritarian regimes, as in Poland and elsewhere, in preference to the liberal regimes that were the legacy of the Revolution. In the twentieth century it had to face the facts: the alternative to liberal democracy was no longer Ancien Regime monarchy, but totalitarian revolution. Hence the high value that Pius XII placed on democracy in his Christmas message of 1944:

> In the sinister light of the war that engulfs them, in the baking heat of the furnace in which they are shut up, people are at last awakening from a protracted slumber. They are adopting a new attitude in the face of

states and governments, questioning, critical, distrustful. Taught by bitter experience, they set their face against dictatorial, unaccountable, and untouchable monopolies on power, and they call for a system of government that is more compatible with the dignity and liberty of citizens.[69]

"Bitter experience" was the decisive factor. In the midst of the Cold War, it led Vatican II to recognize religious liberty, henceforth the cornerstone of the church's political philosophy. It led to the reconciliation between the Catholic Church and the liberal intelligentsia that Michnik observed. John Paul II, who always put great emphasis on human rights, owed something of his political thinking to his experience of totalitarianism and of Solidarity.

In the nineteenth century, the imposing structure of the Catholic Church had been unable to accommodate the democratic order with the same readiness as the Protestant churches. However, in another perspective, that same imposing structure afforded a protective shield against the ideological pressures of one-party states. The rigidity of the Catholic Church, which not long before had made it the enemy of liberal democracy, made it one of its firmest props in the totalitarian era. Overall, the Catholic Church proved more robust than Protestantism in the face of totalitarianism. The importance it attached to its own institutional character, to its hierarchical dimension, and to its unity made it a redoubtable adversary for dictators who wanted to subordinate everything to the state. One need only compare Catholic Poland to East Germany, both under the Soviet yoke for fifty years. While the Polish Catholic Church took a firm stand against the communist regime, the Protestant churches of the German Democratic Republic found it difficult to maintain a sense of their own identity in the face of similar pressures.[70]

Michnik envisaged a more tranquil future: "The concept of a secular state is no longer anticlerical but antitotalitarian. Open conflict between the lay liberal intelligentsia and the church is a closed chapter—forever, we hope!—in European history."[71] Michnik wrote this in 1977. He did not see that, for a decade already, a new front had been opened in that old conflict. The cultural revolution of the 1960s had set the two sides on a collision course. On one side were those who saw the cultural revolution above all in terms of liberation: "women's lib," sexual liberation, and the intensification of individualism and secularization. On the other were those who were disturbed by the direction of moral developments and by what they saw as casual disregard for the rights of the weakest: embryos. The church tended to side with those who were anxious and disturbed. The church stood out against the moral developments of the 1960s, in which it saw not so much liberation as alienation.

The bone of contention was no longer liberal democracy, which the church now supported. It was no longer the fact of political liberalism, but its interpretation. Did the freedom of the individual entail legalizing voluntary termination of pregnancy, euthanasia, and the like? John Paul II was deeply troubled at seeing "crimes against life" interpreted as "legitimate expressions of the freedom of the individual." For him, the problem was not the ideology of human rights but, on the contrary, measures that constituted a "direct threat to the entire culture of human rights." The right to procure the termination of pregnancy was denounced as a radical violation of the most elementary justice: "The 'right' ceases to be a right when it is founded not on the inviolable dignity of the person but on the will of the strongest. Thus democracy, despite its principles, takes on the characteristics of totalitarianism."[72] For the church, when the assertion of the autonomy of the individual will leads to challenging the distinction between the sacred and the profane and to suggesting that all human problems have purely technical solutions, then liberalism starts lurching toward totalitarianism.[73] "The true struggle, in today's society, is the struggle to defend the humanity of the human."[74]

In bourgeois democracies, the issue today is no longer between liberal and illiberal regimes. It is more a matter of which liberal regime is truly liberal. In the sphere of politics, given the choice between liberalism and totalitarianism, the church is firmly on the side of liberalism. But in the moral dimension, the church seems cold, hostile to pleasure and progress, and out of sympathy with liberal public opinion. The church's hostility, however, is not directed toward human rights or political liberalism. What concerns the church are the moral consequences of liberalism envisaged as individual autonomy.

For an element within the Catholic Church, the situation remains one of struggle against a totalitarian threat, only now the crude totalitarianism of the communists has been replaced by a creeping totalitarianism, decked out in the false colors of political liberalism. For an element of the lay intelligentsia, in contrast, the voluntary termination of pregnancy, the ending of suffering through euthanasia, and recent developments in sexual morality have all taken on the character of elementary rights. Those who stand against them are dismissed as fundamentalists. From their point of view, the bourgeois (and, for the most part, Christian) world that was repudiated in the 1960s has come to seem, for all its liberal pretensions, essentially illiberal. Thus, within that perspective, it is crucial to combat the Catholic Church in the name of liberty: the struggle against totalitarianism is to be continued by drastically restricting that church's social and political influence. The Catholic Church is seen not as an ally of liberty but as one of its bitterest enemies, as more interested in constraining freedom than supporting it. It is taken to be an essentially conservative rather than a liberating force, striving to hold back social developments, not to advance them. Benedict XVI, distinguished theologian that he is, appears first and foremost as the intransigent defender of "orthodoxy"—a taboo word in a democratic era infatuated with novelty. His relative lack of charisma (especially in comparison with his predecessor John Paul II) tends to reinforce the sense that the church has set an unpopular course.

Two opposing philosophies have developed, largely in the Anglo-Saxon world, and especially in Great Britain. On one side, the freedom of the individual is taken to consist in choosing for oneself one's own idea of goodness and morality. Its exponents tend to think that asserting an objective concept of the good is the basis of all illiberalism (this is in essence Isaiah Berlin's concept of negative liberty, or Herbert Hart's idea of law). For them, morality is a matter for the individual, not for the state, nor for any other collective institution (such as the church). On the other side, it is argued that individual autonomy must be understood in terms of a moral framework that gives it its meaning and purchase. The exponents of this view, such as Elizabeth Anscombe, Patrick Devlin, and Alasdair MacIntyre, see individual liberty as unintelligible without reference to an objective moral order.[75] For them, it is nonsense to pretend that the state (or other collective institutions) refrain from intervening in moral matters, because that is simply what states do. In their view, the notion that solitary individuals choose their own morality, that morality is entirely a matter of the private sphere, is downright illusory. The Catholic Church is affiliated with this second view, but a vocal section of the secular intelligentsia maintains the first view. The division is seen most clearly over sexual morality.

Today, the criteria for legitimate sexual activity are no longer tied to the institution of marriage and the purposes of reproduction but are held to consist in consent alone. (Marriage, of course, entails consent, but that consent is bound up with the restraint of the promise of fidelity and, in Catholic teaching, with an openness to fertility.) What is forbidden today is not extramarital sexual activity (whether homosexual, premarital, or adulterous) but a much more restricted field of behavior: rape (which by definition excludes consent) and pedophilia (because its victims are not capable of giving consent). Family law as it was still understood but a few decades ago, within a still-Christian context, seems to have abruptly disappeared. The idea of consent involved in the theory of marriage has been systematically subordinated to a different, more subjective, idea of consent, one that requires no institutional authorization. This shift in sexual morality has left the church out on a limb. In retrospect, it seems to have been in practice horribly complacent about certain types of behavior, notably pedophilia. It seems to have been wrong-footed by the change in attitudes toward homosexuality and by the spreading use of contraceptives. The encyclical *Humanae Vitae* (1968), which forbade all artificial means of birth control, had a particularly hostile reception.[76]

In several countries, the Catholic Church has been obliged to close its adoption agencies because it refuses to treat homosexual couples in the same way as heterosexual couples. Despite the fact that homosexual couples can avail themselves of numerous non-Catholic adoption agencies, Catholic agencies are condemned as discriminatory. Moreover, the right of the Catholic Church (and of other religious groups) to teach in its own schools that homosexual acts are sinful could, in time, be challenged. This last issue is particularly sensitive. On one side, it seems self-evident, in the name of nondiscrimination, that it ought to be unlawful to encourage, even indirectly, attitudes of profound disapproval toward homosexual activity. On the other hand, it seems difficult to deny the church the freedom to remain faithful to a morality that it does not believe it has the right to challenge. Can liberal democracy compel the Catholic Church to be silent or to change its moral teaching? Not enough attention has been paid to the way that the notion of nondiscrimination (originally envisaged in terms of race) has changed the nature of liberal democracy, undertaking a radical transformation of society by means of law.

In the past thirty years, the Catholic Church has made an increasing effort to distinguish more sharply between homosexual orientation (which it views as a matter neither for praise nor for blame, but simply for acceptance) and the sexual activity associated with it (of which the church disapproves). For Catholics, this distinction allows it to posit a political rationale for not discriminating against homosexuals: men and women with homosexual tendencies "ought to be treated with respect, compassion, and delicacy; no unfair discrimination should be shown toward them."[77] Nevertheless, it is clear that the fine distinctions drawn in the church's statements are far from satisfactory to those who wish to see a radical alteration in its sexual teaching.

That said, homosexuality is not the key issue: it is the subject of fierce debate within the church itself.[78] But it is representative of the more general issues at stake. In 2002, the Congregation for the Doctrine of the Faith expressed disquiet at "the invocation of tolerance in a dishonest way in the demand that a large number of citizens (among them Catholics) should not base their participation in social and political life on their particular understanding of the human person and the common good."[79] A new debate has opened up on the legitimacy of invoking religious categories of thought in the public sphere. The debate has spread through much of the liberal world.[80] The key question is whether the public expression of religious ideas is or is not, as such, a threat to democratic debate.

As some people now see it, it is not just the state but also society that must be secular. Religion should be confined to the private forum as an entirely personal affair. The idea of confessional political parties (such as the Christian Democrats) over which the church hierarchy might exercise a degree of influence, which until recently seemed entirely compatible with the best traditions of democracy, has come to seem incongruous and illiberal. In the name of a particular understanding of individual autonomy, the separation of the secular from the religious, which, expressed as the separation of the state from society, stood at the heart of classical liberalism, is now being applied within society itself. The citizen is now, bizarrely, being forbidden any longer from speaking on the basis of his or her personal convictions. It is as though the separation of church and state must now be enacted within the individual person. Churches are no longer recognized as having any relevant expertise and are being excluded from participation in the debate, even when it is a question of defending their own liberty. For the churches (whether Catholic or not), this is obviously hardly acceptable, as it entails drastic restrictions on their freedom of action and of expression, for reasons that are not reasons of public order—in principle the only justifiable reasons for such restrictions in a liberal system. Hence the fear of a creeping totalitarianism: the autonomy of the church has been challenged, and thus also, in effect, its very existence as a distinct social and juridical entity. Some Catholics have openly begun to wonder whether they might not face the risk of persecution or even martyrdom. The tension between the new social reality and the teaching of the church calls forth prophets.

Of course, the Catholic Church is anxious that the "good news" it proclaims should not be reduced to a narrow and repressive message about sex (or euthanasia, or abortion). Its mission is to present a positive message that raises wider questions, not simply to promulgate a series of condemnations. Above all, the heart of its message is the death and resurrection of Jesus Christ, the Word of God made flesh. The church does not wish to get bogged down in arguments that run the risk of weakening the overall thrust of its moral and spiritual teaching. It wants to highlight its social teaching, its critiques of economic liberalism, its emphasis on the proper regulation of the economy, and its defense of the poor and of the role of trade unions. The church is swift to denounce the consumer society, which "tends to outdo even Marxism in terms of pure materialism."[81] Yet it is remarkable how the issues it tries to avoid keep resurfacing in public debate. In liberal democracies, the church's social teaching has no purchase on public opinion, partly because it does not challenge contemporary attitudes, and partly because social questions are no longer the center of attention, which instead focuses on problems arising in the area of individual autonomy.

The Catholic Church had long condemned freedom of religion, and thus liberalism, in the name of truth, maintaining that "error has no rights." But at Vatican II the church recognized the right to freedom of religion. The church had not abandoned the idea of truth. The liberalism that it endorsed was a liberalism that allows people to find truth by the light of Christ's teaching. In the decades since the council, the highest authorities in the Curia seem to have grown disenchanted with the formula to which they had in the end rallied. Some official documents, most importantly the encyclical *Veritatis splendor* (1993), have emphasized the importance of truth above all, as if the balance struck in 1965 between freedom and truth had not in practice worked satisfactorily. Thus, for example, Cardinal Ratzinger (later to become Pope Benedict XVI) wrote in 2002:

> It is worth recalling a truth that is not always appreciated today or which is not formulated in an exact manner in current public opinion: the right

to freedom of conscience, and in particular to freedom of religion, proclaimed by the Declaration *Dignitatis humanae* of the Second Vatican Council, is based on the ontological dignity of the human person, and not in any respect upon an equality between religions or human cultural systems which does not in fact exist.[82]

Reconnecting with the traditional Catholic critique of indifferentism, Ratzinger rejected cultural relativism and subjectivism in favor of an objective concept of truth. The historical optimism of some exponents of religious freedom seemed in retrospect exaggerated.[83] Without going back on the great principles set down at Vatican II, John Paul II and Benedict XVI both felt that, in the wake of the council and of the cultural upheavals of 1968, the search for truth had become more and more cut off from the transmission of revelation, with both church and society losing their bearings. They began to wonder whether contemporary Catholicism was not in fact approximating more and more to liberal Protestantism.[84] Without calling into question the acknowledgment of freedom of religion, they were nevertheless disturbed by some of the constructions that had been put upon it. In their eyes, the freedom of the individual had not been properly understood, as was evident from the aforementioned debates over sexual morality and euthanasia.

There is talk today of the Holy See calling Vatican II into question. Whereas at the time of the council the church seemed keen to plunge into the world of democracy and liberalism, the contemporary papacy in contrast seems determined to keep its distance. In the wake of Vatican II, priests sought to blend in with the laity, exchanging the cassock for a smart suit with a discreet cross— and, incidentally, thus retrieving another old Gallican idea: in the nineteenth century, Maret had said that "the cassock is something that fences off and isolates the clergy and divides the people: this division is one of the greatest evils of modern times."[85] Under John Paul II and then Benedict XVI, the cassock has made a comeback, along with the Roman collar, as the sign of a certain separation from society in general. On the whole, the younger bishops are more conservative than their elders, and the younger priests are more conservative still. The future of Catholicism seems to lie in the adoption of an evangelical spirit (in the Protestant sense of that term), which is better suited to the democratic mindset. The "new communities" that have emerged since 1970, such as Charismatic Renewal, the Emmanuel Community, and the Community of the Beatitudes, are among the liveliest and most imaginative elements in the contemporary French Catholic Church. But along with their potential for renewal, they are characterized by a real traditionalism in faith and morals, as well as by a political conservatism. They want to bear witness to their faith, not argue about it.[86] The most dynamic Catholic Churches in the world, those of Africa, America, and Asia, to which the demographic future seems to belong, show similar tendencies. There are three rival interpretations of this postconciliar trend.

The first interpretation holds that the contemporary direction of the Catholic Church is best explained by changes that have taken place since Vatican II. It was only after the council that questions of sexual morality and bioethics pushed the Catholic Church back into a more critical position with regard to progressive opinion in the liberal democracies. This change of style and tone reflects, therefore, not so much a questioning of the council itself as the ephemeral nature of the situation of which "the spirit of Vatican II" was the expression: a moment when the liberal democracies were obviously preferable to the communist bloc they opposed; a moment of unstable equilibrium that saw individual liberty in balance with Christian tradition; a moment in which liberal democracy, though not officially recognizing the authority of the Catholic Church, nevertheless still subscribed to an essentially Christian culture that took account of natural law. It has often been noted that Vatican II was the first general council in church history to take place not in the context of some crisis but at a moment of calm. From this point of view, the council could not have been anything other than an epiphany, significant for the promise of reconciliation that it proffered, but always provisional.

In the second interpretation, local churches and the laity should have taken power in the church but were frustrated by Roman conservatism. The council had emphasized the role of collegiality, but the exponents of this collegiality were always regarded with suspicion from the centralizing perspective of the Curia. One way or another, all subsequent popes have been accused of wanting to go back on Vatican II.

The milder version of this interpretation puts everything down to the sociology of institutions. Executive bodies naturally strive to maximize their own power, and the Holy See, like all other executive authorities, is naturally inclined to make excessive use of that power. It reduces other bishops to dependence on itself, valuing conformism over charisma in episcopal appointments. It undermines national episcopal conferences, which offer the best hope of achieving a level of reasonable yet traditional democracy within the church. It even extends the scope of infallibility to teachings which are not derived directly from revelation.[87]

In its stronger form, this interpretation sees Vatican II in terms of a revolution that was betrayed by the hierarchy. At the highest levels of the church there was, if not a Counter-Revolution, then at least a Thermidor.[88] In certain restricted but vocal circles, it was even thought that the democratic world had made a reality of Christianity, as though Christianity boiled down to the "values"—liberty, equality, fraternity—that modernity embodied, as if it were no longer a religion of interdicts and excommunications, or morality or asceticism, and was simply a matter of "ideals." The "spirit of Vatican II" had aroused an exuberant enthusiasm, refracted through Marxism or related ideologies.[89] Contemporary Catholicism, in contrast, as redefined under John Paul II and Benedict XVI, has broken with that progressivism.[90] Liberation theology was roundly condemned. In the late 1960s and early 1970s, Ratzinger was preoccupied with the emergence of a theology that he thought had become cut off from its roots and contaminated by political aims that were incompatible with the very nature of theological discourse.[91] So a less democratic, less political vision prevailed, to the chagrin of those who had seen the council as an almost Messianic manifestation. There has been a sort of Gallican resurgence against the papacy in recent decades: an *Anti-Roman Complex, Bishops against the Pope.* A good many Catholics have suggested that *Not All Roads Lead to Rome.*[92] The epiphany of Vatican II has led to a novel fusion between the church and democracy, which has in turn led Catholics to identify with their nation just as they did under the Ancien Regime. Catholics agree that there is a crisis, but they disagree over its cause and character. For some, it has arisen from the repudiation of the progressive spirit of Vatican II. For others, it is the result of a syndrome of which that progressive spirit is itself the clinching proof—*a loss of nerve.*

The third interpretation, which is the theme of this book, sets Vatican II in the perspective of the *longue durée.* It proposes that the council was not in fact a fundamental break with tradition, and indeed that it was actually a continuation of the work of Vatican I. The secularization of the state that followed the French Revolution necessitated a change of allegiances. Catholics had to look to Rome for the religious authority that could no longer be found within the framework of the nation, because they sensed the degradation of the body politic in the age of secularization. Catholics would not have attributed such importance to Rome if they had not accepted as a given the passing of the political theology of the Ancien Regime. In this perspective, Vatican II becomes inseparable from Vatican I. The adaptation of the church to the democratic world order came in two stages, at the two councils. The continuities outweigh the discontinuities. There were two stages in the emergence of the new awareness that the church acquired of itself as a distinct society in the light of political developments in Europe. Vatican II has to be understood not in terms of its "spirit" (far too vague a concept) but by reference to what it actually said—which was far more prudent and moderate than is imagined by the more progressive Catholics, and which no pope has felt it necessary to call into question.[93] From Paul VI to Benedict XVI, popes have emphasized their fidelity to Vatican II even as they have insisted on its continuity with Vatican I. The more the two councils are seen in long-term continuity, the less sense there seems to be in the idea of some "betrayal" of Vatican II. The fear of "turning the clock back," of a reaction or a counter-revolution, makes sense only if Vatican II marked some great break with the past. If the two Vatican councils, taken together, constitute a coherent "Vatican reform," then the increasingly Roman temper of the new generation of priests does not necessarily denote a failure to understand the modern world. However, from the other side, the suggestion that Vatican I and Vatican II stand in continuity has sometimes been denounced as a betrayal by Catholics who support radical change.

It is worth underlining that the more importance one attaches to the first of these interpretations (change *since* Vatican II), the less likely one is to credit the stronger version of the second interpretation (Thermidor, or Counter-Revolution). The more the church is haunted by a sense of the intellectual corruption of society, the more it feels the need to refocus itself on the papacy in order to preserve revelation and tradition in their integrity. That is the way that the church forestalls the reduction of doctrine to morality. The more that believers find themselves alienated from society, the more they feel the need for a source of authority that safeguards the "deposit of the faith" and keeps it from adulteration or transformation.

A Positive Idea of Laicity

The rise of a new laicism, or aggressive secularism, cannot be ruled out, because the revolution in morals has fomented growing disquiet in the lay intelligentsia over particular teachings of the Catholic Church. But, by dialectical reflux, this new secularism could soon run up against political constraints. There is talk today of a version of laicity that is clearly more favorable to religion in general and to the Catholic Church in particular: the "positive laicity" that Nicolas Sarkozy has called for in France.[94] This positive conception of "laicity" can be considered in three contexts: with reference to the shifts in Catholic political teaching; with reference to the postmodern crisis of rationalism; and with reference to the reconciliation of classical republicanism with Catholicism in the name of civic and moral virtue.

First of all, it should be noted that the old confrontational secularism was very much the product of particular circumstances that have since disappeared. The founders of the Third Republic dreamed of a democratic and liberal regime that would put into practice the ideals of the Revolution. Ranged against them were highly placed elements in the Catholic Church that distrusted democracy and lent a ready ear to the theorists of the Counter-Revolution. The majority of the French people were Catholics. Laicity was a way of getting round that problem. But laicity of that kind is no longer necessary. On the one hand, the church has reconciled itself to the law of 1905, at least as interpreted in case law, and is even inclined to defend it, seeing it as a guarantee of its own freedom. On the other hand, the church has rallied to the concept of freedom of religion, which it solemnly enshrined in its official teaching at Vatican II. The aggressive secularism of the republicans of the Third Republic has lost its target. Moreover, even republicans can appreciate that the Catholic Church today offers some real advantages. Unlike evangelical Protestantism, the Catholic Church offers some protection against fundamentalism, which is foreign to its tradition. Unlike some strands of political Islam, it offers the prospect of moderation and stability. Catholicism still claims the loyalty of two-thirds of the French population, and it no longer opposes republican government—indeed, quite the contrary.

Second, aggressive laicism long based itself on a brand of rationalism that is today itself in crisis. Its theorists were for the most part positivists or neo-Kantians who looked forward to the displacement of religion by reason. Its guiding principle was the Enlightenment notion that humanity had come of age, had at last taken its destiny into its own hands, and had achieved autonomy. Traditions, customs, and religions depended on outmoded authority figures. In the mythology of the Third Republic, the schoolteacher was contrasted with the parish priest in terms of a conflict between reason and the irrational medievalism of a church that still hankered after the anachronistic alliance between throne and altar. There is little enough of that myth left standing. The ideals of the Enlightenment have themselves been subverted by ever more "advanced" intellects. Since Nietzsche, and more particularly since Foucault, Lyotard, and Derrida, the intelligentsia is supposed to dwell in the postmodern world. The statue of Auguste Comte, the founder of positivism, may still stand in the Place de la Sorbonne—it has not yet been replaced by a statue of Michel Foucault—but his ideas no longer hold sway there. Science itself attracts fewer students than it used to. The French Revolution is no longer regarded as reason incarnate, for the "universal" is simply the mask or cloak of some "particularity" or other, be it bourgeois, sexist, imperialist, or colonialist. Philosophy has turned on itself, and philosophers chase their own tails. One of our culture's favorite fables is on the edge of extinction: the religion of progress, the enchanting myth that captivated the imagination of the intellectuals. Obscurantism has not given way to the luminous reign of the Enlightenment, and prejudices have not been swept away. It is thus that one should understand the apparently slightly inept remark of Nicolas Sarkozy in a speech at the Lateran in December 2007: "In the transmission of values and in inculcating the difference between right and wrong, the schoolteacher will never be able to replace the pastor or the priest, even if it is important that he or she emulate them, because the schoolteacher's vocation can never have the same self-sacrificial dedication or the charisma of a commitment born of hope." In the secularist campaign of the schoolteacher against the parish priest, the former could at one time hope to replace the latter; but now it is clear that this cannot happen. Political interest in religion is reviving as people come to appreciate the limits of the very rationalism that sought to displace it. As Marcel Gauchet has said, for example, "It is the collapse of the militant Enlightenment in the midst of the triumphant Enlightenment that has reshaped the face of democracy. That is what has summoned the religions back into the public square."[95] Positive laicity has been made necessary by the exhaustion of positivist and anticlerical rationalism, which has sapped militant rationalism of its essence and energy. Today, paradoxically, it is the Catholic Church that is most ready to defend natural law and reason against philosophers seduced by nihilism.[96]

Third, positive laicity can be interpreted in the light of the discovery, or recovery, of a degree of convergence between the teaching of the Catholic Church and classical liberalism in the form it has taken on in France since 1880. The radical individualism that holds sway today takes aim not only at the Catholic Church but also at some central characteristics of the republicanism of the Third Republic itself. The attack on moral authority is of course an attack on the magisterium of the Catholic Church. But its field of fire extends to republican education. By a strange paradox, the republicans of 1880 seem in retrospect to have been very close to the Catholics they fought. As a historian of republican education has observed,

> The textbooks of the two educational systems [republican and Catholic] breathed the same air of Francocentric confidence. They praised the same great men and taught the same moral lessons. Because it shared, without realizing it, the same values as its rival, secular education can today sometimes be seen as having represented the culmination, the ironic triumph, of the old educational system of the priests established in the age of classicism.[97]

The republicans wished to rid themselves of the Catholic Church, but they meant to cling on to Christian culture. For Jules Ferry, "secular moral teaching distinguishes itself from religious teaching *without contradicting it.*"[98] Republicans rejected dogma and hierarchy (this was how their teaching was differentiated from that of the church), but they remained faithful to Christian morality. They had no intention of replacing it with a new morality because, for them, there was only one morality. Today the new laicity, aggressive secularism, squares up to a Christian culture and morality with which the old republicanism had no quarrel. From the perspective of classical republicans, the militant existentialism that has transformed education and society since the 1960s would prove pernicious. Equally, however, positive laicity reflects the growing interest of classical republicans in Catholicism. Republicans used to want Christian culture without the Christian faith. Now they are beginning to see that you cannot have one without the other.

The founders of the Third Republic, loyal disciples of Comte, no doubt recalled his dictum that "the only way to avoid being governed by others is to govern oneself." When self-restraint and the sense of civic virtue wither away, then republics subside into Caesarism. Comte again: "The weaker a society's moral regime, the more vital it becomes to reinforce government in material terms, so as to prevent the complete dissolution of the social fabric. . . . In a nation where the indispensable cooperation of individuals in maintaining public order can no longer be presumed on the basis of the voluntary and moral assent granted by each person to a common social doctrine, there is nothing else that can maintain some degree of harmony but the sorry alternatives of force and corruption."[99] Auguste Comte felt the need of a moral order and a spiritual power to ward off administrative despotism and corruption. Paradoxically, the systematic denunciation of authority smooths the way for authoritarianism. Such reflections have long seemed untimely and outmoded. But it could be that the systematic questioning of the idea of moral authority may give the idea of the social role of religion renewed relevance from the point of view of liberalism itself.

The Catholic Church can adapt itself to democracy all the better if, from its point of view, democracy has need of it. The Christian assertion of the autonomy of politics entails a self-denying ordinance that affords some protection against the temptations of boundless pride and inordinate ambition. Civil liberty is not necessarily so much better for the absence of religion. Péguy remarked that "The *de-republicanization* of France is essentially the same movement as the *dechristianization* of France."[100] Dechristianization could undermine the foundations of democracy. Acknowledgment of dependence on God might be the precondition of political independence. "What can be done with a people which is its own master, if it be not submissive to the Divinity?" Tocqueville asked. Of the individual person Tocqueville was inclined to think that "if faith be wanting in him, he must serve, and if he be free, he must believe."[101] The paradox here is that it is often thanks to the authority of revelation that we can avoid authoritarian politics: moral or spiritual authority has the specific advantage that it is indeed moral or spiritual—not physical.

The Catholic Church is favorable to liberal democracy because it sees religious liberty as fundamental to that form of government. It will be markedly less favorable if, in the name of liberalism, strict limits are placed on its own liberty, and society comes to ignore what it regards as the most fundamental laws. The present situation is obviously unstable. One can imagine, on the one hand, a resurgence of profound tension between church and state (in particular over the issue of what the autonomy of the individual means), but it may be, on the other hand, that elements of political convergence will come to the fore. Nor need these two possibilities be mutually exclusive: they could feed off each other. And both could pose serious problems for the Catholic Church. The bishops have no desire to be seen primarily as guardians of moral order against modern individualistic trends. Nor do they want to go back to being the "prefects in purple" of Napoleonic times. It could be difficult for them to speak the language they would like: that of liberty.

To conclude these remarks on positive laicity, it is worth reflecting on the career of a philosopher who is not a believer, but whose successive positions have gradually brought him closer to the Catholic Church: Jürgen Habermas.

For some years now Habermas has opposed more and more openly the idea of restricting public debate in such a way as to exclude the churches, notably the Catholic Church. "When secularized citizens take up their political role," he writes, "they have no right to deny a potential for truth in religious visions of the world, nor to contest the right of their religious fellow citizens to make their contribution to public debates in religious language."[102] For Habermas, the non-believer cannot simply assume that religion rests *a priori* on the irrational. Religion could prove the vehicle of a true rationality, for "reason reflecting on its own deepest foundations discovers that its own origin lies elsewhere."[103] The crisis of positivism renders the church's contribution valuable not in substituting revelation for reason but in providing reason itself with a solid foundation.

It would seem that the development of Habermas's thought can be accounted for at least in part by his fear of a "liberal eugenics."[104] Eugenics has long been excluded from the realm of practical politics as a result of its association in the public mind with Nazism, with all the awful connotations that brings. However, on a philosophical level, it is necessary to enquire into the real reasons for ruling out eugenics. The question has taken on an existential urgency in the contemporary context, in which a radical individualism has prevailed at a time of rapid technological advance in such fields as embryology and fertility treatment. Habermas appreciates that the liberal concept of individual autonomy, prevalent in contemporary political philosophy, is of little help in this area. That, it seems, is why he has taken more interest in Christianity, especially in the Catholic Church. The papacy's decisive rejection of certain developments has made it an obvious ally for opponents of eugenics. Without necessarily adopting the Catholic position, Habermas has at least become aware of its merits. It seems to offer some kind of bulwark against a nihilistic temptation to lose sight of human dignity and thus of one of the possible foundations of political liberalism.

Taken to a radical extreme, the thesis that individuals can do anything they like as long as they do not injure anybody else in the process need not stop with the restructuring of sexual morality. It can also be used to justify euthanasia (the ending of suffering at the request of the one who suffers), termination of pregnancy (it is the right of the woman and does not involve "anybody else"), and even eugenics (one is simply improving the gene pool). Most of the issues that today arouse tension between the secular intelligentsia and the Catholic Church are found in this area. An institution that relies on what it calls "Tradition" can legitimately be charged with conservatism, but it would be a mistake (one made rather often in recent decades) to imagine that it might abandon its traditional principles. The church should, on the contrary, be expected to offer fierce opposition to the moral developments it rejects. For the church, the confrontation with the totalitarian regimes of the twentieth century is the background not only to its own reconciliation with democracy but also to the critiques it persistently advances against certain consequences of the democratic spirit. When the idea of the autonomy of the will goes so far as to call into question the idea of a distinction between the sacred and the profane, and to suggest that everything can be manipulated, that humanity is indefinitely perfectible, it is hard to say whether one is still in a liberal democracy or has in fact already succumbed to totalitarianism.

Conclusion

Over the past two hundred years, the Catholic Church has been confronted with a political system whose triumph it did not foresee, and for which it was therefore ill prepared: liberal democracy. How has it gone about *aggiornamento*? How far has it preserved or recovered its power to inspire and challenge in a world always tempted to ignore the good news it claims to bring? Democracy means the polemical assertion of the sovereignty of the people, and this poses two problems. Insofar as it is *sovereignty*, it is reluctant to acknowledge divine limitations. Insofar as it is *popular*, it is suspicious of anything that smacks of clericalism or hierarchy. To the extent that democracy is liberal, it poses a third problem for the church: freedom of religion can simply engender indifference to truth.

To start with the first problem, the secularization of the state ensures religious freedom for its citizens, with the government adopting a position of neutrality with regard to their various religious beliefs. This secularization is for the most part seen as a stage on the road to "modernity," as liberation from a medieval world. Most liberals are therefore happy to see the state cast off the restraints of an official system of belief. Individual autonomy seems to go hand in hand with the secularization of the public sphere. However, observations such as these touch upon only a part of the truth. It is very easy to overlook the fact that revelation imposed on the confessional state a range of limits that served as safeguards for its citizens. By continually drawing attention to the message of the Gospel, the church imposed salutary constraints in the judicial, moral, and spiritual spheres. These constraints imposed various obligations on rulers and set certain limits on their freedom of action. Rulers could not simply act as they saw fit. Religious constraints hedged them in, defining the norms and conventions that formed the background to political life. This can be seen in reverse, as it were, in the ideologues of the past century's totalitarian states, who were all the more hostile to Christianity because they were bent upon escaping from constraints of that kind. Determined to refashion humanity in their own image, they strove to disencumber themselves of an irksome God who harped on immutable and sacred laws. They did not want anyone putting tedious Christian scruples in the way of their ambitions. Convinced that they had to carry out a thoroughgoing reconstruction of society and that they could govern absolutely every aspect of human life, they had no time for a doctrine that spoke to them of finitude and limitation.

With regard to the second problem, we can start by noting that aristocratic regimes are intrinsically hierarchical. They are pluralist in that they recognize different levels of authority and power. A clerical class fits very easily into such a system as one social "order" alongside others (the nobility and the Third Estate). In such societies, the state can concede a quasi-political authority to the clergy without thereby setting itself in subjection. The monarch can grant the church an official role and even allow the clergy the status of the First Estate without prejudice to his own ultimate primacy. Democratic systems, in contrast, repudiate the heterogeneous nature of the hierarchical worldview. They do not divide society into "orders." This egalitarian denial of all hierarchy has a powerful leveling effect, setting all ways of life on one and the same plane.[1] In this context, the authority of the clergy, however limited, becomes problematic. The people are even more jealous of their sovereignty than were kings (who were jealous enough of theirs). The Civil Constitution of the Clergy provides the perfect illustration of this democratic monism. It sought to bring the religious sphere into line with civil society by imposing on the church the principle of national sovereignty exercised through the electoral process. The revolutionaries could not imagine the church appealing to any other method of legitimation. They could not understand that their political monism was simply unacceptable to the Catholic Church, which could not remain true to its catholicity without insisting on its internal autonomy. The tensions between Christianity and democracy took on a more violent form in Catholic countries than in Protestant ones. Where democracy had not had to establish or defend itself against a Catholic Ancien Regime, anticlericalism appears to have been more limited in scope, notably in the United States (although this observation must not be misunderstood—anti-Catholicism was long a potent force there).

The counter-revolutionary strand in Catholicism offered a radical response to the challenges of anticlericalism and of the nonrecognition of divine law, by diametrically opposing the entire project of modernity. It called upon the papacy to become the arbiter of European political life. The renewed political authority of the papacy would reimpose on secularized states the constraints that they had thrown off. The counter-revolutionary program was not without a degree of coherence, but, overall, ultramontanism was simply too paradoxical. It evidently did not take its departure from any inherent tendency in the modern state toward hierocracy. Reactionary Catholics turned all the more readily to the papacy precisely because they felt that political life was slipping further away from ecclesiastical control. The less open the world became to Counter-Revolution, the more shrill its advocates became in their demands. Their sheer lack of political realism rested ultimately not on a political but on a prophetic foundation. Maistre was awaiting an imminent divine intervention that would see the unification of the human race and put an end to the divisions between

nations. There would be a religious upheaval in response to the political upheavals of the age, a Catholic renewal to match the social revolution.

At first beguiled by the prophetic posturing of Joseph de Maistre, the church
authorities in the end distanced themselves from him. Maistre's project was too
ambitious, counterproductive, and utterly out of step with Catholic tradition,
which in principle repudiated all political theology. Above all, the Catholic
Church found alternative and markedly more satisfactory ways to respond to
the challenges of secularization and anticlericalism. Observation of the democracy of the United States in action led Tocqueville to realize that Christianity
did not need to be established in law in order to exercise a restraining influence
on public life. The "revolutionists of America are obliged to profess an ostensi-
ble respect for Christian morality and equity, which does not easily permit
them to violate the laws that oppose their designs."[2] The secularization of the
state did not necessarily imply the obliteration of Christian influence within it.
Following Tocqueville, Catholics realized that a liberal democracy could still
stay within the orbit of Christendom and be informed by the principles of the
Gospel. They realized that the state did not have to be a confessional state and
that the clergy did not have to exercise an official political function within it.
They understood that lay Catholics, *qua* citizens, could contribute quite as
much as the clergy to the evangelization of society. In sound democratic theory,
there was nothing to prevent the sovereign people from itself recognizing the
sovereignty of God.

Democracy has at its root a striking politicization of human society. Politics
is no longer confined to a little group of oligarchs or aristocrats. The people, as
such, have come onto the scene, and with them a new demand for collective
autonomy as well as a new passion for individual liberty. Accustomed to less
politicized societies, into which governments had integrated its principles, the
Catholic Church now found itself facing societies committed to free public expression, with governments that no longer upheld the truth of Christianity. It
has responded to the challenge by affirming with new vigor the vocation of the
laity to engage actively with the political world. It has thus reappropriated a
tradition that had been first developed over many centuries by the Gallicans, a
tradition that was careful to emphasize both the inherent dignity and the relative autonomy of the political order. This was the first genuinely "lay" tradition,
older than all its Protestant counterparts, but it had the double misfortune of
being distorted first by royal absolutism and then by revolutionary hubris. This
tradition was "lay" not because Christianity was excluded from the temporal
sphere but, on the contrary, because it made itself present and active there. "You
Christians, the most civic of people," wrote Péguy in this lay, Gallican vein.[3]

That brings us to the third problem: religious liberty, which is inextricably
linked to the secularization of the state. The church was in principle hostile to
religious liberty, because it saw no particular merit in the fact that a heretic
could march freely to his own damnation or in the fact that states could foster

indifference to truth and a damaging relativism through standing aloof from religious questions. Liberal democracies focus their energies not on the search for truth and moral excellence but on material comfort and security. The proper function of the state is not to acknowledge or officially privilege revealed truth, but to guarantee public peace and individual liberty. The general tendency of modern political philosophy is to lower its sights in defining the aims of political action: it prefers to talk of interest rather than the good, of opinion rather than theology.[4] Liberal democracies espouse toleration because they set their political sights lower, *prima facie* excluding the religious dimension. However, for the church, the ends of human social life are not compassed merely by the protection of life and liberty. There is also the matter of the *good* life, the life of virtue and moral excellence and the search for ultimate truths.

Confronted with liberal democracy, Catholics were not generally inclined to lower their sights with respect to the ends set for political life. They did not restrict their view to life and liberty at the expense of the good and the true. The counter-revolutionaries took this idea so far that they ended up sacralizing social life and confusing the temporal and spiritual spheres. It was totalitarianism that decisively reorientated Catholic political thought. In the age of the dictators, it became evident that a radical antiliberalism threatened humanity as such. It became equally evident that the liberal lowering of sights constituted a valuable political safety precaution—as long as liberalism itself did not degenerate into a surreptitious totalitarianism. In the great quarrel of the twentieth century, the church initially sided with reactionary regimes against liberal ones. But the church came to realize that no regime could remain reactionary in the face of the leveling tendencies of egalitarianism. Vichy provided an object lesson. Catholic counter-revolutionaries who at first were neither Fascists nor Nazis gradually became indistinguishable from them and ended up selling their souls. Totalitarianism showed that the real danger came not from freedom of religion but from political religions that aimed to take the place of Christianity. Freedom of religion provided the most effective bulwark against political religions.

Faced with the criminal excesses to which modern politics could give rise, it was vital to rediscover a sense of the limits to political aspirations, but this could not be achieved by a return to the confessional state. Faced with secularized states oblivious to the boundaries set by natural law, it was vital to insist unflinchingly on human rights and to confine the state to an appropriately modest sphere of action. Only the liberal suspicion of Utopianism could foster the sense of a natural order that would rein in human ambition. Totalitarianism came not from the liberal advocates of the separation of church and state but from those who sought to fuse the state with the political creeds they offered in place of religion. At Vatican II, the Catholic Church invoked the constitutional principle of limiting the scope of the state and placed freedom of religion at the very heart of its own political teaching. The church did not stop believing that it was the vehicle of truth. But henceforth it insisted upon the *search* for truth. The freedom it endorsed was a personal freedom to seek the truth and to live by it. The state was no longer to stand surety for the true faith or give it its seal of approval. It was no longer, so to speak, to make an act of faith in its own right. The church was neither ignoring scripture nor abandoning tradition; but it was interpreting them in the light of a new political philosophy.

If, over the past two centuries, the Catholic Church has been confronted by a political system—liberal democracy—whose triumph it had not foreseen and for which it was therefore ill prepared, it has nevertheless at last adapted to it. The church has come to appreciate the advantages of a political system of which it was at first suspicious, but without falling prey to a naïve political enthusiasm. It has turned its back on Counter-Revolution. Vatican II emphasized the benefits of democratic government and denounced the dangers of an excessive papalism. A dose of conciliarism was no bad thing for the Catholic Church! In declaring that "on this rock" he would build his church, Jesus did not issue a charter for absolute monarchy. Peter was only *primus inter pares* among the apostles. There was nothing to prevent the emergence of a heretical pope. The bishops, too, were successors of the apostles, and they retained a central role in the life of the church. The bishops' conferences would do well to make this better understood.

It still seems, however, as though the church ought to keep hold of something of nineteenth-century ultramontanism. The heterogeneous and hierarchical society of the Ancien Regime furnished the church with social and political space, whereas democratic society imposes a homogeneity that clearly suits it less well. Catholics have responded to this challenge by renewing their ecclesiology and integrating into it a new form of heterogeneity: the separation of church and state. In the end, paradoxically, nineteenth-century ultramontanism had its place in this process of dissociation. Papal centralism has often been decried as illiberal and antidemocratic, without its having been noticed that it was itself a product of liberalism and democracy. Papal centralism was a symptom of adaptation to the new political order, yet, at the same time, a refusal simply to be assimilated to it. The very externality of the papacy is an affirmation of the limits of even the democratic political order.

The most important of the democratic theorists have claimed that "the general will is always right," and "the people can never be corrupt." However, even democratic societies can perpetrate the direst crimes and abandon themselves to the direst excesses. Catholics turned all the more readily to the papacy because they felt that they could never rely entirely on popular sovereignty, and that democracy, like all political systems, could go wrong. The papacy symbolizes a way of bringing people together that is in marked contrast to the leveling of democratic homogenization. "The Vatican's man in white is a sovereign without a crown, the head of a state with almost no territory."[5] He bears witness to the reality of an order that transcends even the general will. He manifests the

Christian refusal to be entirely swallowed up in the democratic order. That is the church's service to society: to resist the docile conformism to which egalitarianism can lead. In a democratic world that works ceaselessly to eliminate otherness, even (perhaps especially) when it proclaims its commitment to pluralism, believers have an eye to something beyond the society of the here and now, and thus have an escape route from conformism. They form a breakwater against the tide of conformity. They are, par excellence, a sign of contradiction.

The theorists of secularization have portrayed the modern world as substituting political "autonomy" for religious "heteronomy," making democratic politicization part of a struggle against the churches. But perhaps it is precisely acknowledgment of dependence on the divine that, by moderating the tyranny of the majority, makes political liberty possible. Religious life can go together with a wisdom to which democratic life does not give rise on its own, a wisdom that consists in recognizing limits to human autonomy. From the Christian point of view, the autonomy sought by the politicized citizen cannot be attained without God, if it is true that God is "more inward than my inmost heart."[6]

the just man lives forever in our memory
he has nothing to fear from false report

Notes

Introduction

1. B. de Spinoza, *Theological-Political Treatise*, ed. J. Israel (Cambridge: Cambridge University Press, 2007), XIV; John Locke, *Reasonableness of Christianity* (London, 1695); I. Kant, *Religion within the Limits of Reason Alone* [1793]; Karl Barth, *Protestant Theology in the Nineteenth Century* [1947], tr. J. Bowden (London: SCM, 1972); Roger Aubert, "L'enseignement du magistère ecclésiastique au XIXème siècle sur le libéralisme," in R. Aubert et al., *Tolérance et communauté humaine* (Cahiers de l'actualité religieuse; Paris: Casterman, 1952), pp. 75–103.

2. Spinoza, *Ethics*; Tocqueville, *De la démocratie en Amérique*, II, 1, vii ("Of the cause of a leaning to pantheism among democratic nations"), in *Oeuvres complètes*, ed. J.-P. Mayer ([Paris]: Gallimard, 1951–), t. I, vol. 2, pp. 37–38 [*Democracy in America*, ed. Isaac Kramnick (New York: Norton, 2007), II, 1, vii, pp. 397–98)]; and Henri Maret, *Essai sur le panthéisme dans les sociétés modernes* (Paris: Sapia, 1840).

3. On the genesis of liberal democracy, see Pierre Manent, *Histoire intellectuelle du libéralisme* (Paris: Calmann-Lévy, 1987); John Dunn, *Setting the People Free: The story of Democracy* (London: Atlantic, 2005).

4. R. Aubert, *Vatican I* (Paris: L'Orante, 1964); Giuseppe Alberigo, *History of Vatican II* (5 vols. Maryknoll: Orbis, 1995–2006).

5. This book owes a great deal to friends and colleagues who at one time or another have read and commented on it in draft: Vincent Aubin, Alain Besançon, Jean-Marie Donegani, Yann Fauchois, Raymond Geuss, Patrice Gueniffey, Rita Hermon-Belot, Russell Hittinger, Lucien Jaume, Cécile Laborde, André Manaranche, Pierre Manent, Jean-Marie Mayeur, Jim Murphy, Aidan Nichols, Thomas Pink, Philippe Portier, Jean-Yves Pranchère, Philippe Raynaud, Catherine Séguier-Leblanc, Paul Thibaud, and Paul Valadier—not to mention one who must never be forgotten. May this serve as an expression of my gratitude to you all.

Chapter 1

1. Jean Gaudemet, *Les élections dans l'Eglise latine des origines au XVIème siècle* (Paris: Lanore, 1979).

2. Emmanuel Siéyes, *Qu'est-ce que le Tiers Etat?* [1789], ed. R. Zapperi (Geneva: Droz, 1970), p. 124, note.

3. Rousseau, *Contrat social*, II.3. See *The Social Contract and the Discourses*, tr. G. D. H. Cole (London: Dent, 1973), p. 185.

4. Michel Vovelle, *Religion et Révolution: la déchristianisation de l'an II* (Paris: Hachette, 1976), and *1793, la Révolution contre l'Eglise: de la Raison à l'Etre suprême* (Brussels: Complexe, 1988).

5. Jean de Dieu-Raymond de Boisgelin, speech of 29 May 1790 on the Civil Constitution of the Clergy, in *Archives parlementaires de 1787 à 1860*, ed. M. J. Mavidal and M. E. Laurent (Paris: Dupont, 1879–), t. 15, p. 729.

6. *Ibid.*, t. XVI, p. 156.

7. Henri Jabineau, *Réplique au développement de M. Camus sur la constitution civile du clergé* (Paris, 1791), p. 37.

8. Germaine de Staël, *Considérations sur les principaux événements de la Révolution françoise* (3 vols. Paris: Delaunay, Bossange & Masson, 1818), part 2, ch. 13 (t. 1, p. 361).

9. The *Reflections on the Revolution in France* of Edmund Burke, who proposed this interpretation, appeared in November 1790, and was much influenced by the debate over the Civil Constitution of the Clergy.

10. Alphonse Aulard, "Les origines de la séparation des Eglises et de l'Etat: la laïcisation de l'état civil," *La Révolution française* 49 (1905): 289–315.

11. Pius VI, *Quod aliquantum* [1791], in *Droits de l'Eglise et droits de l'homme: le bref Quod aliquantulum et autres textes*, ed. J. Chaunu (Limoges: Critérion, 1989).

12. César-Guillaume de La Luzerne, *Examen de l'instruction de l'Assemblée nationale sur l'organisation prétendue civile du clergé* (Paris: L'ami du roi, n.d. [1791]), p. 25.

13. Peter Garnsey, *Ideas of Slavery from Aristotle to Augustine* (Cambridge: Cambridge University Press, 1996), pp. 157–219.

14. Machiavelli, *Discourses on Livy*, II, 2. Cf. D. Hume, *Natural History of Religion* [1757], chap. 10; Rousseau, *Contrat social*, IV.8; R.-A. Gauthier, *Magnanimité: l'idéal de la grandeur dans la philosophie païenne et dans la théologie chrétienne* (Paris: Vrin, 1951).

15. J. de Maistre, "Discours à la marquise de Costa" [1794], in *Œuvres complètes de J. de Maistre* (14 vols. Lyon: Vitte et Perrussel, 1884–86), t. VII, p. 249.

16. Jacques Maritain, *L'homme et l'Etat* [1953], in *Œuvres complètes* (15 vols. Fribourg: Editions universitaires, 1982–95), t. IX, pp. 513–39. Thomas Aquinas discusses the "prince," not the "sovereign."

17. Jean-Marie Lustiger, "L'Eglise, la Révolution et les droits de l'homme," in *Dieu merci, les droits de l'homme* (Paris: Critérion, 1990), p. 119.

18. Augustine, *City of God*, V.17; Rousseau, *Contrat social*, IV.8 (*Social Contract*, p. 274).

19. Jean-Baptiste Treilhard, speech of 30 May 1790 on the Civil Constitution of the Clergy, *Archives parlementaires*, t. XV, p. 749; Armand-Gaston Camus, speech of 31 May, *Archives parlementaires*, t. XVI, pp. 6–7. Treilhard's speech, along with one by Boisgelin, is reprinted unabridged in François Furet and Ran Halévi, *La monarchie républicaine: la constitution de 1791* ([Paris]: Fayard, 1996), pp. 498–530.

20. François Fénelon to the Duke of Chevreuse, 4 Aug. 1710, in *Ecrits et lettres politiques*, ed. C. Urbain (Paris: Bossard, 1920), p. 180.

21. Victor Martin, *Le gallicanisme politique et le clergé de France* (Paris: Picard, 1929), pp. 25–40.

22. Ibid., pp. 314–22; Pierre Blet, "Jésuites gallicans au XVIIème siècle?" *Archivum Historicum Societatis Jesu* 29 (1960): 55–84.

23. Claude Fleury, *Discours sur les libertés de l'Eglise gallicane* [1723], in M. Tabaraud, *Histoire critique de l'assemblée générale du clergé de France en 1682, suivie du discours de M. l'abbé Fleury sur les libertés de l'Eglise gallicane* (Paris: Baudouin, 1826), pp. 333–34.

24. Bossuet, *Politique tirée de l'écriture sainte* (1709), I.vi: "De l'amour de la patrie" (cf. I.ii). Bossuet goes on to refer to Mathatias. Cf. Norman Ravitch, *The Catholic Church and the French Nation, 1589–1989* (London: Routledge, 1990), pp. 1–41.

25. "Among all writers," wrote Paul Valéry, "I see none greater than Bossuet; none more exact in his words, none stronger in his verbs, none more forceful nor more subtle in all his utterances, none bolder nor to better effect in his syntax; in short, none more master of his words, which is to say, more master of himself." See his "Sur Bossuet," *Variété*, in P. Valéry, *Œuvres*, ed. J. Hytier (2 vols. [Paris]: Gallimard, 1959–60), t. 1, p. 498. For Bossuet's encomium of the French language, see his *Discours de réception à l'Académie française* (1671).

26. Bossuet, *Politique tirée de l'écriture sainte*, VII.vi, proposition 14.

27. Joseph R. Strayer, "France: the Holy Land, the Chosen People and the Most Christian King," in T. Rabb et J. Seigel (eds.), *Action and Conviction in Early Modern Europe* (Princeton: Princeton University Press, 1969), pp. 3–16; Colette Beaune, *Naissance de la nation France* (Paris: Gallimard, 1985), pp. 75–229.

28. Aryeh Graboïs, "Un mythe fondamental de l'histoire de France au Moyen Age: le roi David précurseur du roi très chrétien," *Revue historique* 287 (1992): 29–30; Jacques Krynen, *L'empire du roi: idées et croyances politiques en France, XIIIème–XVème siècle* (Paris: Gallimard, 1993), pp. 339–414; J. N. Figgis, *The Divine Right of Kings* (2nd ed. Cambridge: Cambridge University Press, 1896).

29. Bossuet, *Politique tirée de l'écriture sainte*, III.2. Cf. Aimé-Georges Martimort, *Le gallicanisme de Bossuet* (Paris: Cerf, 1953).

30. Ernst Kantorowicz, "Mysteries of State: An Absolutist Concept and Its Late Medieval Origins," *Harvard Theological Review* 48 (1955): 65–91, at p. 66. Kantorowicz explored these ideas further in his classic study, *The King's Two Bodies* (Princeton: Princeton University Press, 1957). See also G. Lacour-Gayet, *L'éducation politique de Louis XIV* (Paris: Hachette, 1898), pp. 330–38.

31. H. Jabineau et al., *Mémoire à consulter et consultation sur la compétence de la puissance temporelle* (Paris: Desaint, 1790), p. 4. Cf. Malebranche, *Traité de morale* (1684), II.ix, §vii: "As church and state are made up of the same people, who are at the same time Christians and citizens, children of the church and subjects of the prince, it is not possible for these two powers, which ought to show mutual respect, and which ought to be sovereign and autonomous in the exercise of their respective functions, to fulfill those functions and to carry out the will of their common master, if they are not in perfect harmony with each other."

32. François Fénelon, "Plans de gouvernement dits Tables des Chaulnes (novembre 1711)," in *Œuvres*, ed. J. Le Brun (2 vols. [Paris]: Gallimard, 1983–97), t. II, p. 1095. For an alternative view, see Voltaire: "It is not in the least because Henri IV was anointed at Chartres that obedience was owed to him, but because the indefeasible right of his birth conferred upon him a crown which he then proved by his courage and goodness that he deserved" (*Traité sur la tolérance*, ch. XI).

33. Bossuet, *Politique tirée de l'Ecriture sainte*, book VII, art. 5, proposition 18.

34. Martin, *Le gallicanisme politique et le clergé de France*, pp. 268–70. See also his *Les origines du gallicanisme* (2 vols. Paris: Bloud et Gay, 1939), t. I, pp. 209–39.

35. P. Blet, *Les assemblées du clergé et Louis XIV de 1670 à 1693* (Rome: Università Gregoriana Editrice, 1972).

36. Cited by André Latreille, "Les nonces apostoliques en France et l'Eglise gallicane sous Innocent XI," *Revue d'histoire de l'Eglise de France* 41 (1959): 226.

37. Among the "patriot" clergy, see in particular Richard Chaix d'Est-Ange, *De l'influence de la religion sur le patriotisme et la liberté* (Paris, n.d. [1789]).

38. P. T. Durand de Maillane, *Histoire apologétique du comité ecclésiastique de l'Assemblée nationale* (Paris: F. Buisson, 1791), p. 41.

39. Maistre, *Considérations sur la France*, ch. 5, in *Oeuvres complètes*, t. I, p. 56. On Maistre, see especially Jean-Yves Pranchère, *L'autorité contre les Lumières. La philosophie de Joseph de Maistre* (Geneva: Droz, 2004); Philippe Barthelet (ed.), *Joseph de Maistre* (Lausanne: L'Age d'homme, 2005); and Pierre Glaudes (ed.), *Dictionnaire Joseph de Maistre*, in *Joseph de Maistre. Œuvres* (Paris: Laffont, 2007), pp. 1115–1310.

40. It is worth comparing Maistre with Condorcet. For Condorcet, France remained an exception, but for rationalism rather than religiosity. In his *Esquisse d'un tableau historique des progrès de l'esprit humain* (Paris: Agasse, 1794), Condorcet charted a path that led from Socrates via Descartes to the foundation of the French Republic. In the final stage of the *Tableau*, France bore alone and unaided the universal destiny of the human spirit.

41. René Taveneaux, *Jansénisme et politique* (Paris: A. Colin, 1965); Dale Van Kley, *The Religious Origins of the French Revolution* (New Haven: Yale University Press, 1996).

42. Arlette Jouanna, "L'édit de Nantes et le processus de sécularisation de l'Etat," in P. Mironneau and I. Pébay-Clottes (eds.), *Paix des armes, paix des âmes* (Paris: Imprimerie nationale, 2000), pp. 481–89; Roland Mousnier, "L'édit de Nantes," in C.E.J. Caldicott, H. Gough, and J.-P. Pittion (eds.), *The Huguenots and Ireland* (Dun Laoghaire: Glendale, 1987), pp. 17–35; Martin, *Le gallicanisme politique et le clergé de France*, pp. 25–86 and 323–25.

43. Cited by Jean Orcibal in *Louis XIV et les protestants* (Paris: Vrin, 1951), p. 131.

44. Machiavelli, *The Prince*, ch. XXI. Edgar Quinet: "While with the Florentine writer one enjoys at least the anxieties of the tyrant, one feels a kind of horror on seeing Bossuet's king become a despot over a scruple of conscience." Quinet, *Le christianisme et la Révolution française*, in *Œuvres complètes* (10 vols. Paris: Pagnerre, 1857–58), t. III, p. 202.

45. On the homogenizing tendencies of absolutism, see Heinz Schilling, *Konfessionskonflikt und Staatsbildung* (Gütersloh: Gütersloher Verlagshaus, 1981); and Heinz Schilling and Wolfgang Reinhard (eds.), *Die katholische Konfessionalisierung* (Münster: Aschendorff, 1995).

46. Ernest Lavisse, *Histoire de France depuis les origines jusqu'à la Révolution* (9 vols. in 18. Paris: Hachette, 1906), t. 7, part 2, p. 42.

47. Michel de l'Hospital, *Œuvres complètes* (3 vols. Paris: Boulland, 1824), t. 1, p. 452.

48. Claude Fleury, *Discours sur les libertés de l'Eglise gallicane*, p. 339.

49. Thus, one scholar has even written of "nationalism" at Constance: George C. Powers, *Nationalism at the Council of Constance (1414–1418)* (Washington, D.C.: Catholic University of America, 1927).

50. William F. Church, *Richelieu and Reason of State* (Princeton: Princeton University Press, 1972); Jörg Wollenberg, *Les trois Richelieu: servir Dieu, le roi et la raison* [1977], tr. E. Husson (Paris: F. de Guibert, 1995).

51. Walter Ullmann, *Principles of Government and Politics in the Middle Ages* (London: Methuen, 1961), p. 139.

52. Innocent Gentillet, *Discours d'Etat sur les moyens de bien gouverner* (1576); F. de Gravelle, *Politiques royales* (1596). Cf. Robert Bireley, *The Counter-Reformation Prince: Anti-Machiavellianism or Catholic Statecraft in Early Modern Europe* (Chapel Hill: University of North Carolina Press, 1990); and Lucien Jaume, "Fénelon critique de la dérai-

son d'Etat," in Y.-C. Zarka (ed.), *Raison et déraison d'Etat* (Paris: Presses universitaires de France, 1994), pp. 395–422. Bossuet's library contained the complete works of Machiavelli as well as two separate copies of *The Prince*.

53. Bossuet, *Politique tirée de l'écriture sainte*, IV.i and VIII.ii. This was the distinction classically drawn by absolutist thinkers (e.g., Bodin and Loyseau). Cf. Fanny Cosandey and Robert Descimon, *L'absolutisme en France: histoire et historiographie* (Paris: Seuil, 2002), pp. 51–93. Before the age of absolutism, Claude de Seyssel emphasized that royal power was restrained by three "bridles": the Christian faith, justice, and the customs of the realm (*La grande monarchie de France* [1519], I, 9–11).

54. Bossuet, *Politique tirée de l'écriture sainte*, V.1.xiv.

55. Machiavelli, *The Prince*; Pierre Bayle, *Dictionnaire historique et critique* (1697); Voltaire, *Dictionnaire philosophique* (1764).

56. Maistre to Blacas, 22 May 1814, in *Œuvres complètes*, t. XII, pp. 428–29.

57. J. de Maistre, *Du pape*, book 2, ch. 4, in *Œuvres complètes*, t. II, p. 182.

58. Maistre, *Du pape*, II.4 (*Œuvres complètes*, t. II, p. 181).

59. Maistre, *Du pape*, II.10 (*Œuvres complètes*, t. II, p. 265).

60. Maistre, *Considérations sur la France*, ch. 8 (*Œuvres complètes*, t. I, pp. 89 and 90; and at end of paragraph, p. 56).

61. J.-J. Rousseau, *Lettre à Christophe de Beaumont*, in *Œuvres complètes*, ed. B. Gagnebin and M. Raymond (5 vols. [Paris]: Gallimard, 1959–95), t. IV, p. 967.

62. Jean Starobinski, "La mise en accusation de la société," in J. Starobinski, J.-L. Lecercle, H. Coulet, and M. Eigeldinger (eds.), *Jean-Jacques Rousseau* (Neuchâtel: La Baconnière, 1978), p. 20.

63. Maistre, *Examen d'un écrit de J.-J. Rousseau*, in *Œuvres complètes*, t. VII, p. 563 (and more generally, pp. 537–55). Cf. Antoine Compagnon, *Les antimodernes: de Joseph de Maistre à Roland Barthes* ([Paris]: Gallimard, 2005), pp. 88–110, and Carl Schmitt, *Théologie politique* [1922], tr. J.-L.Schlegel ([Paris]: Gallimard, 1988), pp. 64–67. For Schmitt, whose work was inspired by Maistre, "all true political theories postulate a fallen humanity, that is to say, a dangerous and dynamic being, nothing but trouble." See Schmitt, *La notion de politique* [1932], tr. M.-L. Steinhauser ([Paris]: Flammarion, 1992), p. 105.

64. Maistre, *Du pape*, II.12 (*Œuvres complètes*, t. II, pp. 295–96).

65. Maistre *Du Pape*, II.3 (*Œuvres complètes*, t. II, p. 179).

66. Maistre, *Considérations sur la France*, citations from chs. VIII, V, and VI respectively (*Œuvres complètes*, t. I, pp. 111, 56, and 71).

67. Louis de Bonald, *Observations sur l'ouvrage de madame la baronne de Staël* (Paris: Le Clere, 1818), p. 95.

68. Louis de Bonald, *Législation primitive, considérée dans les derniers temps par les seules lumières de la raison*, t. II, in *Œuvres de M. de Bonald* (11 vols. Paris: Le Clere, 1817–19), t. III, p. 127.

69. Juan Donoso Cortès, *Essai sur le catholicisme, le libéralisme et le socialisme* (Liège: Lardinois, 1851), p. 8.

70. Maistre, *Considérations sur la France*, ch. 5 (*Œuvres complètes*, t. I, p. 56).

71. Kant, *What Is Enlightenment?* (1783); Thomas Paine, *The Age of Reason* (1794). Compare Bonald, "Sur les préjugés" [1810], in *Œuvres*, t. XI, pp. 514–26.

72. Bonald, *Législation primitive*, t. II (*Oeuvres*, t. III, pp. 129–30).

73. Maistre, *Considérations sur la France*, ch. 5 (*Œuvres complètes*, t. I, p. 57).

74. Bonald, "Sur les Juifs," in *Oeuvres*, t. XI, p. 270.

75. Félicité de Lamennais, *Essai sur l'indifférence en matière de religion* (Paris: Tournachon, 1817).

76. Maistre to Costa de Beauregard, 21 Jan. 1791, in *Œuvres complètes*, t. IX, p. 11. Cf. Robert Triomphe, *Joseph de Maistre: étude sur la vie et sur la doctrine d'un matérialiste mystique* (Geneva: Droz, 1968), pp. 138–40 and 166–70.

77. Maistre, *De l'Eglise gallicane*, I.12 (*Œuvres complètes*, t. III, p. 83, note 1).

78. Bonald, "De l'alliance des gens de lettres et des gens du monde," in *Œuvres*, t. XI, pp. 581–93. Cf. Burke, *Reflections on the Revolution in France* (1790), "Thoughts on French Affairs" (1791), "Three Letters to a Member of the Present Parliament, on Proposals of Peace with the Regicide Directory of France" (1796). On the tradition of counter-revolutionary analysis, see in particular Augustin Cochin, *Les sociétés de pensée et la démocratie* (Paris: Plon, 1921); and Reinhart Koselleck, *Le règne de la critique* [1959], tr. H. Hildenbrand (Paris: Minuit, 1979).

79. Maistre, *Du pape*, I.11 (*Œuvres complètes*, t. II, p. 89). Cf. Michèle Sacquin, *Entre Bossuet et Maurras: l'antiprotestantisme en France de 1814 à 1870* (Paris: H. Champion, 1998).

80. Maistre, *Considérations sur la France*, ch. 5 (*Œuvres complètes*, t. I, p. 55).

81. Maistre, *Considérations sur la France*, ch. 1 (*Œuvres complètes*, t. I, p. 7).

Chapter 2

1. Fénelon, "Plans de gouvernement dits Tables des Chaulnes (novembre 1711)," t. II, pp. 1096–97. Compare Saint Bernard's *De consideratione*.

2. Fénelon, "Plans de gouvernement dits Tables des Chaulnes," t. II, p. 1097. "After a certain point, the "liberties of the Gallican Church" (with respect to the papacy) would have been better termed "liberties of the Crown." P. E. Lemontey, *Essai sur l'établissement monarchique de Louis XIV*, in *Œuvres* (7 vols. Paris: Mesnier et al., 1829–32), t. V, p. 26.

3. Claude Fleury, *Discours sur les libertés de l'Eglise gallicane*, p. 400. Cf. Montesquieu, *Mes pensées*, 2039 and 2040, in *Œuvres complètes*, ed. R. Caillois (2 vols. [Paris]: Gallimard, 1949–51), t. I, pp. 1520–21. The "quarrel over the sacraments" in the 1750s and 1760s was a sort of dry run for the quarrel over the Civil Constitution of the Clergy. Cf. Dominique Julia, "Les deux puissances: chronique d'une séparation de corps," in K. M. Baker (ed.), *The Political Culture of the Old Regime* (Oxford: Pergamon, 1987), pp. 293–310.

4. Emile Ollivier, *1789 et 1889. La révolution et son œuvre sociale, religieuse et politique* [1889] (Paris: Aubier, 1989), pp. 167–85; and Yann Fauchois, "La difficulté d'être libre: les droits de l'homme, l'Eglise catholique et l'assemblée constituante (1789–1791)," *Revue d'histoire contemporaine* 48 (2001): 71–101.

5. Treilhard, speech of 18 April 1791, in *Archives parlementaires*, t. XXV, p. 182.

6. G. N. Maultrot, *Les vrais principes de l'Eglise, de la morale et de la raison sur la constitution civile du clergé* (Paris: Dufrene, 1791), p. 243.

7. Henri Grégoire, *Légitimité du serment civique exigé des fonctionnaires ecclésiastiques* (Paris: Imprimerie nationale, 1791), p. 5. Cf. Rita Hermon-Belot, *L'abbé Grégoire: la politique et la vérité* (Paris: Seuil, 2000), pp. 228–50.

8. Albert Mathiez, *La Révolution et l'Eglise* (Paris: A. Colin, 1910), p. ix (see also pp. 1–25 and 148–96). The separation of church and state effected during Thermidor was not so much a policy decision as a necessity imposed by events. In 1795, the Convention simply recognized reality: the civic cult had been swept away with the Terror; church and state were de facto separate.

9. A. Thiers, *Histoire du consulat et de l'empire* (20 vols. Paris: Paulin, 1845–62), t. III, pp. 211–22.

10. Jean-Etienne-Marie Portalis, "Observation sur les demandes du pape," in *Discours, rapports et travaux inédits sur le Concordat de 1801* (Paris: Joubert, 1845), pp. 294–95.

11. Portalis, "Discours sur l'organisation des cultes. 15 Germinal an X," in *Discours*, pp. 24–25.

12. Edouard Laboulaye, *De l'Eglise catholique et de l'Etat: à l'occasion des attaques dirigées contre les articles organiques du Concordat de 1801* (Paris: Bureau de la Revue de législation et de jurisprudence, 1845), p. 21.

13. Thiers, *Histoire du consulat et de l'empire*, t. III, p. 223. Cf. Jean Jaurès, *Histoire socialiste de la Révolution française* (4 vols. Paris: Rouff, 1901–3), t. I, pp. 532–33.

14. Portalis, "Discours sur l'organisation des cultes," *Discours*, p. 41.

15. P. S. Ballanche, *Essai sur les institutions sociales* [1818], in *Œuvres de M. Ballanche* (4 vols. Paris: Barbezat, 1830), t. II, pp. 322 and 323.

16. Charles de Montalembert, *Discours de M. Montalembert sur la question religieuse en France* (Gand: Vanryckegem, 1844), p. 19. Cf. André Latreille, *Napoléon et le Saint-Siège* (Paris: F. Alcan, 1935); Jacques-Olivier Boudon, *Napoléon et les cultes* (Paris: Fayard, 2002). On the captivity of the pope, it is worth resorting to a source of an entirely different genre, Paul Claudel's play, *L'otage* (1909).

17. François-René de Chateaubriand, "Opinion sur la Résolution relative au clergé" [1816], in his *Ecrits politiques (1814–1816)*, ed. C. Smethurst (Geneva: Droz, 2002), p. 346. Cf. Hyppolite Taine, *Les origines de la France contemporaine*, III, 5.

18. E. Daudet, *Joseph de Maistre et Blacas: leur correspondance inédite et l'histoire de leur amitié* (Paris: Plon-Nourrit, 1908).

19. Ercole Consalvi, *Mémoires du cardinal Consalvi* (2 vols. Paris: Plon, 1864), t. I, pp. 345–46.

20. Camille Latreille, *L'opposition religieuse au Concordat de 1792 à 1803* (Paris: Hachette, 1910); and *Après le Concordat: l'opposition de 1803 à nos jours* (Paris: Hachette, 1910).

21. Abbé Barruel, *Du Pape et de ses droits religieux à l'occasion du Concordat* (2 vols. Paris: Crapart, 1803), t. I, p. xx. Klaus Schatz, a more emollient figure than Barruel, and writing moreover with the benefit of hindsight, has put it in almost exactly the same terms: *La primauté du pape: son histoire des origines à nos jours* (Paris: Cerf, 1992), p. 213.

22. Ernest Renan, "La crise religieuse en Europe" [1874], in *Mélanges religieux et historiques* (Paris: Calmann Lévy, 1904), p. 6.

23. Bruno Neveu, "Pour une histoire du gallicanisme administratif de l'an IX à nos jours," in Jean Gaudemet et al., *Administration et Eglise: du Concordat à la Séparation de l'Eglise et de l'Etat* (Geneva: Droz, 1987), pp. 66–77; A.-G. Martimort, *Le gallicanisme* (Paris: Presses universitaires de France, 1973), pp. 113–22.

24. Maistre to Lamennais, 1 May 1820, in *Œuvres complètes*, t. XIV, p. 226.

25. Maistre, *De l'Eglise gallicane*, II.13 (*Œuvres complètes*, t. III, pp. 236–37).

26. Maistre, *De l'Eglise gallicane*, II.15 (*Œuvres complètes*, t. III, p. 260). Cf. Bonald, *Observations sur l'ouvrage de Madame la baronne de Staël*, p. 99.

27. Maistre, *Du pape*, II.12 and III.2 (*Œuvres complètes*, t. II, pp. 281–98 and 337–48); F. de Lamennais, *Des progrès de la révolution et de la guerre contre l'Eglise* (Paris: Belin-Mandar & Devaux, 1829); J. Görres, *Athanasius* (Regensburg: Manz, 1838); H. E. Manning, *Caesarism and Ultramontanism* (London: Burns & Oates, 1874).

28. F.-D. Montlosier, *Mémoire à consulter sur un système religieux et politique tendant à renverser la religion, la société et le trône* (Paris: Dupont & Roret, 1826).

29. In his pamphlet, *Des moyens de gouvernement et d'opposition dans l'état actuel de la France* (Paris: Ladvocat, 1821), Guizot rebuked the government for ignoring "new interests" that were well and truly established, even if the government preferred to ignore them. The government could not pretend that the secularized church lands had not been sold or that liberty of conscience had not been introduced.

30. Odilon Barrot, *Mémoires posthume* (4 vols. Paris: Charpentier, 1875), t. I, pp. 61, 62, and 63. Cf. J. Lecler, "Les controverses sur l'Eglise et l'Etat au temps de la Restauration (1815–1830)," in M. Nédoncelle et al., *L'ecclésiologie au XIXème siècle* (Paris: Cerf, 1960), pp. 297–307.

31. F. de Lamennais, *De la religion considérée dans ses rapports avec l'ordre politique et civil* (Paris: Mémorial catholique, 1826), p. 97.

32. Alexis de Tocqueville to Henry Reeve, 7 Oct. 1856, in *Correspondance anglaise*, in *Œuvres complètes*, t. VI, part 1, p. 199. For ultramontanism as seen by the ultramontanes themselves, see Justin Fèvre, *De la restauration du droit pontifical en France* (Paris: Delhomme & Briguet, 1893). For a Gallican view of ultramontanism, see Henry Maret, *Du Concile général et de la paix religieuse* (2 vols. Paris: Plon, 1869), t. II, pp. 301–56. Among church historians, see R. Aubert, *Le pontificat de Pie IX: 1846–1878* (Paris: Bloud & Gay, 1952); and Austin Gough, *Paris and Rome: The Gallican Church and the Ultramontane Campaign, 1848–1853* (Oxford: Clarendon Press, 1986).

33. *Decrees of the Ecumenical Councils*, ed. N. P. Tanner (2 vols. London: Sheed & Ward, 1990), vol. II, p. 816.

34. Wilfrid Ward, *William George Ward and the Catholic Revival* (London: Macmillan, 1893), p. 14.

35. Yves Congar, "L'ecclésiologie de la Révolution française au concile du Vatican sous le signe de l'affirmation de l'autorité," in Nédoncelle et al., *L'ecclésiologie au XIXème siècle*, pp. 77–114. Or, in a quite different genre, see Stendhal, *Le rouge et le noir*, I.26.

36. Tocqueville, *L'Ancien Régime et la Révolution* book II, ch. 11, in *Oeuvres complètes*, t. II, vol. 1, p. 171.

37. Pierre-Paul Royer-Collard's speech of 15 May 1821 on the proposed law regarding ecclesiastical pensions, cited by Léon Vingtain (who gives the complete text of a number of speeches) in *Vie publique de Royer-Collard* (Paris: M. Lévy, 1858), p. 202.

38. E. Ollivier, *L'Eglise et l'Etat au concile du Vatican* (2 vols. Paris: Garnier, 1879), t. I, pp. 132–36 and 282–98; and t. II, pp. 515–24; Brigitte Basdevant-Gaudemet, *Le jeu concordataire dans la France du XIXème siècle: le clergé devant le Conseil d'Etat* (Paris: Presses universitaires de France, 1988).

39. Tocqueville, *Ecrits et discours politiques*, in *Œuvres complètes*, t. III, vol. 2, p. 493.

40. Louis Trichet, *Le costume du clergé* (Paris: Cerf, 1986).

41. Philippe Levillain, Philippe Boutry, and Yves-Marie Fradet (eds.), *150 ans au cœur de Rome: le Séminaire français, 1853–2003* (Paris: Karthala, 2004).

42. Royer-Collard's speech against the so-called law of sacrilege (12 April 1825), in *Vie publique de Royer-Collard*, pp. 272–73. Cf. Henry Maret, *L'Eglise et l'Etat, cours de Sorbonne inédit, 1850–1851*, ed. C. Bressolette (Paris: Beauchesne, 1979), pp. 171–72; Félix de Mérode, "De l'athéisme légal," *Nouvelle revue de Bruxelles* 3 (Jan. 1845): 1–8; A. Leroy-Beaulieu, *La Révolution et le libéralisme. Essais de critique et d'histoire* (Paris: Hachette, 1890), pp. 219–27.

43. Montesquieu, *Esprit des lois*, XXIV.5.

44. Charles de Rémusat, "Du traditionalisme," *Revue des deux mondes*, May 1857, p. 247.

45. Tocqueville, *L'Ancien Régime et la Révolution*, book 1, ch. 2, *Oeuvres complètes*, t. II, vol. 1, p. 84. Cf. E. Ollivier, *L'Eglise et l'Etat au concile du Vatican*, t. II, pp. 485–512.

46. Tocqueville, *De la démocratie en Amérique*, II, 2, viii, *Oeuvres complètes*, t. I, vol. 1, pp. 127–30 [*Democracy in America*, II, 2, viii, pp. 462–64].

47. Montesquieu, *De l'esprit des lois*, III.10.

48. Aristotle, *Politics*, I, 1253a2–3. Nevertheless it should be noted that, in comparison with Aristotle, Thomas Aquinas minimizes the political dimension.

49. Dogmatic Constitution on the Catholic Faith, "Dei Filius" (24 April 1870), ch. IV, in *Decrees of the Ecumenical Councils*, t. II, pp. 808–9.

50. Thomas Aquinas, *Summa theologiae*, II-II, q. 12, art. 2. Elsewhere Thomas wrote: "The spiritual power and the secular power alike derive from the divine power; and that is why the secular power is not subordinate to the spiritual power except insofar as it has been subordinated to it by God, that is, in the sphere of what concerns the salvation of the soul. Thus, it is necessary, in that sphere, to obey the spiritual power rather than the secular. But *in that which concerns the civil order, it is necessary to obey the secular power rather than the spiritual*" (*Sent.* II, d. 44, *exp. text.*, ad 4; emphasis added).

51. Pius VI, *Quod aliquantum* [1791], in Chaunu, *Droits de l'Eglise et droits de l'homme*, p. 99.

52. Yann Fauchois, "Les évêques émigrés et le royalisme pendant la Révolution française," in François Lebrun and Roger Dupuy (eds.), *Les résistances à la Révolution* (Paris: Imago, 1987), pp. 386–95. The two preceding citations are both from Fauchois.

53. Royer-Collard's speech against the so-called law of sacrilege (12 Apr. 1825), cited in Vingtain, *Vie publique de Royer-Collard*, pp. 265–66.

54. Augustin Fliche, *La réforme grégorienne* (3 vols. Louvain: Spicilegium, 1924–37). Compare what Maistre and Bossuet say about Gregory VII: Maistre, *Du pape*, II.7 (*Oeuvres complètes*, t. II, pp. 231–37); and Bossuet, *Défense de la déclaration de l'Assemblée du clergé de France de 1682*, I.i, chs. 7–13; I.ii, ch. 24; III, chs. 2–4 (1745 edition). The Orthodox schism and the Protestant Reformation arose from divergent evaluations of the prospect and the outcome of the Gregorian Revolution. The Orthodox schism (1054) preceded the election of Gregory VII (1073). But at its root lay the principles of the Gregorian Revolution. The orthodox did not want the reforms that were already being formulated. See Yves Congar, *Neuf cents ans après: notes sur le Schisme oriental* (Chevetogne: Editions de Chevetogne, 1954), pp. 78–79. The starting point of the Reformation in the West was the real or apparent failure of the Gregorian reform program. Far from having succeeded in reforming morals and discipline, the building up of ecclesiastical

hierarchy and papal primacy seemed, by the start of the sixteenth century, simply to have entrenched corruption—hence the anticlericalism and antipapalism of the Protestants.

55. Russell Hittinger, "Introduction to Modern Catholicism," in John Witte and Frank Alexander (eds.), *Teachings of Modern Christianity, on Law, Politics, and Human Nature* (2 vols. New York: Columbia University Press, 2006), vol. I, pp. 3–38.

56. V. Martin, *Le gallicanisme et la réforme catholique* (Paris: A. Picard, 1919), pp. 211–70; Camille Latreille, *Joseph de Maistre et la papauté* (Paris: Hachette, 1906), pp. 209–38.

57. Portalis, *Discours*, p. 39.

58. Lamennais, *Des progrès de la révolution*, pp. 105–6.

59. Ibid., p. 50.

60. Ibid., pp. 99–100.

61. Lamennais, "Les doctrines de l'Avenir," *Journaux ou articles publiés dans le Mémorial catholique et l'Avenir*, in *Œuvres complètes* (12 vols. Paris: Daubrée et Cailleux, 1836–37), t. X, p. 197.

62. Henri-Dominique Lacordaire, "De la liberté de la presse," *L'Avenir*, 12 June 1831, in *Articles de l'Avenir* (Louvain, 1831), t. IV, pp. 505 and 506. What kind of bishops did the new regime want? "Obedient deputies of the bureaucracy" (Lamennais, "De la position de l'Eglise de France," 6 Jan. 1831, *Articles de l'Avenir*, t. II, p. 152).

63. Jacques Gadille, "Emile Ollivier et l'Eglise catholique," in Anne Troisier de Diaz (ed.), *Regards sur Emile Ollivier* (Paris: Sorbonne, 1985), p. 288.

64. Emile Ollivier, *L'Eglise et l'Etat au concile du Vatican*, t. I, pp. 399–400 (session of 10 July 1868). Cf. Ollivier, *L'Empire libéral: études, récits, souvenirs* (17 vols. Paris: Garnier, 1895–1918), t. X, pp. 589–604; and his *Journal: 1846–1869*, ed. T. Zeldin and A. Troisier de Diaz (Paris: Julliard, 1961), t. II, pp. 331–33.

65. Ollivier, *Nouveau manuel de droit ecclésiastique français* (Paris: Garnier, 1907), t. II, p. 10. Noël Abrieu (a pseudonym of Louis Canet, a leading Gallican official): "If there was any desire to save what remained of the Gallican tradition after the Concordats of 1516 and 1801, then in 1870 we should have listened to Count Daru rather than Emile Ollivier, and allowed Duke Albert de Broglie to go on the diplomatic mission that he was ready to undertake; or better still, if we had been prepared to be brutal, recalled M. de Banneville [the ambassador], as urged by Monsignor Darboy [the Gallican archbishop of Paris, of whom more shortly], and withdrawn the French garrison from Rome. For by the withdrawal of our troops and the recall of our ambassador, any definition [of infallibility] would have been precluded." ("Le dixième anniversaire du code ecclésiastique," *Revue de Paris*, 15 Jan. 1928, p. 426).

66. Ollivier, *L'Eglise et l'Etat au concile du Vatican*, t. I, pp. 328–29.

67. Ollivier, *L'empire libéral*, t. XIII, p. 154.

68. Ibid., t. X, p. 588. Cf. Aubert, *Vatican I*, pp. 50–51 and 86–89.

69. E. Renan, "L'avenir religieux des sociétés modernes," in *Questions contemporaines* (Paris: M. Lévy, 1868), p. 378; and "La crise religieuse en Europe" [1874], in *Mélanges religieux et historiques* (Paris: Calmann Lévy, 1904), p. 63. Gallicans had long been mistrustful of a papacy they saw as too Italian. Napoleon dreamed of transferring the papal see to Paris so that the temporal master of the world could keep a close eye on its spiritual master. But he forgot that it was easier to reach an understanding with a papacy that was not too near, provided that it was politically reasonable. Thiers, the historian of the Napoleonic empire, saw more clearly than Napoleon: "The head [the pope] is reproached

with being a foreign sovereign. Indeed this head is foreign, and we should thank heaven. What! Does anyone think that a figure of such authority could be tolerated next door to the government of a state? United with the government, that authority would rival the despotism of the Porte; if it was separated from the government, or hostile to it, the result would be an intolerable rivalry. The pope is outside of Paris, and that is good; he is neither in Madrid nor Vienna [France's leading Catholic rivals], and that is why we support his spiritual authority." Thiers, *Histoire du consulat et de l'empire*, t. III, p. 219. Sheer physical distance could foster the separation. Rome took hold of more spiritual power, and nation-states were less able to take hold of it.

70. John Emerich Edward Dalberg Acton, "The Next General Council" [1867], in H. A. MacDougall (ed.), *Lord Acton on Papal Power* (London: Sheed & Ward, 1973), p. 115. Cf. Félix Dupanloup, *Lettre de Mgr l'évêque d'Orléans au clergé de son diocèse relativement à la définition de l'infaillibilité au prochain concile* (Paris: C. Douniol, 1869), pp. 20–29.

71. Maret, *Mémoire à l'Empereur* [1867], in G. Bazin, *Vie de Mgr Maret* (3 vols. Paris: Berche & Tralin, 1891), t. II, p. 399.

72. Cited in E. Lecanuet, *Montalembert* (3 vols. Paris: Poussielgue, 1901), t. III, pp. 430–31.

73. Léon Duguit, *Le régime du culte catholique antérieur à la séparation et les causes juridiques de la séparation* (Paris: Sirey, 1907), pp. 3–4 (see also pp. 33–37).

74. Ollivier, *L'Empire libéral*, t. XIII, pp. 201–2. It also met with the disapproval of the majority of the episcopate, as well as of the government. See Jean Maurain, *La politique ecclésiastique du Second Empire* (Paris: F. Alcan, 1930), pp. 885–87 and 951. However, Falloux approved of it (*L'Empire libéral*, t. X, p. 598), and so, up to a point, did *Civiltà cattolica* (article of 6 Feb. 1869, translated in Aubert, *Vatican I*, pp. 261–69).

75. Manning, *Caesarism and Ultramontanism*, pp. 40 and 58–59. Manning's pamphlet was a response to criticisms advanced by Gladstone in *The Vatican Decrees and Their Bearing on Civil Allegiance* (London: John Murray, 1874).

76. Papal allocution of 20 July 1871, cited by Ollivier, in *L'Eglise et l'Etat au concile du Vatican*, t. II, p. 374. See also his *Nouveau manuel de droit ecclésiastique* (Paris: Garnier, 1886), p. 626.

77. Cited by Ollivier, *L'Eglise et l'Etat au concile du Vatican*, t. II, p. 383.

78. Armand de Melun, as cited in Jean-Rémy Palanque, *Catholiques libéraux et gallicans en France face au Concile du Vatican, 1867–1870* (Aix en Provence: Ophrys, 1962), p. 190.

79. Brian Tierney, *Origins of Papal Infallibility, 1150–1350* (Leiden: Brill, 1972), and, for a broader perspective, Schatz, *La primauté du pape*, pp. 179–86.

80. G. Bazin, *Vie de Mgr Maret*, t. III, p. 218. Cf. M. O'Gara, *Triumph in Defeat: Infallibility, Vatican I and the French Minority Bishops* (Washington, D.C.: Catholic University of America Press, 1988), p. xvii, n. 11.

81. C. Maréchal, *La jeunesse de La Mennais* (Paris: Perrin, 1913), pp. 393–412.

82. Jean-Louis Harouel, *Les désignations épiscopales dans le droit contemporain* (Paris: Presses universitaires de France, 1977), p. 99.

83. Martin, *Le gallicanisme et la réforme catholique*, pp. 400–405. Cf. René Rémond, *Religion et société en Europe* (Paris: Seuil, 1998), pp. 92–96 and 240–50.

84. Montalembert, speech of 26 Apr. 1844, p. 11.

85. Bruno Horaist, *La dévotion au pape et les catholiques français sous le pontificat de Pie IX, 1846–1878* (Rome: Ecole française de Rome, 1995).

86. John P. Boyle, 'The Ordinary Magisterium: Towards a History of the Concept,' *Heythrop Journal* 20 (1979): 380–98 and 21 (1980): 14–29.

87. *Code of Canon Law* (1917), canon 218. Cf. *Code of Canon Law* (1983), canon 331, and Vatican I, *Pastor Aeternus*, ch. 3.

88. Aubert, *Vatican I*, pp. 215–35.

89. Schatz, *La primauté du pape*, p. 10.

90. Portalis, *Discours*, p. 96.

91. Ibid., p. 4.

92. Ibid., p. 8.

93. Ibid., p. 33.

94. "Monseigneur Darboy et le Saint-Siège: documents inédits," *Revue d'histoire et de littérature religieuse* 12 (1907): 251–53.

95. K. Schatz, *Vaticanum I (1869–1870)* (3 vols. Paderborn: Schöningh, 1992–93), t. I, pp. 52–72, and t. II, pp. 23–55.

96. Jacques-Olivier Boudon, *L'épiscopat français à l'époque concordataire 1802–1905* (Paris: Cerf, 1996), pp. 37–62. An opponent of papal infallibility alluded with distaste to "the dangers of an episcopate of commoners, ambitious fanatics trading Church and fatherland for papal favor." See Jean Wallon, *La vérité sur le concile* (Paris: Sandoz et Fischbacher, 1872), p. vi.

97. There is a distinction to be made between liberals of Dupanloup's stamp, who were opposed to collaboration with the empire, and those who, like Maret, favored it.

98. Bruno Neveu, *Les facultés de théologie catholique et l'Université de France, 1808–1885* (Paris: Klincksieck, 1998).

99. On liberal Gallicanism it is worth reading Emile Appolis, *Le "Tiers Parti" au XVIIIème siècle* (Paris: Picard, 1960), pp. 513–70; Stanley Mellon, *The Political Uses of History: A Study of Historians in the French Restoration* (Stanford: Stanford University Press, 1958); and Boudon, *L'épiscopat français à l'époque concordataire*, pp. 253–64. See also Denis Affre, *De l'appel comme d'abus. Son origine, ses progrès et son état présent* (Paris: Le Clere, 1845).

100. Maret, *L'Eglise et l'Etat*, p. 158. The idea that, notwithstanding the Concordat, church and state were in reality separated, did not command universal assent. See, for example, Frédéric Bastiat, "Lettre à un ecclésiastique" [1848], in his *Oeuvres complètes* (7 vols. Paris: Guillaumin, 1862–64), t. VII, p. 353.

101. Monsignor Parisis, *Lettre de Mgr l'évêque de Langres à M. le comte de Montalembert sur la part que doivent prendre aujourd'hui les laïques dans les questions relatives aux libertés de l'Eglise* (Paris: Lecoffre, 1845).

102. Claude Bressolette, *L'abbé Maret: le combat d'un théologien pour une démocratie chrétienne, 1830–1851* (Paris: Beauchesne, 1977).

103. Tocqueville, *De la démocratie en Amérique*, I, 2, ix ("Principal causes which make religion powerful in America"), *Oeuvres complètes*, t. I, vol. 1, p. 309 [*Democracy in America*, I, xvii, p. 251].

104. H.-D. Lacordaire, "Discours de réception à l'Académie française prononcé le 24 janvier 1861," in *Notices et panégyriques*, in *Œuvres* (9 tomes in 5. Paris: Poussielgue, 1872–1877), t. VIII, p. 327. See Tocqueville's letter to Mme Swetchine, 26 Feb. 1857. After all, the question of the sincerity of faith was not necessarily what really mattered from the point of view of political philosophy: "I do not know whether all the Americans have a sincere faith in their religion; for who can search the human heart? But I am

certain that they hold it to be indispensable to the maintenance of republican institutions," he wrote in *De la démocratie en Amérique*, I, 2, ix ("Indirect influence of religious opinions upon political society in the United States"), *Oeuvres complètes*, t. I, vol. 1, p. 306 [*Democracy in America*, I, xvii, p. 249].

105. Tocqueville to Edouard de Tocqueville, 6 Dec. 1843, in *Correspondance familiale*, in *Œuvres complètes*, t. XIV, p. 236. See also his letter to Corcelle, 15 Nov. 1843, in *Correspondance d'Alexis de Tocqueville et de Francisque de Corcelle*, in *Oeuvres complètes*, t. XV, pp. 172–75.

106. Tocqueville, *L'Ancien Régime et la Révolution*, book II, ch. 11, in *Oeuvres complètes*, t. II, vol. 1, pp. 172–73. The Tocquevilles were cousins of César-Guillaume de la Luzerne (1738–1821), one of the most able churchmen of the time, bishop of Langres from 1770. A member of the Assembly of Notables (1788), and an active member of the Constituent Assembly, he had emigrated in 1791, before becoming, at the Restoration, a Peer of France, minister of state, and cardinal.

107. Tocqueville, *L'Ancien Régime et la Révolution* (travaux préparatoires), in *Oeuvres complètes*, t. II, vol. 2, p. 318.

108. Maistre to Blacas, 24 Dec. 1811–5 Jan. 1812, in Daudet, *Joseph de Maistre et Blacas*, p. 156.

109. Tocqueville, article of 7 March 1845 in *Le commerce*, in *Ecrits et discours politiques*, in *Œuvres complètes*, t. III, vol. 2, p. 605.

110. An Anglican historian of political thought reckoned that "Probably the most revolutionary official document in the history of the world is the decree of the Council of Constance asserting its superiority to the Pope." J. N. Figgis, *From Gerson to Grotius, 1414–1625* (Cambridge: Cambridge University Press, 1907), p. 35.

111. Tocqueville, *De la démocratie en Amérique*, I, 2, ix ("Indirect influence of religious opinions upon political society in the United States"), in *Oeuvres complètes*, t. I, vol. 1, p. 306 [*Democracy in America*, I, xvii, p. 249]. Compare Orestes A. Brownson, "Catholicity necessary to Sustain Popular Liberty," in *Essays and Reviews: Chiefly on Theology, Politics and Socialism* (New York: Sadlier, 1852), pp. 368–86.

112. Tocqueville, *Ecrits et discours politiques*, in *Œuvres complètes*, t. III, vol. 2, p. 519.

113. Tocqueville, *De la démocratie en Amérique*, I, 2, ix ("Indirect influence of religious opinions upon political society in the United States"), in *Oeuvres complètes*, t. I, vol. 1, p. 306 [*Democracy in America*, I, xvii, p. 249].

114. Pierre Manent, *Tocqueville et la nature de la démocratie* (Paris: Fayard, 1993), pp. 134–35. For context, see Paul Thureau-Dangin, *L'Eglise et l'Etat sous la monarchie de Juillet* (Paris: Plon, 1880), pp. 90–122. A Jansenist tone has been discerned in Tocqueville. See Lucien Jaume, *Tocqueville: les sources aristocratiques de la liberté* ([Paris]: Fayard, 2008), pp. 217–61.

115. Norbert Elias, *La civilisation des mœurs* [1939] (Paris: Calmann-Lévy, 1973) and *La dynamique de l'occident* [1939], tr. P. Kamnitzer (Paris: Calmann-Lévy, 1976).

116. Montesquieu, *De l'esprit des lois*, XXIV, 14. Portalis wrote in in his "Discours sur l'organisation des cultes," p. 16: "It is above all in free states that religion is needful. This, Polybius says, is because in order to avoid having to entrust a dangerous degree of power to men, the most powerful fear has to be that of the gods." During the French Revolution, the theme surfaced frequently in the writings of patriot priests who hoped to see a close connection between Christianity and the new regime. See, for example, the three speeches of Claude Fauchet on "French liberty." The same theme appears in the writings

of Necker, Mme de Staël, Constant, and Guizot (all of them Protestants). See B. Constant, *De la religion* (5 vols. Paris: Bossange, 1824–31), t. I, pp. 84–94: unlike "religious forms," "religious sentiment" was favorable to liberty. But for a different perspective, see L. de Bonald, *Théorie du pouvoir politique et religieux* (1796), I, 5 ("Religion publique, forme de gouvernement"): "the feebler the government, the more repressive religion will become."

117. Tocqueville, *De la démocratie en Amérique*, I, 2, ix ("Indirect influence of religious opinions upon political society in the United States"), and II, 1, v ("Of the manner in which religion in the United States avails itself of democratic tendencies"), in *Oeuvres complètes*, t. I, vol. 1, p. 306, and vol. 2, p. 29 [*Democracy in America*, I, xvii and II, 1, v, pp. 249 and 392].

118. Tocqueville, *Ecrits et discours politiques*, in *Œuvres complètes*, t. III, vol. 2, p. 494.

119. Tocqueville, *De la démocratie en Amérique*, II, 1, v, in *Oeuvres complètes*, t. I, vol. 2, p. 29 [*Democracy in America*, II, 1, v, p. 392].

120. Tocqueville to Edouard de Tocqueville, 6 Dec. 1843, in *Correspondance familiale*, in *Œuvres complètes*, t. XIV, p. 237.

121. Felix Dupanloup, *Lettre de Mgr l'évêque d'Orléans aux prêtres de son diocèse pour leur donner communication de son avertissement à M. Louis Veuillot* (Paris: Douniol, 1869).

122. Tocqueville to Mme Swetchine, 20 Oct. 1856, in *Œuvres complètes*, t. XV, vol. 2, pp. 296–97.

Chapter 3

1. Antoine de Baecque et al. (eds.), *L'an 1 des droits de l'homme* (Paris: CNRS, 1988), p. 175. The member in question was Rabaut Saint-Etienne, a Protestant pastor.

2. Henri Grégoire, *Histoire des sectes religieuses* (6 vols. Paris: Baudouin, 1828), t. I.

3. Mathiez, *La Révolution et l'Eglise*, p. 150.

4. Edgar Quinet, *L'ultramontanisme ou l'Eglise romaine et la société moderne* [1844], in *Œuvres complètes*, t. II; Jules Michelet, "Notre nationalité non catholique," in *Cours au Collège de France, 1838–1851*, ed. P. Viallaneix et al. (2 vols. [Paris]: Gallimard, 1995), pp. 155–61.

5. Jacob L. Talmon, *Political Messianism: The Romantic Phase* (London: Secker & Warburg, 1960); Paul Bénichou, *Le temps des prophètes: doctrines de l'âge romantique* ([Paris]: Gallimard, 1977); François Furet, "L'idée française de la Révolution," *Le débat* 96 (Sept.–Oct. 97): 13–31, at pp. 25–30.

6. A. Comte, *Physique sociale: cours de philosophie positive, leçons 1 à 45*, ed. J.-P. Enthoven (Paris: Hermann, 1975), leçon 55, pp. 380–464; and *Système de politique positive* (4 vols. Paris: Librairie Scientifique-Industrielle, 1854), t. III, ch. 7, and t. IV, ch. 5.

7. A. Comte, "Considérations sur le pouvoir spirituel" [1826], in "Appendice général du système de politique positive," part 5, *Système de politique positive*, t. IV, pp. 177–216, at p. 204.

8. Comte, *Physique sociale: cours de philosophie positive*, leçon 46, p. 30.

9. Comte, "Considérations sur le pouvoir spirituel," *Système de politique positive*, t. IV, p. 197. Cf. Léon Brunschvicg, *Le progrès de la conscience dans la philosophie occidentale* (2 vols. Paris: F. Alcan, 1927), t. II, pp. 511–34; and Robert A. Nisbet, *The Sociological Tradition* (New York: Basic Books, 1966).

10. Louis Legrand, *L'influence du positivisme dans L'œuvre scolaire de Jules Ferry* (Paris: Rivière, 1961); Claude Nicolet, *L'idée républicaine en France (1789–1924): essai d'histoire critique* (Paris: Gallimard, 1982), pp. 187–277. Among the tutelary deities of the new republic, one should also number Renan and Renouvier.

11. Ferdinand Buisson, *La foi laïque: extraits de discours et d'écrits, 1878–1911* (Paris: Hachette, 1912).

12. Lucien Jaume, *L'individu effacé ou le paradoxe du libéralisme français* ([Paris]: Fayard, 1997), pp. 238–78.

13. Stéphane Douailler, Christian Mauve, et al., *La philosophie saisie par l'Etat: petits écrits sur l'enseignement philosophique en France, 1789–1900* (Paris: Aubier, 1988).

14. Emile Durkheim, "L'Etat" [1900–1905], in *Textes* (3 vols. Paris: Minuit, 1975), t. III, p. 178. See Cécile Laborde, *Critical Republicanism: The Hijab Controversy and Political Philosophy* (Oxford: Oxford University Press, 2008), pp. 101–24.

15. Gambetta, speech of 4 May 1877 to the Chamber of Deputies, in Joseph Reinach (ed.), *Discours et plaidoyers politiques de M. Gambetta* (11 vols. Paris: G. Charpentier, 1881–85), t. VI, p. 351. Cf. Emile Littré, "Du principe de la séparation de l'Eglise et de l'Etat" [1877], in *De l'établissement de la Troisième République* (Paris: Bureaux de la philosophie positive, 1880), pp. 393–99; and Jules Ferry, *Discours et opinions de Jules Ferry*, ed. P. Robiquet (7 vols. Paris: A. Colin, 1893–98), t. VI, pp. 27–28.

16. Léon Duguit, *Traité de droit constitutionnel* (5 vols. Paris: Boccard, 1924–25), t. V, p. 628.

17. L. V. Méjan, *La séparation des Eglises et de l'Etat: L'œuvre de Louis Méjan* (Paris: Presses universitaires de France, 1959), p. 27 (for Méjan's own, contrary, opinion, see pp. 19 and 49).

18. Jacqueline Lalouette and Jean-Pierre Machelon (eds.), *1901, les congrégations hors la loi?* (Paris: Letouzey et Ané, 2002); Patrick Cabanel and Jean-Dominique Durand, *Le grand exil des congrégations religieuses française, 1901–1914* (Paris: Cerf, 2005); J.-P. Machelon, *La République contre les libertés? Les restrictions aux libertés publiques de 1879 à 1914* (Paris: FNSP, 1976), pp. 352–98.

19. Méjan, *La séparation des Eglises et de l'Etat*, p. 36.

20. G. Clémenceau, in *L'Aurore*, 30 Nov. 1904, cited in Méjan, *La séparation des Eglises et de l'Etat*, p. 136 (see also pp. 229–30). Cf. Maurice Larkin, *Church and State after the Dreyfus Affair* (London: Macmillan, 1974), pp. 126–41.

21. Maurice Larkin, *Religion, Politics and Preferment in France since 1890* (Cambridge: Cambridge University Press, 1995), pp. 3–28.

22. Léon Noël, "Le statut de l'Eglise de France après la Séparation: l'affaire des associations diocésaines," *Revue d'histoire diplomatique* 94 (1980): 5–69, at pp. 18–20. More generally, Emile Poulat, *Les diocésaines: République française, Eglise catholique; loi de 1905 et associations cultuelles, le dossier d'un litige et de sa solution, 1903–2003* (Paris: Documentation française, 2007).

23. Portalis, *Discours*, p. 275.

24. Treilhard, speech of 30 May 1790 on the Civil Constitution of the Clergy, *Archives parlementaires*, t. XV, pp. 746–47.

25. Jean Jaurès, *Histoire socialiste de la Révolution française* (Paris: Rouff, 1901), t. 1, pp. 521–48; Albert Mathiez, *Rome et le clergé français sous la Constituante* (Paris: A. Colin, 1911).

26. Jean-Louis Ormières, "Les rouges et les blancs," in Pierre Nora (ed.), *Les lieux de mémoire* (6 vols. [Paris]: Gallimard, 1984–92), t. III, pt. 1, pp. 259–65.

27. Emile Combes, *Une campagne laïque, 1902–1903* (Paris: Empis, 1904), p. 253.

28. Ollivier, *Nouveau manuel de droit ecclésiastique français*, t. II, pp. 49–50. See Jules Simon, *Dieu, patrie, liberté* (Paris: Calmann-Lévy, 1883), pp. 290–93.

29. Paul Nourrisson, *Trois précurseurs de la liberté d'association: Berryer, Montalembert, Lamartine* (Paris: Sirey, 1922); Pierre Rosanvallon, *Le modèle politique français: la société civile contre le jacobinisme de 1789 à nos jours* (Paris: Seuil, 2004).

30. Maret, *L'Eglise et l'Etat*, p. 132. Cf. Pius VI, *Quod aliquantum* [1791], in Chaunu, *Droits de l'Eglise et droits de l'homme*, pp. 104–8; and César-Guillaume de La Luzerne, *Instruction pastorale sur le schisme de France* (Langres: Laurent-Bournot, 1805).

31. Combes, *Une campagne laïque, 1902–1903*, p. 354.

32. Aristide Briand, *La Séparation des Eglises et de l'Etat: rapport fait au nom de la Commission de la Chambre des députés* (Paris: Cornély, 1905), pp. 60–61; John Courtney Murray, "The Church and Totalitarian Democracy," *Theological Studies* 13 (1952): 525–63. His title alludes to J. T. Talmon's *The Rise of Totalitarian Democracy* (Boston: Bacon Press, 1952).

33. C. Constantin, "Constitution civile du clergé," in *Dictionnaire de théologie catholique*, ed. A. Vacant, E. Mangenot, and E. Amann (18 vols. Paris: Letouzey et Ané, 1923–72), t. III, col. 1562.

34. Patrick Granfield, "Church as *Societas Perfecta* in the *Schemata* of Vatican I," *Church History* 48 (1979): 431–46; Roland Minnerath, *L'Eglise et les Etats concordataires, 1846–1981: la souveraineté spirituelle* (Paris: Cerf, 1983), pp. 60–63.

35. Lucien Laberthonnière, *Critique du laïcisme ou comment se pose le problème de Dieu* (Paris: Vrin, 1948); Charles Taylor, *A Secular Age* (Cambridge, Mass.: Harvard University Press, 2007), pp. 556–69.

36. Jules Ferry, *Lettres de Jules Ferry, 1846–1893* Paris: (Calmann-Lévy, 1914), p. 337 (letter of late July 1883). Cf. Jean-Marie Mayeur, "Jules Ferry et la laïcité," in F. Furet (ed.), *Jules Ferry, fondateur de la République* (Paris: EHESS, 1985), pp. 147–60.

37. Littré, "Le catholicisme selon le suffrage universel" [1879], in *De l'établissement de la Troisième République*, pp. 496–502. On the distinction between punitive and preventive measures, see Jean Rivero, *Les libertés publiques. 1. Les droits de l'homme* (Paris: Presses universitaires de France, 1991), pp. 209–34.

38. Ferry, *Lettres*, pp. 387–88 (letter of 5 Dec. 1885).

39. Pierre Chevalier, "Jules Ferry et le Saint-Siège," in Furet, *Jules Ferry, fondateur de la République*, pp. 171–89.

40. Leo XIII, *Au milieu des sollicitudes* (1892).

41. Aristide Briand, *La Séparation: discussion de la loi, 1904–1905* (Paris: Fasquelle, 1908).

42. A. Leroy-Beaulieu, *Les doctrines de la haine: l'antisémitisme, l'antiprotestantisme, l'anticléricalisme* (Paris: Calmann-Lévy, 1902).

43. Paul Bureau, *Quinze années de séparation: étude sociale documentaire sur la loi du 9 décembre 1905* (Paris: Bloud & Gay, 1921); Jean Rivero, "De l'idéologie à la règle de droit: la notion de laïcité dans la jurisprudence administrative," in A. Audibert et al., *La laïcité* (Paris: Presses universitaires de France, 1960), pp. 263–83.

44. Anatole France drew the conclusions of his analysis in his pamphlet in support of the separation of church and state, *L'Eglise et la République* (Paris: Pelletier, 1904). Zola's

novel, *La conquête de Plassans* (1874), completes the picture sketched out in *L'Orme du mail*.

45. Hippolyte Hemmer, *Politique religieuse et séparation* (Paris: Alphonse Picard, 1905), pp. 10–11. Cf. J.-M. Mayeur, *La séparation des Eglises et de l'Etat* (Paris: Éditions ouvrières, 1991), pp. 31–34. Compare Albert de Mun, *Contre la séparation* (Paris: Poussielgue, 1905), pp. 74–75. Jules Ferry was sensitive to the problem posed by the idea of a "committee of ten freethinkers gathering around a card table to pick bishops." See *Discours et opinions de Jules Ferry*, t. VII, p. 22.

46. *Codex iuris canonici* (Rome: Typis polyglottis Vaticanis, 1917), p. 70, canon 329 §2 (canon 377 §1 of the 1983 Code of Canon Law), emphasis added. Cf. Carlo Fantappié, *Chiesa romana e modernità giuridica. Il Codex iuris canonici (1917)* (Milan: Giuffre, 2008).

47. Giorgio Feliciani, "Les nominations épiscopales entre liberté de l'Eglise et intervention de l'Etat: la prénotification officieuse," *Revue de droit canonique* 46 (1996): 345–58.

48. Cardinal Gasparri, "Aide-Mémoire" addressed to France in 1921. The text is found in V. Martin, "Le choix des évêques dans l'Eglise latine," *Revue des sciences religieuses* 4 (1924): 249. Emphasis added. Cf. Minnerath, *L'Eglise et les Etats concordataires, 1846–1981*, pp. 299–312.

49. Vatican II, *Christus Dominus*, ch. 2, §20 [*The Documents of Vatican II*, ed. W. M. Abbott (London: Geoffrey Chapman, 1966), p. 411].

50. Under some popes (e.g., Paul VI), there has been a tendency toward self-selection on the part of the local episcopate. Under others (e.g., Pius XI and John Paul II), the Curia has played a greater role. The one major exception to this process is China. See *A Collection of Documents on the History of the 60 Years of Sino-Vatican Diplomatic Relations* (Taipei: Fu-Jen Catholic University, 2002) and, for the historical background, Jacques Gernet, *Chine et christianisme: action et réaction* (Paris: Gallimard, 1982), pp. 143–89.

51. Bruno Neveu, "Louis Canet et le service du conseiller technique pour les Affaires religieuses au Ministère des Affaires étrangères," *Revue d'histoire diplomatique* 82 (1968): 134–80, at p. 155.

52. François Méjan, "La solution concordataire d'ensemble," in Audibert et al., *La laïcité*, p. 419. On the Concordat project, see Jean-Marie Mayeur, *La question laïque (XIXème–XXème)* (Paris: Fayard, 1997), pp. 177–91. Significantly, Méjan considered that laicity stood in a direct line of descent from the Gallicanism of the Ancien Regime: F. Méjan, *L'esprit laïc* (Paris: Sudel, 1956), pp. 68–71, et "La laïcité de l'Etat en droit positif et en fait," in Audibert et al., *La laïcité*, pp. 202–7. On the traces of Gallicanism evident in General de Gaulle, see Mayeur, "De Gaulle et l'Eglise catholique," in *De Gaulle en son siècle* (8 vols. Paris: Plon, 1991–93), t. 1, pp. 444–45.

53. Alfred Loisy, *L'Eglise et la France* (Paris: Nourry, 1925), p. 123.

54. Jacques Gadille, *La pensée et l'action politiques des évêques français au début de la Troisième République* (2 vols. Paris: Hachette, 1967).

55. Littré, "Un triomphe clérical" [1875], in *De l'établissement de la Troisième République*, pp. 268–85.

56. Littré, "Le catholicisme selon le suffrage universel," pp. 490–91, 489–90, and 507. Compare Jean-Marie Donegani, *La liberté de choisir. Pluralisme religieux et pluralisme politique dans le catholicisme français* (Paris: FNSP, 1993), pp. 425–72. The author shows

that it is necessary not only to analyze the "vote of the Right" but also positions within the church in terms of political affiliation. See also Philippe Portier, "Catholicisme et politique dans la France contemporaine. Un état de la recherche," in B. Pellistrandi (ed.), *L'histoire religieuse en France et en Espagne* (Madrid: Casa de Velasquez, 2004), pp. 77–106. Compare also the primacy of the political as expounded by Stathis Kalyvas, "Unsecular Politics and Religious Mobilization," in Thomas Kselman and Joseph A. Buttigieg (eds.), *European Christian Democracy: Historical Legacies and Comparative Perspectives* (Notre Dame: University of Notre Dame Press, 2003), pp. 293–320.

57. Littré, "Le catholicisme selon le suffrage universel," p. 491.

58. It is worth noting that Littré ended up on better terms with the church and may indeed have died a Catholic. See Jean-François Six, *Littré devant Dieu* (Paris: Seuil, 1962).

59. Georges Clémenceau, "Discours pour la liberté," 17 Nov. 1903, in Yves Bruley (ed.), *1905. La séparation des Eglises et de l'Etat* (Paris: Perrin, 2004), pp. 117–23.

60. On the church's reconciliation with the new regime, see André Latreille, "L'Eglise catholique et la laïcité," in his *La laïcité* (Paris: Presses universitaires de France, 1960), pp. 59–97; Philippe Portier, "L'Eglise catholique face au modèle français de laïcité," *Archives de sciences sociales des religions* 129 (2005): 117–34; J.-M. Lustiger, "L'Eglise, la Révolution et les droits de l'homme," in *Dieu merci, les droits de l'homme*, pp. 111–35.

61. E. Renan, *Souvenirs d'enfance et de jeunesse* (Paris: Calmann-Lévy, 1883), p. 345. For an alternative view, see Charles Renouvier, *Uchronie: esquisse historique apocryphe du développement de la civilisation européenne tel qu'il n'a pas été, tel qu'il aurait pu être* (Paris: Bureau de la critique philosophique, 1876).

62. C. Maurras, *Kiel ou Tanger: la République française devant l'Europe* (Paris: Nouvelle librairie nationale, 1910). (Maurras was not a Catholic, but he had a substantial following among Catholics.)

63. Contribution of Deputy Isaac at the National Assembly, *Journal officiel de la République française. Débats parlementaires . . . Chambre des députés*, session of 11 Dec. 1921, p. 4917.

64. [*Translator's note*: Shakespeare's well-known tag (*Hamlet* IV.5.123) is the best way to render Bossuet's "Je ne sais quoi de divin s'attache au prince," which is cited in the author's original French text from Bossuet's *Politique tirée de l'Ecriture sainte*, V.4.i (itself an allusion to Psalm 138, which Shakespeare also implicitly invokes).] See also L. Jaume, *Le discours jacobin et la démocratie* ([Paris]: Fayard, 1989), pp. 368–85.

65. Charles Péguy, *Notre Jeunesse* [1910], in *Œuvres en prose complètes*, ed. R. Burac ([Paris]: Gallimard), 1987–), t. III, p. 22 [C. Péguy, *Temporal and Eternal*, tr. A. Dru (London, 1958), p. 33].

66. Péguy, *Dialogue de l'histoire et de l'âme charnelle* [1912], in *Œuvres en prose complètes*, t. III, p. 668 (see also p. 1071) [*Temporal and Eternal*, p. 115]. Cf. Geraldi Leroy, *Péguy entre l'ordre et la Révolution* (Paris: FNSP, 1981), pp. 123–33.

67. Péguy, *Notre Jeunesse*, p. 74 [(Charles Péguy, *Men and Saints: Prose and Poems*, tr. A. and J. Green (London: Kegan Paul, 1947), p. 127].

68. Augustine, *City of God*, XIX.13.

69. Péguy, *Dialogue de l'histoire et de l'âme charnelle*, pp. 626 and 629 [*Temporal and Eternal*, pp. 91 and 92].

70. Péguy, *Notre Jeunesse*, p. 76.

71. Péguy, *Notre Jeunesse*, p. 101 [*Temporal and Eternal*, p. 66].

72. Péguy, *Dialogue de l'histoire et de l'âme charnelle*, p. 640 [*Temporal and Eternal*, p. 96]. On Péguy's complex relationship with the Catholic Church, see Bernard Guyon, *Péguy devant Dieu* (Paris: Desclée de Brouwer, 1974); and Hans Urs von Balthasar, *The Glory of the Lord*, ed. J. Riches (7 vols. Edinburgh: T. & T. Clark, 1982–91), vol. III, pp. 400–517.

73. Péguy, *Dialogue de l'histoire et de l'âme charnelle*, p. 631 [*Temporal and Eternal*, p. 93; for the previous two sentences, see *Temporal and Eternal*, pp. 96–97].

74. Péguy, *Dialogue de l'histoire et de l'âme charnelle*, p. 647 [*Temporal and Eternal*, p. 101].

75. Péguy, *Dialogue de l'histoire et de l'âme charnelle*, p. 651–52 [*Temporal and Eternal*, p. 104].

76. Péguy, *Notre Jeunesse*, p. 99 [*Temporal and Eternal*, p. 64].

77. Rousseau, *Contrat social*, IV, 8 (*Social Contract*, p. 270). Cf. Machiavelli, *The Prince*, 15.

78. Péguy, *Dialogue de l'histoire et de l'âme charnelle*, p. 632 [*Temporal and Eternal*, pp. 93–94].

79. Péguy, *Notre Jeunesse*, p. 42 [*Temporal and Eternal*, p. 45].

80. Péguy, *Cahiers de la quinzaine*, V, xii [1904], in *Œuvres en prose complètes*, t. I, p. 1342.

81. Rousseau, *Contrat social*, IV.8 (*Social Contract*, p. 274).

82. Augustine, *Letter 138* (411–12).

83. Péguy, *Notre Jeunesse*, p. 101 [*Temporal and Eternal*, p. 67].

84. Péguy, *Notre Jeunesse*, p. 37 [*Temporal and Eternal*, p. 42].

85. Cited in E. Kantorowicz, "*Pro patria mori* in Medieval Political Thought," *American Historical Review* 56 (1951): 472–92, at p. 484.

86. Joan of Arc was beatified in 1909 and canonized in 1920.

87. Péguy, *Notre Jeunesse*, p. 23 [*Temporal and Eternal*, p. 34].

88. Péguy, *Clio: Dialogue de l'histoire et de l'âme païenne*, p. 1131 et 1129.

89. Péguy, *Notre Jeunesse*, p. 45 [*Temporal and Eternal*, pp. 31 and 48].

Chapter 4

1. Etienne Fouilloux, *Une Eglise en quête de liberté: la pensée catholique française entre modernisme et Vatican II* (Paris: Desclée de Brouwer, 1998), pp. 71–72.

2. Gaston Fessard, *De l'actualité historique. Progressisme chrétien et apostolat ouvrier* (Paris: Desclée de Brouwer, 1960), pp. 33–48; Thierry Keck, *Jeunesse de l'Eglise, 1936–1955: aux sources de la crise progressiste en France* (Paris: Karthala, 2004); Emile Poulat, *Les prêtres-ouvriers: naissance et fin* (Paris: Cerf, 1999). More generally, social Catholicism was rooted in the counter-revolutionary critique of the world of capitalist, liberal, bourgeois individualism. See J.-M. Mayeur, *Catholicisme social et démocratie chrétienne* (Paris: Cerf, 1986).

3. André Laudouze, *Dominicains français et Action Française (1899–1940). Maurras au couvent* (Paris: Éditions ouvrières, 1989); François Leprieur, *Quand Rome condamne: Dominicains et prêtres-ouvriers* ([Paris]: Plon-Cerf, 1989). See, for example, Marie-Dominique Chenu, *La "doctrine sociale" de l'Eglise comme idéologie* (Paris: Cerf, 1979).

4. Th.-M. Pègues, "La théorie du pouvoir dans saint Thomas," *Revue thomiste* 19 (1911): 591–616. The article begins, "We could have entitled this essay, "'Was Saint Thomas a democratic republican?'" and ends with an encomium of Saint Louis.

5. Louis Althusser, "Une question de faits," *Jeunesse de l'Eglise* 10 (1949): 13–24.

6. Paul Vigneron, *Histoire des crises du clergé français contemporain* (Paris: Téqui, 1976).

7. On liberation theology, see Gustavo Gutiérrez, *Textos esenciales: acordarse de los pobres* (Lima: Fondo Editorial del Congreso del Perú, 2004).

8. On what was with hindsight the prototypical path of Lamennais, see Louis Bouyer, *La décomposition du catholicisme* (Paris: Aubier-Montaigne, 1968), pp. 81–90; and Alain Besançon, *La confusion des langues* (Paris: Calmann-Lévy, 1978), pp. 17–31.

9. Eric Voegelin, *The New Science of Politics* (Chicago: University of Chicago Press, 1952); Henri de Lubac, *La postérité spirituelle de Joachim de Flore* (Paris: Lethielleux, 1978).

10. Maret, *Essai sur le panthéisme dans les sociétés modernes* [1840] (3rd rev. ed. Paris: Méquignon, 1845), p. xxiii.

11. Leo XIII, *Rerum novarum* (1891); John Paul II, *Centesimus annus* (1991).

12. Maritain, *Humanisme intégral* (Paris: Aubier, 1936); Lubac, *Le drame de l'humanisme athée* (Paris: Spes, 1945) and *Résistance chrétienne au nazisme* (Paris: Cerf, 2006); Fessard, *Pax nostra: examen de conscience international* (Paris: Grasset, 1936), *France, prends garde de perdre ton âme* (Cahier du Témoignage chrétien, 1941), and *France, prends garde de perdre ta liberté!* (Paris: Éditions du Témoignage chrétien, 1945).

13. Jacques Maritain, *Primauté du spirituel* (Paris: Plon, 1927). Cf. J. Prévotat, *Les catholiques et l'Action française: histoire d'une condamnation (1899–1939)* ([Paris]: Fayard, 2001).

14. Pius XI, *Mit brennender Sorge* and *Divini Redemptoris* (1937); Eric Voegelin, "The Origins of Totalitarianism," and Arendt's reply, in the *Review of Politics* 15 (1953): 68–85. Cf. Xavier de Montclos, *Les Chrétiens face au nazisme et au stalinisme: l'épreuve totalitaire, 1939–1945* (Paris: Plon, 1983); Jean Chaunu, *Christianisme et totalitarismes en France dans l'entre-deux-guerres, 1930–1940* (3 vols. Paris: F.-X. de Guibert, 2007–9).

15. Marcel Lefebvre, *Mes doutes sur la liberté religieuse* (Étampes: Clovis, 2000); Y. Congar, *La crise dans l'Eglise et Mgr Lefebvre* (Paris: Cerf, 1977); John Courtney Murray, *Religious Liberty: Catholic Struggles with Pluralism* (Louisville, Ky.: John Knox Press, 1993); Dominique Gonnet, *La liberté religieuse à Vatican II: la contribution de John Courtney Murray* (Paris: Cerf, 1994).

16. Compare J. Maritain, *Antimoderne* (Paris: Éditions de la Revue des jeunes, 1922) and *L'homme et l'Etat* (Paris: Presses universitaires de France, 1953). See also Yves Simon, *Philosophy of Democratic Government* (Chicago: University of Chicago Press, 1951). Simon denounces the corruption of the elites who betrayed the people they ought to have served, notably at the time of the rise of Nazism (pp. 93, 98–99, and 221–22). He looks to Catholic critiques of the divine right of kings (Bellarmine and Suarez, pp. 158–76) to furnish a basis for democratic political thought: it's a long way from Bossuet.

17. J.-M. Mayeur, *Des partis catholiques à la démocratie chrétienne (XIXème–XXème siècles)* (Paris: A. Colin, 1980); Michael Burleigh, *Sacred Causes: Religion and Politics from the European Dictators to Al Qaeda* (London: HarperPress, 2006), pp. 284–313.

18. Leo XIII, *Longinqua Oceani*, 6 Jan. 1895. Cf. Robert D. Cross, *The Emergence of Liberal Catholicism in America* (Cambridge, Mass.: Harvard University Press, 1958), pp. 182–205.

19. De Mun, *Contre la séparation*, p. 113; and, more generally, pp. 76–77 and 113–21.

20. C. de Montalembert, *Des intérêts catholiques au dix-neuvième siècle* (Paris: Lecoffre, 1852).

21. C. Falconi, *Documents secrets du Concile: première session* (Monaco: Éditions du Rocher, 1965), pp. 105–13.

22. Vatican II, *Lumen Gentium*, ch. 4, §31 [*Documents of Vatican II*, p. 57]. Cf. Y. Congar, *Jalons pour une théologie du laïcat* (Paris: Cerf, 1953); Vatican II, *Gaudium et Spes*, §§36 and 43; John Paul II, *Christifideles laici* (1988), §42; *Catechism of the Catholic Church*, §2105.

23. Compare Yves Déloye, *Les voix de Dieu: pour une autre histoire du suffrage électoral; Le clergé catholique français et le vote (XIXème–XXème siècle)* ([Paris]: Fayard, 2006); and Gustave Martelet, "L'Eglise et le temporel: vers une nouvelle conception," in G. Barauna (ed.), *L'Eglise de Vatican II: études autour de la constitution conciliaire sur l'Eglise* (Paris: Cerf, 1966), t. 2, pp. 517–39.

24. *The Code of Canon Law* (London: Collins, 1983), §§285.3 and 287.2. These provisions had no precedents in the code of 1917. Laypeople were not invited to replace the clergy in the latter's proper sphere of activity. See Hans Küng, "La participation des laïcs aux décisions de l'Eglise: une lacune dans le Décret sur l'apostolat des laïcs," in Y. Congar (ed.), *L'apostolat des laïcs: décret Apostolicam actuositatem; texte et commentaire* (Paris: Cerf, 1970), pp. 285–308.

25. Some American bishops forbid the administration of communion to Catholic politicians who consistently favor abortion rights. However, first, this practice is by no means universal but is restricted to the most conservative bishops; second, it relates to a purely religious issue (communion) that only touches politics *indirectly*.

26. J. H. Newman, *A Letter Addressed to His Grace the Duke of Norfolk on the Occasion of Mr Gladstone's Recent Expostulation* (London: Pickering, 1875), p. 57, cited in the *Catechism of the Catholic Church* (London: Chapman, 1994), §1778. Cf. Sheridan Gilley, *Newman and His Age* (London: Darton, Longman and Todd, 1990), pp. 363–81.

27. Bossuet, *Defensio*, books I to IV; Fleury, *Discours sur les libertés de l'Eglise gallicane*, pp. 3, 4, 5, 7, and 12; Denis Affre, *Essai historique et critique sur la suprématie temporelle du Pape et de l'Eglise* (Amiens: Caron-Vitet, 1829). Cf. Martin, *Le gallicanisme politique et le clergé de France*, pp. 25–40.

28. H. de Lubac, "Le pouvoir de l'Eglise en matière temporelle," *Revue des sciences religieuses* 12 (1932): 329–54, at p. 335. Cf. Y. Congar, "Eglise et Etat," in *Sainte Eglise: études et approches ecclésiologiques* (Paris: Cerf, 1963), pp. 393–410.

29. Jean Mesnard, "La monarchie de droit divin, concept anti-clérical," in Gérard Ferreyrolles (ed.), *Justice et force: politiques au temps de Pascal* (Paris: Klincksieck, 1996), pp. 111–38; J. Leclerc, "Anticléricalisme," dans G. Jacquemet (ed.), *Catholicisme* (Letouzey et Ané, 1948), t. 1, col. 633–38.

30. George de Lagarde, *La naissance de l'esprit laïque au déclin du Moyen Age* (6 vols. Paris: Presses universitaires de France, 1934–42). See also Martin, *Le gallicanisme politique et le clergé de France*. Charles Taylor insists on the "affirmation of everyday life" against the primacy of monastic life: the sanctification of ordinary life, of work and marriage, of production and reproduction. C. Taylor, *Sources of the Self: The Making of the Modern Identity* (Cambridge: Cambridge University Press, 1989), pp. 211–33.

31. Marsilius of Padua, *Defensor pacis*; Hobbes, *Leviathan*, III and IV; Spinoza, *Theological-Political Treatise*, XIX; Locke, *Second Treatise of Civil Government*.

32. Many of the defenders of the Civil Constitution insisted on the role that it conferred upon the laity. See J.-B. Bordas-Demoulin, *Œuvres posthumes*, ed. F. Huet (2 vols. Paris: Ladrange, 1861). See also Pierre Leroux, *De l'origine démocratique du christianisme* (Boussac: Leroux, 1848), a book "written as a refutation of [Maistre's] *Du pape*.

33. Carl Schmitt, "La formation de l'esprit français par les légistes," in Schmitt, *Du politique* (Puiseaux: Pardès, 1990), pp. 177–210.

34. Bossuet, *Défense de la déclaration de l'Assemblée du clergé de France de 1682*, book I, section II, ch. 32. Or again, book 1, section II, ch. 14: "as religion does not exist in order to disturb governments, it leaves them in the situation in which the law of the people of each particular nation has set them."

35. Lamennais, *Des progrès de la révolution*, pp. 47, 49–50, 56–57.

36. Justin Fèvre, *Histoire critique du catholicisme libéral jusqu'au pontificat de Léon XIII* (Saint-Dizier: Thévenot, 1897), pp. 6, 8, and 5. See also pp. 58–80.

37. Edgar Quinet, *Le christianisme et la Révolution française*, in *Œuvres complètes*, t. III, pp. 206–7 (lecture 12).

38. Maret, *L'Eglise et l'Etat*, p. 113.

39. Maret, *Mémoire au ministre des cultes sur l'état de l'Eglise catholique de France* [1857], in Bazin, *Vie de Mgr Maret*, t. II, p. 32. Compare Abbé Grégoire's similar effort, *Essai historique sur les libertés de l'Eglise gallicane* (Paris: Baudouin, 1820), pp. 562–63.

40. Maret, *L'Eglise et l'Etat*, p. 125.

41. Ollivier, *Nouveau manuel de droit ecclésiastique français*, t. II, pp. 34–35.

42. John Paul II, *Centesimus annus*, §47.

43. Augustine, *City of God*, XIX.17.

44. Pierre Manent, *Enquête sur la démocratie* ([Paris]: Gallimard, 2007), p. 18.

45. Schmitt, *La notion du politique*. As already noted, Schmitt drew his inspiration from Maistre.

46. Manent, "Loi morale et droits de l'homme," an unpublished working paper for the bishops of the Ile de France, 2000, p. 13.

47. Thomas Nipperdey, "Les partis chrétiens," in *Réflexions sur l'histoire allemande*, tr. C. Orsoni (Gallimard, 1992), pp. 178–97.

48. Hans Maier, *Revolution und Kirche: Studien zur Frühgeschichte der christlichen Demokratie (1789–1901)* (Freiburg im Breisgau: Rombach, 1965); David Sorkin, *The Religious Enlightenment: Protestants, Jews, and Catholics from London to Vienna* (Princeton: Princeton University Press, 2008), pp. 261–310.

49. Y. Congar, *Entretiens d'automne* (Paris: Cerf, 1987), pp. 9–12.

50. Joseph Lecler, "L'œuvre ecclésiologique du Concile du Vatican, une tâche inachevée," *Etudes* 307 (Oct.–Dec. 1960): 289–306; Jacques Gadille, "Vatican I, concile incomplet?" in *Le deuxième concile du Vatican: Actes du colloque organisé par l'Ecole française de Rome* (Rome: Ecole Française de Rome, 1989), pp. 33–45; Gérard Philips, *L'Eglise et son mystère au deuxième concile du Vatican: texte et commentaire de la constitution Lumen Gentium* (2 vols. Paris: Desclée, 1968), t. II, pp. 291–96.

51. René Metz, "Les organismes collégiaux," in Gabriel Le Bras and Jean Gaudemet (eds.), *Le droit et les institutions de l'église catholique latine de la fin du XVIIIème siècle à 1978: organismes collégiaux et moyens de gouvernement* (Histoire du droit et des institu-

tions de l'Eglises en Occident, t. XVII; Paris: Cujas, 1982), pp. 96–112 ("Les conférences épiscopales").

52. G. Feliciani, "Les conférences épiscopales de Vatican II au code de 1983," in Hervé Legrand, J. Manzanares, and A. Garcia y Garcia (eds.), *Les conférences épiscopales* (Paris: Cerf, 1988), pp. 42–43; Henri de Lubac, *Entretien autour de Vatican II* (Paris: Cerf, 1985), pp. 52–69.

53. "Bossuet's Gallicanism was essentially a vindication of the independent power of bishops," wrote Y. Congar, *L'Eglise: de saint Augustin à l'époque moderne* (Paris: Cerf, 1970), p. 398.

54. Thomas Aquinas, *Summa theologiae*, IIa-IIae, q. 10, a. 8, *Utrum infideles compellendi sint ad fide?* (whether those without faith are to be brought to it by force).

55. Vatican I, "First Schema on the Church," ch. XIII, French translation in Aubert, *Vatican I*, pp. 270–73 (p. 272 for this quotation; cf. pp. 173–75).

56. Vatican II, *Declaration on Religious Freedom*, ch. 2, §13 [*Documents of Vatican II*, p. 694].

57. Ibid., ch. 1, §2 [*Documents of Vatican II*, p. 679].

58. Etienne Gilson, *Introduction à l'étude de saint Augustin* (2nd ed. Paris: Vrin, 1943), pp. 185–216; J. Maritain, "L'idée thomiste de la liberté," *Revue thomiste* 45 (1939),: 440–59.

59. Montalembert, *Des intérêts catholiques au dix-neuvième siècle* [1852], in *Œuvres* (Paris: Lecoffre, 1860), t. 5, p. 87. See also Lord Acton, "The History of Freedom in Christianity" [1877], in *The History of Freedom and Other Essays* (London: Macmillan, 1907), pp. 30–60.

60. Vatican II, *Declaration on Religious Freedom*, ch. 1, §1 [*Documents of Vatican II*, p. 677]. Cf. *Wisdom*, 8:1. C. Montalembert, *L'Eglise libre dans l'Etat libre* (Paris: Douniol & Didier, 1863), p. 90: "Force can never persuade anyone; it produces only hypocrites." John Locke, *A Letter Concerning Toleration* (London: Churchill, 1689), p. 40: "The truth certainly would do well enough if she were once left to shift for herself . . . if Truth makes not her way into the understanding by her own light, she will be but the weaker for any borrowed force violence can add to her."

61. The debates can be found in Basile Valuet, *La liberté religieuse et la tradition catholique* (3 vols. in 6. Le Barroux: Abbaye Sainte-Madeleine du Barroux, 1995–98).

62. Cf. Avery Dulles, "*Dignitatis Humanae* and the Development of Catholic Doctrine," in Kenneth L. Grasso and Robert P. Hunt (eds.), *Catholicism and Religious Freedom: Contemporary Reflections on Vatican II's Declaration on Religious Liberty* (Lanham, Md.: Rowman & Littlefield, 2006), pp. 43–67; and Russell Hittinger, "*Dignitatis Humanae*, Religious Liberty, and Ecclesiastical Self-Government," in *The First Grace: Rediscovering the Natural Law in a Post-Christian World* (Wilmington, Del.: I.S.I. Books, 2003), pp. 215–41.

63. Royer-Collard, speech of 12 April 1825, against the so-called law of sacrilege; cited in Vingtain, *Vie publique de Royer-Collard*, p. 274.

64. Vatican II, *Declaration on Religious Freedom*, ch. 1, §6 [*Documents of Vatican II*, p. 685].

65. John Paul II, *Centesimus annus* (1991), §5.

66. Augustine, *City of God*, XIX.12.

67. Augustine, *City of God*, V.17.

68. Adam Michnik, *L'Eglise et la gauche. Le dialogue polonais* [1977], tr. A. Slonimski (Paris: Seuil, 1979), p. 141, pp. 27 and 170.

69. Pius XII, *Sur la démocratie. Radio-message au monde. 24 décembre 1944* (Paris: Cèdre, 1969), pp. 9–10. [*Translator's note*: For an English version, see "Democracy and Peace," in *Selected Letters and Addresses of Pius XII* (London: Catholic Truth Society, 1949), pp. 301–18.] Differently translated, the passage cited here is at pp. 302–3.

70. Burleigh, *Sacred Causes*, pp. 168–213 and 428–49.

71. Michnik, *L'Eglise et la gauche*, p. 129.

72. John Paul II, *Evangelium vitae* (1995), §§4, 18, and 20. On the significance of the 1960s for the churches, see Hugh McLeod, *The Religious Crisis of the 1960s* (Oxford: Oxford University Press, 2007).

73. Leszek Kolakowski, "The Revenge of the Sacred in Secular Culture," in *Modernity on Endless Trial* (Chicago: University of Chicago Press, 1990), pp. 63–74. On the rise of a democratic totalitarianism, see in particular Aurel Kolnai, *Privilege and Liberty and Other Essays in Political Philosophy* (Lanham, Md.: Lexington Books, 1999) and *Political Memoirs* (Lanham Md.: Lexington Books, 1999). Kolnai (1900–1973), a Jew who converted to Catholicism, offers illuminating insights on his times.

74. Lustiger, *Dieu merci, les droits de l'homme*, p. 25.

75. Isaiah Berlin, *Four Essays on Liberty* (Oxford: Oxford University Press, 1969); H. L. A. Hart, *Law, Liberty and Morality* (Oxford: Oxford University Press, 1963); G. E. M. Anscombe, "Modern Moral Philosophy" [1958], in *Ethics, Religion and Politics* (Oxford: Blackwell, 1981), pp. 26–42; Patrick Devlin, *The Enforcement of Morals* (Oxford: Oxford University Press, 1965); Alasdair MacIntyre, *After Virtue* (London: Duckworth, 1981). It is worth noting that Anscombe, Devlin, and MacIntyre are all Catholics. One might add the name of the anthropologist Mary Douglas, also a Catholic.

76. Reactions to this encyclical were collected in Fernando Vittorino Joannes (ed.), *L'Humanae vitae* (Milan: Mondadori, 1969).

77. Congregation for the Doctrine of the Faith, *Considérations à propos des projets de reconnaissance juridique des unions entre personnes homosexuelles* (2003), §4; and *Catechism of the Catholic Church*, §2358. In the great debate on the legal status of homosexuality that took place in Great Britain during the 1950s and 1960s, for example, the Catholic Church was in favor of decriminalization.

78. Charles E. Curran, *Loyal Dissent: Memoir of a Catholic Theologian* (Washington, D.C.: Georgetown University Press, 2006).

79. Congregation for the Doctrine of the Faith, *Note doctrinale sur quelques questions concernant la participation des catholiques dans la vie politique* (2002), §2. In some important Catholic circles, the Buttiglione affair (2004) was seen as bearing out these fears. Nominated for the position of European Commissioner for Justice, Liberty, and Security, Rocco Buttiglione, an intellectual and a politician with links to the Vatican, came under heavy fire for his position on homosexual activity (which he considered, from the moral point of view, sinful), despite the fact that he distinguished clearly between the fields of law and morality. Buttiglione was obliged to withdraw his candidacy.

80. For example, Robert Audi, "The Separation of Church and State and the Obligations of Citizenship," *Philosophy and Public Affairs* 18 (1989): 259–96, and 20 (1991): 52–65.

81. John Paul II, *Centesimus annus*, §19.

82. Congregation for the Doctrine of the Faith, *Note doctrinale concernant certaines questions sur l'engagement et le comportement des catholiques dans la vie politique*, §8.

83. The work of Courtney Murray is characterized by a historical optimism that has not lasted well.

84. Danièle Hervieu-Léger, *Catholicisme: la fin d'un monde* (Paris: Bayard, 2003). This recapitulates the Maistre thesis: the French Revolution is in effect the Reformation.

85. Cited in Trichet, *Le costume du clergé*, p. 180.

86. Olivier Landron, *Les communautés nouvelles. Nouveaux visages du catholicisme français* (Paris: Cerf, 2004). On the shift since 1975, see Gérard Cholvy and Yves-Marie Hilaire, *Le fait religieux aujourd'hui en France. Les trente dernières années (1974–2004)* (Paris: Cerf, 2005). More generally, see Peter Berger (ed.), *The Desecularization of the World: The Resurgence of Religion in World Politics* (Grand Rapids, Mich.: Eerdmans, 1999), pp. 1–18.

87. Jean-François Chiron, *L'infaillibilité et son objet: l'autorité du magistère infaillible de l'Eglise s'étend-elle sur des vérités non-révélées?* (Paris: Cerf, 1999).

88. Paul Ladrière, "Le catholicisme entre deux interprétations du concile Vatican II. Le synode extraordinaire de 1985," *Archives des sciences sociales des religions* 62 (1986): 9–51; René Luneau (ed.), *Le rêve de Compostelle: vers la restauration d'une Europe chrétienne?* (Paris: Centurion, 1989).

89. Denis Pelletier, *La crise catholique: religion, société, politique en France, 1965–1978* (Paris: Payot, 2002).

90. Joseph Ratzinger, *Libertatis nuntius* (1984); and "Eschatology and Utopia," in *Church, Ecumenism and Politics*, tr. R. Nowell (Slough: St Paul, 1988), pp. 237–54 .

91. Joseph Ratzinger, *Milestones: Memoirs, 1927–1977*, tr. E. Leiva-Merikakis (San Francisco: Ignatius, [1998]), *pp. 132–51.*

92. Hans Urs von Balthasar, *Le complexe anti-romain* [1974] (Montréal: Editions Paulines, 1976); François-Georges Dreyfus, *Des évêques contre le pape* (Paris: Grasset, 1985); R. Luneau and Patrick Michel (ed.), *Tous les chemins ne mènent plus à Rome: les mutations actuelles du catholicisme* (Paris: A. Michel, 1995); Hans Küng, *Infallible? An Enquiry*, tr. E. Mosbacher (London: Collins, 1971).

93. J. Ratzinger (with Vittorio Messori), *The Ratzinger Report* [1985] (Leominster: Fowler Wright, 1985), pp. [27–59]. The great history of the council put together under the editorship of Giuseppe Alberigo—*Histoire du Concile Vatican II* (Paris: Cerf, 1997–2004)—has been criticized for its excessive emphasis on the "spirit" of the council. See Agostino Marchetto, *Il Concilio ecumenico Vaticano II: Contrappunto per la sua storia* (Città del Vaticano: Libreria Editrice Vaticana, 2005).

94. N. Sarkozy, *La république, les religions, l'espérance* (Paris: Cerf, 2004).

95. Marcel Gauchet, *La religion dans la démocratie. Parcours de la laïcité* ([Paris]: Gallimard, 1998), p. 103. See also Paul Valadier, *Détresse du politique, force du religieux* (Paris: Seuil, 2007).

96. John Paul II, *Fides et ratio* (1998).

97. Mona Ozouf, *L'école, l'Eglise et la République, 1871–1914* ([Paris]: Cana, 1982), p. 8. Laicist republicans and Catholics in the tradition of Péguy can easily join hands today: Philippe Raynaud and Paul Thibaud, *La fin de l'école républicaine* (Paris: Calmann-Lévy, 1990).

98. Jules Ferry, Decree of 27 July 1882 setting out the pedagogical organization and curriculum of public primary schools, *Journal Officiel du 2 août 1882*, covered especially in Ferdinand Buisson's article "Laïcité," in the *Dictionnaire de pédagogie et d'instruction primaire* (Paris: Hachette, 1888), part I, t. II, p. 1473 (emphasis added).

99. Auguste Comte, "Considérations sur le pouvoir spirituel" [1826], in *Appendice général du système de politique positive* (Paris, 1854), pp. 188–89.

100. Péguy, *Notre Jeunesse*, p. 42 [*Temporal and Eternal*, p. 23].

101. Tocqueville, *De la démocratie en Amérique*, I, 2, ix ("Indirect influence of religious opinions upon political society in the United States"), in *Oeuvres complètes*, t. I, vol. 1, p. 308 [*Democracy in America*, I, xvii, p. 251]; and II, 1, v ("Of the manner in which religion in the United States avails itself of democratic tendencies"), in *Oeuvres complètes*, t. I, vol. 2, p. 29 [*Democracy in America*, II, 1, v, p. 392].

102. Jürgen Habermas, "Pluralisme et morale," *Esprit* 306 (July 2004): 6–18, at p. 18. See also his *Between Naturalism and Religion: Philosophical Essays*, tr. C. Cronin (Cambridge: Polity, 2003), pp. 251–311.

103. Habermas, "Pluralisme et morale," p. 14.

104. J. Habermas, *The Future of Human Nature* (Cambridge: Polity, 2003).

Conclusion

1. This is of course a theme developed by Tocqueville in *De la démocratie en Amérique* and *L'Ancien Régime et la Révolution*; by Hyppolite Taine, in *Les origines de la France contemporaine* (Paris: Hachette, 1876); and by Louis Dumont in *Homo Hierarchicus* ([Paris]: Gallimard, 1967) and *Homo Aequalis* (2 vols. [Paris]: Gallimard, 1985–91).

2. Tocqueville, *De la démocratie en Amérique*, I, 2, ix ("Indirect influence of religious opinions upon political society in the United States"), in *Oeuvres complètes*, t. I, vol. 1, p. 306 [*Democracy in America*, I, xvii, p. 249].

3. Péguy, *Dialogue de l'histoire et de l'âme charnelle*, p. 632 [*Temporal and Eternal*, p. 93]. Catholic politicians in the democratic era have reaffirmed their independence vis-à-vis the clergy. J. F. Kennedy's address to a Protestant gathering at Houston in September 1960 was the American equivalent of the first article of the declaration of 1682: "I believe in an America where the separation of church and state is absolute; where no Catholic prelate would tell the President—should he be Catholic—how to act . . . ; where no public official either requests or accepts instructions on public policy from the pope, the National Council of Churches or any other ecclesiastical source." For the background, see Dorothy Dohen, *Nationalism and American Catholicism* (New York: Sheed & Ward, 1967).

4. Leo Strauss has put the lowering of political sights at the center of his history of political thought. See, for example, *Natural Rights and History* (Chicago: University of Chicago Press, 1953), pp. 165–251.

5. Alphonse Dupront, *Puissances et latences de la religion catholique* ([Paris]: Gallimard, 1993), p. 29.

6. Augustine, *Confessions*, III.6: *tu autem eras interior intimo meo*.

Index